HANDBOOK OF CONVEYANCING PRACTICE IN SCOTLAND

HANDBOOK OF CONVEYANCING PRACTICE IN SCOTLAND

Fifth Edition

John Henderson Sinclair BA (QUB), LLB (Glas)
Emeritus Professor of Conveyancing Practice
and former Director of Legal Practice in the
University of Strathclyde and Glasgow Graduate School of Law
Formerly Clerk Treasurer and Fiscal, now an Honorary Member of
the Royal Faculty of Procurators in Glasgow

Euan Fraser Fitzpatrick Sinclair LLB (Dundee),
MBA (Edin), LLM (Strathclyde) WS
Solicitor in Scotland
Writer to the Signet

Published by

Tottel Publishing Ltd	Tottel Publishing Ltd
Maxwelton House	9-10 St Andrew Square
41-43 Boltro Road	Edinburgh
Haywards Heath	EH2 2AF
West Sussex	
RH16 1BJ	

ISBN 13: 978-1-84592-287-0
ISBN 10: 1-84592-287-5
First published by Butterworths & Co 1985
Second edition 1990
Third edition published by LexisNexis Butterworths 2000
Fourth edition 2002
© John Sinclair and Euan Sinclair 2006
Fifth edition published by Tottel Publishing Ltd 2006

British Library Cataloguing-in-Publication Data
A catalogue record for this book is available from the British Library

Typeset by Marie Armah-Kwantreng, Dublin, Ireland
Printed and bound in Great Britain by
M & A Thomson Litho Ltd., East Kilbride, Glasgow

For Fleur Valerie Sinclair
"Let the deed show"

PREFACE

Many years ago, I was thrust into a Conveyancing Department, without any knowledge of the subject whatsoever. Sensing my bafflement a kindly soul set a chapter of the then standard text on Conveyancing before me with an assurance that if I read that, all would become clear. Far from it, the text might as well be written in Sanskrit for all the enlightenment it brought. I wondered then why no one had written a book in relatively straightforward English explaining what the various steps were, from the time someone woke up and said "I must move house urgently" until the final steps.

Nobody obliged, and that was how I came to write the first edition of this book. There have been several editions since, all setting out the various changes that had taken place in the subject, particularly the emergence of Land Registration as the dominant form of registration.

This, the Fifth Edition, hopefully reflects the major changes that have taken place in conveyancing in this century, particularly the abolition of the Feudal System, which had overstayed its welcome by several hundred years, and the increase in regulation that has occurred.

This book is, hopefully, written in a reader friendly style. Several characteristics of legal textbooks are avoided for greater readability; for instance there are no intrusive footnotes, and certain statutes are represented only by self explanatory initials instead of cluttering the text with the full title. Sentences and paragraphs, following the advice given in Chapter 2, are hopefully kept short. I'm afraid, however, that there will be several instances of "do as I say, not as I do."

The unstinting thanks of my co-author and myself are given to all who helped in the writing of this book – whether knowingly or otherwise. Particular thanks are given to the Registers of Scotland Executive Agency for all their help, to Michael Samuel, Dean of the Royal Faculty of Procurators in Glasgow for the provision of the Glasgow Standard Offer, and to Murray Donald, Drummond Cook, Solicitors, St. Andrews, for supplying the house particulars which appear, heavily disguised, in the book.

Most of all I owe thanks to Euan Sinclair, my co-author, who has kept me abreast of changes in the subject and without whom this text could not have been written.

John H. Sinclair
September 2006

CONTENTS

Contents

Contents

Table of Statutes

Table of Orders, Rules and Regulations

Table of European Legislation

Table of Cases

Procedural Tables

PROCEDURAL TABLE I

CHRONOLOGICAL STEPS IN A TRANSACTION INVOLVING THE FIRST REGISTRATION OF DOMESTIC PROPERTY IN THE LAND REGISTER

Note: This example includes repayment of the sellers' loan and the constitution of the purchasers' loan.

SELLERS	PURCHASERS
R1 Ideally the sellers inform their solicitors of intention to sell. Solicitors then: (a) inform lenders of clients' intention and asks for the title deeds; and (b) obtain the writs referred to for burdens (or quick copies) if these are likely to be required and are not with the title deeds, and request property enquiry certificates (sometimes known as a property clearance certificate) *re* roads and planning; (c) send form 10 in DUPLICATE and form P16 to Keeper of Land Register or searchers requesting reports. (**Note**: P16 report is not necessary for flats.) **R2** The solicitors may or may not act in the marketing of the property. If instructed to act, advertisements are placed, property is registered with the property centre, enquiries answered, and arrangements made to show potential buyers round the property. If the solicitors do not act at this stage, they may not be instructed until the purchaser has been found, in which case steps R1(a), R1(b) and R1(c) are taken now or at the earliest opportunity.	

2

SELLERS	PURCHASERS
R1 (continued)	

Tip: Many private searching companies now provide a multi-search service, including form 10A/P16 reports, property enquiry certificate and a free form A equivalent.

R3 Purchasers inspect property and consult their solicitors, who intimate purchasers' interest to selling agents. Purchasers' solicitors enquire if there is a closing date for offers. Further details of the property are obtained at this stage, and preferably a copy of the particulars of the property, for particular reference to moveables included in the sale. Solicitors enquire if property is already registered—if in doubt an enquiry to the Keeper can be made on a form 10 or 14.

R4 Purchasers are advised to contact lenders *re* loan. If lenders are satisfied as to purchasers' income and credit rating, they will arrange to have property valued. If the valuation covers the amount of the loan, the lenders will make an offer of loan.

R5 Once the purchasers' finances are seen to be in order, solicitors submit offer on behalf of purchasers.

R6 (a) Offers are considered and sellers' instructions taken. Best offer is accepted conditionally or unconditionally, and others are informed. Advertisements are cancelled, property centre informed and boards removed. Building insurance is maintained, unless in special circumstances.

SELLERS	PURCHASERS
R6 (continued)	

(b) Lenders are informed of sale and date of entry, and are asked to state how much is to be repaid at the date of entry.

(c) Diary entries as to various steps in transaction are made.

Tip: It is good practice to send a copy of the redemption statement to the clients for approval. This may save any shocks after settlement if the clients are unaware of an early redemption penalty.

Lenders send loan offer to purchasers and a copy to their solicitors with instructions to act on behalf of the lenders. If the finance is not arranged by this stage, purchaser's solicitors should ensure that any offer made is conditional on finance being arranged. *Condition of missives.*

R7 Purchasers' solicitors accept sellers' qualifications and generally ensure that parties are completely in consensus and there are no loose ends in agreement. Due consideration should be given to any time limits in the acceptance, within which the purchasers' solicitors must satisfy themselves as to conditions of title. Temporary insurance cover is arranged, unless sellers accept responsibility in terms of missives. Diary entries are made.

Golden rule: Buildings insurance is cheap, and double insurance is always better than no insurance.

R8 Sellers' solicitors send purchasers' solicitors (a) title deeds; (b) form 10A and P16 reports; (c) draft form 11; (d) draft discharge of security; (e) draft letter of obligation; (f) the search but without a draft memorandum for its continuation; (g) draft state for settlement and all relative receipts; (h) any timber preservation reports and/or guarantees; (i) any building or development control documentation; (j) property enquiry certificates and (k) any other information that may be useful.

4

SELLERS

PURCHASERS

R9 (a) Purchasers' solicitors examine title, approve or revise sellers' drafts, and draft disposition in favour of purchasers and forms 1 and 4.

(b) Carefully peruse lenders' loan instructions, with reference to the online CML Handbook, if necessary (www.cml.org.uk), and accordingly draft standard security and form 2 (Blue) in respect of the standard security which is treated as being the first dealing in registered land.

(**Note**: Where the same solicitors act for purchasers and lenders, it is only necessary to prepare one Form 4—to include the standard security—in duplicate.) If loan is taken in one name only, or in the names of two persons who are engaged, or who have the potential of being married, the appropriate affidavit(s) under MH(FP)(S)A 1981, as amended, and Civil Partnership Act 2004, is prepared to protect lenders' interest.

(c) The draft disposition and draft forms 1 and 4, the title deeds, and all other papers are returned to the sellers' solicitors.

Purchasers' solicitors also make observations on title at this stage.

R10 Purchasers' solicitors make any enquiries that the sellers' solicitors have not undertaken in missives (eg roads certificates et cetera).

R11 Solicitors report to clients on any important title conditions or other important matters of title.

R12 Sellers' solicitors serve notice of redemption of feuduty if this has not already been attended to and contact council tax office of the local authority to intimate change of ownership; also remind the sellers to

SELLERS	PURCHASERS
R12 (continued) contact gas, electricity and telephone companies to arrange final readings.	

R13   (a) Sellers' solicitors revise disposition and forms 1 and 4 and send these to purchasers' solicitors, answering observations on title at the same time.

(b) Discharge of loan is typed and sent to lenders with letter asking them to execute this and return it on the undertaking by sellers' solicitors to hold it as undelivered pending repayment of loan.

(c) Check lender's redemption statement.

Tip: Try to arrange execution of the discharge as early as possible. The discharge attracts an abated fee if it is presented contemporaneously with the purchaser's application.

R14   (a) Disposition is engrossed, compared with draft and returned to sellers' solicitors for signature, with the draft for comparison.

(b) Forms 1 and 4 are typed, the latter in DUPLICATE.

(c) Standard security and appropriate affidavits are signed/sworn in good time for settlement.

(d) Report on title and request of cheque is sent to lenders, allowing at least five days for return. Purchasers are requested to provide balance of price in order to have cleared funds ready at settlement.

(e) Prepare SDLT (return for client's approval).

SELLERS	PURCHASERS
R15 Sellers' solicitors either get keys or arrange for their transfer on date of entry. The engrossed disposition is compared with draft, and signed by sellers together with any affidavit. Draft disposition is returned to purchasers' agents. Solicitors ensure discharge of security is available, put in a testing clause and prepare Form 2 for discharge. Letter of obligation is typed.	
R16 Once everything is ready, sellers' solicitors arrange settlement. Have letter of obligation signed (see **para 8.40**). The sellers should also arrange for a form 11A Report to be sent by the Keeper or purchaser just prior to settlement (allow five working days). If short of time, a faxed report may be obtained, at an additional fee.	**R16** Purchasers' solicitors having ensured there are sufficient funds in clients' account to settle, and that no points are outstanding, requisition cheque, have this signed and arrange settlement. If posting the settlement cheque, ensure that this is done in good time to arrive at the sellers' solicitors' office on the date of settlement. Make sure you stipulate in the covering letter that the cheque is to be held as undelivered pending your confirmation that the settlement items are in order.
R17 *Settlement* Sellers' solicitors hand over: 1. keys (or have arranged for their collection by purchasers); 2. signed disposition and draft and particulars of signing (if not already returned); 3. deliverable title deeds and writs referred to for burdens; 4. letter of obligation and draft; 5. feu duty redemption receipt; 6. receipted state for settlement and draft; 7. any matrimonial or family homes affidavit and draft; 8. discharge of standard security and draft and form 2 for discharge (signed by sellers' solicitor).	**R17** *Settlement* (a) Purchasers' solicitors hand over cheque. Check all items handed over, with drafts where appropriate, and return drafts to sellers' solicitors. If settlement items have been posted, check these and once satisfied, telephone the sellers' solicitors to confirm that the cheque can be treated as delivered. (b) Submit the Land Transaction Return to HM Revenue and Customs.

SELLERS	PURCHASERS

R17 (continued)
9. clear form 11A report;
(**Note**: The discharge is registered in the Land Register.)

R18 (a) Testing clause is added to disposition (if appropriate).
(b) Check all deeds and forms to ensure that testing clauses are correct, all signatures of granters and witnesses are furnished, and that the form 1 is signed and dated.
(c) Application for registration is sent to the Land Register, including:
1. signed and dated form 1;
2. form for (in duplicate);
3. cheque for registration dues (if not payable by direct debit);
4. all items mentioned in the form 4 including the relevant title deeds, matrimonial and family home affidavit(s) or renunciation(s) and the SDLT certificate, which should have arrived, the discharge of the sellers' loan, which may have arrived, together with relative form 2 and cheque for registration dues (if applicable) and form 4 in duplicate.
(d) Purchasers' solicitors ensure that buildings insurance arrangements have been confirmed.
(e) Notify lenders of completion of transaction and encashment of cheque.

R19 (a) Loan is repaid once the settlement cheque has cleared.
(b) Having deducted the loan, all fees and outlays, sellers' solicitors send cheque for proceeds to sellers with statement of account. Alternatively payment may be made to sellers' bank or as otherwise instructed (ensuring that cheque is designated with sellers' names), or proceeds applied to purchase of a new house.

SELLERS	PURCHASERS
R19 (continued) (c) Fire insurance is cancelled and all standing orders for premiums and rates etc. If sending a cheque in redemption, ensure that the additional daily rate specified in the redemption is added for the time it will take for the cheque to arrive and/or clear.	**R19** Purchasers' solicitors should send statement of account showing receipts and payments, fees and outlays to client with explanatory letter. Fee note should include land registration dues for disposition and standard security.

R20 BOTH PARTIES SHOULD NOW CHECK FILE AGAIN FOR ANY LOOSE ENDS.

	R21 Purchasers' solicitors await any observations from Land Register. If any are received these are dealt with if possible or referred to sellers' solicitors for clarification under terms of letter of obligation.
Tip: Registration of title can take up to two years to complete. Some solicitors retain some money from the sale proceeds to ensure that any requisitions by the Keeper can be dealt with speedily (you have 60 days from the date of the requisition or the Keeper's decision to cancel the registration. If you are going to do this, it need hardly be said that you would need your clients' agreement.	
	R22 Eventually the land certificate and charge certificate are received together with documents submitted to Land Register. Both are checked for any exclusion of indemnity or other irregularity. Upon satisfaction, the letter of obligation is returned to sellers' solicitors. Land certificate and charge certificate and any other certificates (eg NHBC, roads, planning, woodworm treatment et cetera)

SELLERS	PURCHASERS
	R22 (continued) are sent to lenders with life policy, assignation and receipted intimation of assignation. Any writs referred to for burdens which were borrowed from a third party are returned to the sellers' solicitors.
R23 Discharge is received with a note from Registers to say that the tile has been registered.	
R23 REPAY ANY BALANCE TO CLIENTS AND BOTH FILES ARE CLOSED AND PUT AWAY. **Note:** The Land Registers (Scotland) Act 1995 provides that registration fees will be payable at the time of presentation of the deeds to the Register.	

PROCEDURAL TABLE II

CHRONOLOGICAL STEPS IN A TRANSACTION INVOLVING A SECOND OR SUBSEQUENT REGISTRATION OF DOMESTIC PROPERTY

Note: This transaction closely resembles the First Registration in Procedural Table I, and many steps are given only by reference to Procedural Table II to avoid repetition.

SELLERS	PURCHASERS
SR1 Ideally the sellers inform their solicitors of intention to sell. Solicitors then: (a) inform lenders of clients' intentions and ask for the Land Certificate and Charge Certificate, and any other papers that were sent (see **R22**); (b) obtain property enquiry certificate, and (c) send form 12 in duplicate requesting report. (**Note:** Transfers of a plot may require a P17 report.) (see Tip at R2)	
SR2 as in **R2**	
	SR3 as in **R3**.
	SR4 as in **R4**.
	SR5 as in **R5**.
SR6 as in **R6**.	
	Conclusion of missives **SR7** as in **R7**.
SR8 Sellers' solicitors send purchasers' solicitors (a) land certificate and charge certificate; (b) form 12A report; (c) draft Form 13;	

11

SELLERS

PURCHASERS

SR8 (continued)
(d) draft discharge of security; (e) draft letter of obligation; (f) draft state for settlement and all relative receipts; (g) any further preservation reports and/or guarantees; (h) any building and/or development control documentation; and (i) any other information that may be useful.

SR9 (a) Purchasers' solicitors examine the land certificate and charge certificate, approve or revise sellers' drafts and draft disposition and form 2 (Blue) if the whole of the registered holding is being transferred or form 3 (green) if only part of a registered holding (eg a new house on a building estate) and form 4.
(b) Carefully peruse lenders' loan instructions with reference to the online CML Handbook if necessary (www.cml.org.uk) and accordingly draft standard security, form 2 (blue) in respect of the standard security. (**Note:** Where same solicitors act for purchasers and lenders it is only necessary to prepare one form 4, incorporating the standard security, in duplicate. If purchase is taken in one name only, the appropriate affidavit(s) under MH(FP)(S) Act 1981, as amended, and Civil Partnership Act 2004 is prepared to protect lenders' interest.)
(c) The draft disposition and draft Form 2 or 3 and Form 4, the land and charge certificates and all other papers are returned to the sellers' solicitors. Purchasers' solicitors also make observations on title at this stage.

SR10 as in **R10**.

SR11 as in **R11**.

SELLERS	PURCHASERS

SELLERS

SR12 R12 (redemption of feu duty) is no longer appropriate as this will have been done, unless the feu duty is unallocated in which case it will remain in force until voluntarily redeemed. Sellers' solicitors contact council tax office of the local authority to intimate change of ownership.

SR13 (a) Sellers' solicitors revise disposition and Form 2/3 and 4 and send these to purchasers' solicitors, answering observations on title at the same time; (b) as in **R13**(b).

PURCHASERS

SR14 (a) Disposition is engrossed, compared with draft and returned to sellers' solicitors for signature, with the draft for comparison.
(b) Forms 2/3 and 4 are typed, the latter IN DUPLICATE. (c), (d) and (e) as in **R14**(c), (d) and (e).

SR15 as in **R15**.

SR16 as in **R16** (except read form 13A Report for form 11A, which is only competent on first registration).

SR16 as in **R16**.

SR17 Sellers' solicitors hand over:
1. keys (or have arranged for their collection);
2. signed disposition and draft (if not already returned);
3. land certificate and change certificate;
4. letter of obligation and draft;
5. receipted state of settlement and draft;
6. any matrimonial or family homes affidavit and draft;
7. discharge of standard security and draft and form 2 for discharge; and
8. Form 13A report.

SELLERS	PURCHASERS
	SR18 (a) Testing clause is added to disposition (if appropriate).
	(b) All deeds are checked before dispatch to ensure that testing clauses are correct, all signatures of granters and witnesses are furnished, and that the form 2/3 is signed and dated.
	(c) Application for registration is sent to the Land Register, including:
	1. signed and dated form 2/3;
	2. form 4 in duplicate;
	3. cheque for registration dues (if not payable by direct debit);
	4. all items mentioned in the form 4, including the relevant title deeds, matrimonial and family homes affidavits or renunciation(s) and the SDLT certificate which should have arrived.
	The discharge of the seller's loan, which may have arrived, together with relative form 2 and cheque for registration dues (if applicable) and form 4 (in duplicate).
	(d) Purchasers' solicitors ensure that buildings insurance arrangements have been made.
	(e) Notify lenders of completion of transaction and encashment of cheque.
SR19 as in **R19**.	**SR19** as in **R19**.

SR20 BOTH PARTIES SHOULD NOW CHECK FILE AGAIN FOR ANY LOOSE ENDS.

	SR21 as in **R21**.
	SR22 as in **R22**.
SR23 REPAY ANY BALANCE TO CLIENTS AND BOTH FILES ARE CLOSED AND PUT AWAY.	

Notes: See Notes under First Registration above.

Part One
Introduction

Chapter 1

WELCOME TO TESCOLAW (?)

'Legal advice will be "just like buying a tin of beans".' (Headline in *Daily Telegraph*, 18 October 2005, after the Lord Chancellor announced reforms to legal regulation in England and Wales)

'When a big new branch of Sainsbury's opened on the site the old Victoria bus station a couple of years ago, Pimlico shopkeepers had two choices: they could whinge about supermarkets destroying local trade, sit back and watch themselves go out of business, or they could see what the supermarket was not providing and stay in business by providing it.

Two who took the latter course are family owned independent chemists. I always shop in them, because they stock everything I want, from the slightly obscure brand of contact lens solution I favour to a particular type of cough medicine.

The staff are friendly, helpful and knowledgeable. They greet you as you enter the shop, they offer advice and suggestions and will often recommend a cheaper generic product over the more expensive product you were thinking of buying. In short they are prospering because they offer what the supermarket cannot—old fashioned service.'

(*Rachel Simhon, The Telegraph*)

'There is only one boss. The customer. And he can fire everyone in the company from the chairman on down simply by spending his money elsewhere.'

(*Sam Walton, founder of Wal-Mart Asda Supermarkets*)

'Carly Fiorina (former Chief Executive of Hewlett Packard) studied law to please her father. It was a decision she regretted. "I had a blinding headache every day" she later told Stanford University students. Then in a shower one day, Fiorina decided to rebel. "It's my life, I can do what I want." She began as a receptionist at an estate agency opposite Hewlett Packard's headquarters and became the first outsider to run HP, the first female to run HP, and the first woman executive in the world to earn $77,000 a day.'

1.01 A conveyancer is, at present, a solicitor or the employee of a solicitor, who deals in practice mainly with the purchase and sale of heritable property. A solicitor in Scotland, is a person who is qualified and licensed to practise as such by having obtained a law degree (or passing equivalent examinations assessed by the Law Society of Scotland), a Diploma in Legal Practice, and then having served a two-year traineeship in a solicitor's office, attending a professional competence course, and completing a test of professional competence to prove that the lessons have been learnt. This rigorous basic training occupies at the very least six years, which is the equivalent of the basic medical training. The aspiring Scottish solicitor must also be shown to be a fit and proper person to be admitted as a solicitor.

The solicitor is governed by the Solicitors (Scotland) Acts 1980 and 1988, which supersede the Solicitors (Scotland) Act 1949, the foundation Act which set up the Law Society of Scotland as the governing body for the profession. Section 5 of the 1980 Act continues to empower the Council of the Law Society of Scotland to make regulations, with the concurrence of the Lord President of the Court of Session. Many of these regulations will be referred to throughout this chapter and are printed in full in the *Parliament House Book* (W Green, looseleaf) or in the offprint known as *Solicitors' Compendium* (W Green). The council is now permitted to delegate functions to committees, sub-committees or individuals in terms of the Council of the Law Society Act 2003.

A practising solicitor must be a member of the Law Society of Scotland under the Solicitors (Scotland) Act 1980, s 4 (unlike English solicitors in England who need not be a member of their Law Society), and must hold a practising certificate in terms of the Solicitors (Scotland) Practising Certificate Rules 1988.

1.02 The reasons for entering the profession are perceived to be: (a) it should ensure a comfortable life style and a safe job for life, although it is doubtful that any such thing now exists; (b) despite the comments of the media, it is a profession that still inspires a certain amount of respect in the general public especially in smaller communities; (c) there is a genuine sense of satisfaction in helping people out in the biggest events in their lives, although it is to be noted that even the nicest clients can turn into monsters in a crisis, and that a good job well done does not necessarily imply your fee will be unquestioningly paid; (d) law can become a totally absorbing discipline and a great deal of intellectual stimulation can be obtained from solving its complexities; and (e) if it all gets too much, the lawyer is well qualified to turn to another career in, for example, commerce, industry, or politics. Many public figures are lawyers.

What of the disadvantages? You have chosen one of the most tightly regulated of occupations, and it is predicted to become worse. The main problem is that the solicitor handles huge amounts of clients' money—even a small practice can have an annual turnover of several millions in clients' money in its clients' account every year—and many solicitors are not particularly good at handling such sums. This can breed problems, which in turn breeds regulation.

Where there is money, there is temptation for the dishonest, the weak, and the badly organised. The *Journal of the Law Society of Scotland* (JLSS) regularly carries a dismal little column detailing the offences of solicitors who have come to grief through misuse of their clients' account, as does the *Annual Report* of the Solicitors Disciplinary Tribunal. While some offences are hair-raising in their dishonesty, the majority are committed by people who have simply got out of their depth with the regulations concerning the keeping of proper accounts. Fortunately, due to the vigilance of the Law Society, the latter far outnumber the former. The *Journal* also maintains a website (www.journalonline.co.uk) setting out the latest tribunal cases. Currently there is nothing relating to dishonesty, and the sentences passed are fairly lenient. There is nothing like some of the older cases of dishonesty—the solicitor who plundered an executry, resulting in the Law Society paying for a lifeboat which should have been paid for by a legacy from that executry; or the bank which supplied a solicitor with a chequebook and authorise him to write cheques for bridging loans without further reference to the bank—he did, but mainly for his own purposes; or the solicitor who obtained powers of attorney in his favour from elderly clients, and then proceeded to pay himself large sums from the clients' accounts. Hopefully these days are over.

What is even more alarming is where solicitors have entrusted the running of their cashroom to a cashier, who has then done the embezzling. If the cashier embezzles not only are the partners liable to reimburse the clients who have suffered, but the solicitors face a charge under the Accounts Rules of the Law Society. Just such a situation arose many years ago—when the cashier told the partners of the firm that she was going 'on a holiday of a lifetime', to visit a relative in Australia. She asked for extra holiday leave to make it all worthwhile. The partners readily agreed, threw a farewell party and waved her off at the airport. Needless to say, that was the last they saw of her, and the several thousand pounds she had embezzled. Nowadays the Law Society requires firms to nominate a cashroom partner, who is responsible for the running of the cashroom. In one case in 1993, the discipline tribunal ruled that 'even although an established shortfall may be attributable to the dishonesty of a member of a solicitor's staff, such circumstances do not necessarily provide an answer to a charge of professional misconduct on the basis that it always remains the solicitor's duty to take all reasonable steps to ensure that clients' funds are safeguarded'.

At the time of writing (April 2006) the Law Society has objected viqurously to the Legal Practice and Legal Aid (Scotland) Bill. The two strands of objection are: if the limit of compensation available to clients will be raised from the present £5,000 to a jaw-dropping £20,000; and (2) the lack of independent appeals process. The fear is that the former will mean that legal firms will desist from practising in the areas most likely to induce a claim. As to the latter, even lawyers have human rights.

Even the most trusted members of staff, if left entirely to their own devices, can all too easily turn dishonest. It usually starts in a small way, by the taking of a small 'loan'. If this is not detected, the temptation the next week is to take a slightly larger sum, and so it goes on. In no time at all a great sum has been taken, especially if gambling is involved. Now that one can play poker on the internet, the possibility of huge losses is large. The newspapers recently carried the story of a Halifax agent, who borrowed £7m from the bank and left an IOU for that sum in the safe. When arrested, he complained that he was not allowed a week to get the money back on a number of 'sure things'. That is the way the mind of a compulsive gambler works. At some stage it is going to come out in the open, with disastrous consequences for employer and employee alike. That is the only 'sure thing.'

The requirements of your firm's business insurance policy about cash handling procedures, should be scrupulously followed. It is bad enough to be robbed, and perhaps have a colleague injured, without the insurers then turning down a claim because proper procedures were not followed.

There are many instances where a trusted cashier has yielded to the temptation of too much freedom, and it is essential that a close check be kept on all cash handling staff to make sure that a minor defalcation is not allowed to grow into something more serious. This is the only fair procedure from the point of view of both employer and employee.

1.03 The Law Society of Scotland (hereinafter referred to—following the practice of good conveyancing – 'the Law Society' or the 'Society'— although this name, without territorial designation, officially belongs to its English counterpart) governs the actions of Scottish solicitors from its stately offices at 26 Drumsheugh Gardens, Edinburgh EH3 7YR (tel: 0131 226 7411). The Law Society also has an expanding website, full of useful information (do not miss the conveyancing essentials page) at www.lawscot.co.uk

In terms of the Solicitors (Scotland) Act 1980, s 1(2), the objects of the Law Society shall include the promotion of: (a) the interests of the solicitors' profession in Scotland; and (b) the interests of the public in relation to that profession. It might be said that these two objects are in conflict with each other, but this proposition demands rather closer examination.

The Law Society has to walk a very thin line between representing the interests of its members, and representing the interests of members of the public who think, rightly or wrongly, that they may have been ill-served by their solicitor. Thus, while many lay persons might think of the Law Society as being 'a lawyers' trade union', many solicitors would equally think of the Society as a body which exists to wrap the solicitor in a web of petty regulations, and to punish the solicitor for any minor transgression of these.

The Society has, quite honourably, managed to tread through these conflicting duties, but, by and large, have pleased neither one side or the other. After years of refusal of any suggestion that the disciplinary function be transferred to an independent outside body, the Society announced in November 2005 that it asked the Scottish Executive to create an independent body to investigate complaints against solicitors. As Emeritus Professor Robert Black QC of Edinburgh University said: 'From a public relations point of view [the Society's] handling of complaints looks wrong. Whether they are doing the job properly or not, they are not the right people to do it.'

The proposition will require an amendment of the Solicitors (Scotland) Act 1980, the setting up of the independent body, the redeployment of some 40 Society complaints staff, and will therefore take some time. Bitter experience suggests that the cost of such a body will be huge (cf the Child Support Agency, which cost £12m, to collect £8m) and that solicitors will be expected to pay at least most of it, but at least it will put a stop to the perpetual moans of those who do not like lawyers—or will it, we shall see.

It is no surprise, therefore, that many partnerships are now converting their businesses into limited liability practices (LLPs) in an attempt to limit the liability of the partners (members) (see **1.11(e)**).

1.04 The Law Society, as part of the first object of its duty under the Solicitors (Scotland) Act 1980, is responsible, among other things, for the training and admission of solicitors, continuing professional development, legal education, practice development, maintaining links with other societies, publications, giving advice on numerous professional topics through a network of specialist committees and the secretariat, scrutinising proposed legislation and making representations as necessary, ensuring that accounting rules and the regulations under the Financial Services Act 1986 are observed, liaising with the Scottish Executive and the Scottish Law Commission, corporate public relations and advertising, arranging mediation proceedings through an organisation called 'Accord' and negotiating professional indemnity insurance through the Society's block policy.

1.05 The Law Society, as part of the second object of the Solicitors (Scotland) Act 1980, maintains a client care committee and secretariat, which runs several Clients Relation Committees considering complaints received from members of the public against solicitors. Where the Society concludes that there has been inadequate professional service (IPS), which means very much what it says, it may modify a solicitors fee or order the solicitor to correct the fault, or pay for having it corrected by someone else.

The Law Reform (Miscellaneous Provisions) (Scotland) Act 1990 places a statutory duty on the Society to investigate complaints, which means that all mail received has to be analysed and categorised. Many complaints can be dealt with by the secretariat, but those that cannot are referred to one of the complaints committees. These committees are made up of lawyers but with the majority being lay members on each committee. This blend apparently worked well, but not in the view of the profession's critics, which has caused the Law Society to ask the Scottish Executive to appoint an outside body to consider complaints against solicitors.

Of course, not all complaints are justified, usually by professional complainers, and many are dismissed causing great ill-will against the profession, because justice has not been perceived to have been done, whether justified or not.

1.06 In serious cases of professional misconduct arising from complaints received, or from the investigations of the Society, principally under the Solicitors (Scotland) Accounts Rules, Accounts Certificate Rules, Professional Practice Rules, or the Guarantee Fund Rules, the Law Society may make a complaint to the Solicitors Discipline Tribunal. This body operates under the Scottish Discipline Tribunal Procedures Rules 1989 and its members are appointed by the Lord President of the Court of Session. The members are made up from lay people and lawyers who must not be members of the Law Society Council, lest the Society be thought to be both judge and prosecutor.

The tribunal has the power to order a solicitor's name to be struck off the roll of practising solicitors, or to suspend or restrict their practising certificates quite independently of any criminal prosecution there may be. A right of appeal exists against the decisions of the Tribunal to the Court of Session, not the Appeal Court of the High Court of Justiciary.

1.07 Disgruntled members of the public who cannot be appeased by any of these means, may make a complaint to the Scottish Legal Ombudsman. The Ombudsman replaced the Lay Observer as a result of the Law Reform (Miscellaneous Provisions) (Scotland) Act 1990, s.34(1) which gave the Ombudsman wider powers than the former Lay Observer including a power to raise a matter in the discipline tribunal, and a jurisdiction over advocates for the first time.

The Ombudsman has proved to be generally critical of the Law Society in respect of its client claims handling. She thinks that the Law Society should be a more active regulator, and should inspect solicitors records to see if they are providing an adequate professional service (see article in *The Scotsman*, 26 July 2005) instead of sitting back and waiting for complaints. She also recommended that the Law Society should see whether there is a pattern of complaints, and the Society has agreed to do that.

The Scottish Parliament, through its Justice 1 Committee has also been critical of the Society's complaints handling, and issued a critical report in November 2002. It is therefore not surprising that the Society has finally bowed to political pressures, and decided to let some other body handle these.

1.08 Although one might form a contrary conclusion, a very small proportion of the many transactions that must be carried out by solicitors every year in Scotland actually result in a complaint to the Law Society. It is a matter of pride that this is so, and the standard should be maintained and improved in the interests of the profession. The Society now requires each firm to have a designated partner to handle all complaints. Many can be sorted out quite easily—often a statement of regret (without admitting liability), or a modification of the fees charged. It should be remembered that there is a requirement for a high degree of regulation in the profession, and that the disciplinary functions of the Society are in the interests of the whole profession, however irksome they may seem, as it is important that bad apples be thrown out quickly before they rot the whole barrel.

Nevertheless many solicitors feel that in the event of their getting into trouble, there is nobody to look after their interests, and they may feel that the Law Society has deserted them in spectacular fashion, and is indeed prosecuting them. They can turn to various other bodies for help—first there is the Legal Defence Union (LDU), which is analogous to the well-established Medical and Dental Defence Union (MDDU), which represents the interest of doctors and dentists who are in trouble, and meets their costs. In the medical world, the disciplinary function is dealt with by the General Medical Council (GMC), and the doctors' 'trade union' is the vociferous British Medical Association (BMA). There is thus a disciplinary function (GMC), a trade union function (BMA), and an insurance function (MDDU) in the medical professions, while in the legal profession the first two functions are dealt with by one body.

The Scottish Law Agents Society, incorporated by Royal Charter in 1884 provides a well-supported, independent, body to foster and protect the interests of the profession and articulates its view, which is often quite different from that of the regulatory body, the Law Society, and is free to do so without the restriction of s 1 of the Solicitors (Scotland) Act 1980. Additionally, local faculties can provide much advice and support for the solicitor with professional problems.

1.09 The solicitors' profession was the last of the non-specialising professions, and a solicitor is still qualified to advise on a great number of matters, although, inevitably, with the greater complexity of matters, a degree of specialisation is becoming more prevalent and desirable. Thus you get 'chambers' solicitors who handle only for example commercial conveyancing, employment law, family law etc. It is very difficult to combine 'chambers' work with litigation, as attendance at court can take up so much of the working day. The solicitor, like other agents, is bound by duties of agent to client imposed by the common law of agency, which although often woven into modern statutory duties, remain as clear duties and should not be forgotten:

(a)   the agent must carry out the principal's instructions.

(b)   the agent is in a personal relationship with the principal, and must not delegate the duties of the principal to another, without the principal's instructions.

(c)   the agent must keep the money and property of the principal separate from the agent's own money and property, and keep accounts of dealings with it.

(d)   the agent must give the principal the full benefit of contracts made with third parties, and any secret commission must not be gained without the principal's consent.

In return for these duties, the agent is entitled to receive a reasonable remuneration, reimbursement of expenses, to be relieved of all liabilities incurred in the performance of the agency, and to the agent's lien over the property of the principal in the agent's hands in the course of the agency, until remuneration has been received.

1.10 To the law of agency there must now be added various regulatory controls, principally under the Law Society Regulations, and under the Financial Services Act 1986 (as amended by the Financial Services and Markets Act 2000), and various other statutes. There is no point in complaining about these regulatory controls; they are designed to protect the general public from people who would cheerfully skin them alive, and are a feature of 21st century living.

The financial services provisions are particularly important, and are designed to protect investors from obtaining incompetent or dishonest advice from incompetent and dishonest advisers and dealers, of whom there is no apparent shortage. While the Acts are framed on the basis that investors must accept responsibility for the risk involved in every investment to be made, and are thus not protected from the consequence of their own folly, they are nevertheless entitled to the benefit of sound and impartial advice, from someone who is skilled at giving such advice. This is known technically as 'best advice' and the concept is not greatly different from that laid down by the law of agency.

Best advice is therefore precisely what every competent solicitor, registered as a financial adviser under the Act, would, or should, have offered anyway. The Act is aimed at rather more 'colourful' figures on the financial spectrum. Nevertheless solicitors who give financial advice, as do most, are inevitably brought into the regulatory net and, again, this involves the Law Society which is the regulatory body for the profession under the umbrella of the Financial Services Authority (FSA).

The solicitor who gives any form of financial advice must now be registered as a financial adviser under the Act. The giving of financial advice, without registration, is a criminal offence, punishable by up to two years in prison. Sales of heritable property are not covered by the Act, but often the solicitor will be asked for financial advice by clients as part of a sale or purchase.

The solicitor who is not registered should avoid even discussing certain stocks or shares, as a criminal offence might be committed.

Under the Solicitors (Scotland) (Conduct of Investment Business) Practice Rules 1994 and the Solicitors (Scotland) (Incidental Investment Business) Practice Rules 2001, solicitors who give financial advice must comply with these rules, and submit to regular inspection to ensure compliance.

Thus, solicitors must be able to show that they have given 'best advice' taking into account the clients' means and needs, and that the product recommended is best suited to these circumstances, taking into account other products offered on the market. The clients' instructions must also be shown to have been followed through on the best basis—the 'best execution' rule. Records must be kept to prove compliance with the best advice and best execution rules, and these records are frequently inspected by the Law Society.

All of these requirements under the FSA 1986 naturally are expensive, and solicitors who do not do much financial business are therefore well advised to refer their business elsewhere, and not to register under the Act. There is certainly no compulsion to do so, but unregistered solicitors are reminded, again, not to offer any form of financial advice.

1.11 Other duties incumbent on the solicitor are:

(a)   To effect through the Law Society's nominated broker and its Master Policy, professional indemnity insurance covering the solicitor's clients against any loss caused by the solicitor's negligence (Solicitors (Scotland) Professional Indemnity Insurance Rules 1995). As a guideline, the maximum payment from the policy is £1.5 million per claim, unless an additional premium is paid, which may be justified for a large firm, or for a small firm with an exceptionally large transaction. The premium is calculated having regard to: the number of partners; the ratio of partner to staff; the fee income of the firm as a proportion of the whole profession; and the firm's claim experience in the last five years. Many solicitors may feel that they could reach a better bargain through their own broker, but this is doubtful, bearing in mind the Society's negotiating experience and formidable market presence. In fact, they have been able to negotiate reductions in the annual premiums in certain years.

(b)   To contribute to the Solicitors' Guarantee Fund, which reimburses persons who have been defrauded by their solicitors (Solicitors' (Scotland) Accounts, Account Certificates, Professional Practice and Guarantee Fund Rules 2001). The amount payable by each solicitor depends on the amounts paid out by the Fund in the previous period. The compensation paid for the financial year 2004/2005 was £214,000, much less than it has been in previous years, when the Law Society was less vigilant.

(c)   To observe the Solicitors' (Scotland) (Advertising and Promotion) Practice Rules 1995. Advertising was formerly strictly forbidden by the Law Society, but is now allowed in the interests of informing the general public the contact details and specialities of the solicitors advertising. Such advertising is useful, but not, by and large, particularly entertaining. These Regulations were amended by a Practice Rule approved at the Law Society AGM in 2006. The principal changes are the removal of the prohibitions on claims of superiority and comparison of fees. The prohibition on inaccurate and misleading advertising, unsurprisingly, remains.

(d)   To observe the Accounts etc Rules mentioned above. The general reminder is merely given that 'each partner of a firm shall be responsible for ensuring compliance by the firm with the provisions of these Rules'. The operation of this rule is slightly relaxed for junior partners who are not given responsibility in accounting matters (*Sharp v Council of the Law Society of Scotland 1984 SLT 313* at 316), but basically solicitors cannot wash their hands of accountancy matters, muttering how they are 'men of letters' and therefore quite innumerate.

The Accounts Rules are a separate and very important study. The Solicitors Discipline Tribunal Report for 1993 devoted a whole chapter to cases before it which concerned a failure to comply with the Rules. Reliance on staff, or on computer programmes, without understanding them, and the particularly distressing case of a solicitor who committed his firm's clients account to a withdrawal of almost three million US dollars, for a scheme which promised untold riches, but was just too good to be true. Needless to say this was done without knowledge of the other partners of the firm, who nevertheless were all declared bankrupt.

Some larger practices now employ chartered accountants as their partnership accountants or secretaries, and they may employ other professional people, such as chartered surveyors or social workers, to deal with specialist functions within the firm. The names of such persons may be printed on the firm's stationery, provided that the public are not misled as to the status of the individual within the firm or to think that they are solicitors (Solicitors (Scotland) (Associates, Consultants and Employees) Practice Rules 2001. A smaller practice could not possibly justify having a chartered accountant in the practice, but might consider having access to the services of a competent bookkeeper, who will probably be trained by the excellent Society of Law Accountants in Scotland (SOLAS).

(e)   To accept unlimited liability for the debts of the partnership, and even, in extreme cases, of the other partners. The financial obligations of this requirement are, however, to some extent mitigated by: (1) the possibility of forming a limited liability partnership (LLP) under the provisions of the Limited Liability Partnership Act 2000 and the similarly titled Regulations of 2001 or a limited company in terms of the Companies Acts. An LLP is a corporate body and not a partnership, and the LLP has unlimited liability, but the partners do not, an LLP is a separate entity and actions are raised against it and not the partners, annual accounts have to be lodged showing the income of the highest paid member of an LLP, but an LLP is taxed as a partnership. In 2006, the Professional Practice Committee of the Law Society reported that there were 69 incorporated practices: 40 LLPs and 29 Limited companies. This number although growing, is still dwafted by almost 1,200 traditional practice units (either sole practitioners or partnerships). (2) the cover against defaulting partners offered by the compulsory professional indemnity policy (see *infra*).

An LLP is a very suitable status for a very large firm, of accountants or lawyers, who may have claims against them for several millions, whether justified or not.

In the case of major embezzlement by a partner in a firm, which cannot be met by the firm itself, the Law Society will appoint a trustee to run the business, and will settle immediately all claims by clients for moneys lost from the Guarantee Fund. The Society will then look to the firm itself and then the partners of the firm (unless it is an LLP) for recompense of sums paid out by the Fund. The professional indemnity policy will cover the partners for the first £3,000 per partner, capped at £45,000 for firms of 15 or more partners , but that may not protect them from being declared bankrupt, and their assets seized and sold. Any balance, after the firm and its partners, have been bled dry, will then be met by the Guarantee Fund, and thus the rest of the profession.

(f) Not to act in the same matter for two parties who might have conflicting interests (Solicitors (Scotland) Practice Rules 1986). Formerly a solicitor might have acted, and often did, for both seller and purchaser in a house transaction. In most cases, where there was no substantial conflict of interest, the result was usually, somehow, satisfactory to both parties. But, if one considers a court case, where the one solicitor acts for both parties, one quickly realises how unrealistic it is to expect one person to represent both sides fairly. There is basically a conflict of interest where one person is buying and another selling— even in a marriage there can be a conflict of interest when one person acts for both husband and wife (see ch 10).

Having said that, there is considerable difficulty in country areas, where there are few solicitors, and consulting another solicitor may entail a journey of many miles. Certain exceptions are therefore made to the broad rule that a solicitor cannot act for both parties—to cover transactions between parties who are related, where both parties are established clients of the same solicitor, or where there is no other solicitor in the area whom the client could reasonably be expected to consult.

Probably the most major exemption from the general rule is that a solicitor may act for the purchaser of property, and the lender who funds the purchase. This exemption is dealt with under r 5(f) of the 1986 Practice Rules. In commercial transactions the lenders tend to instruct their own, separate, solicitors, but in residential transactions lenders are willing to instruct the purchasers' solicitors, provided they are on the lenders' 'panel of solicitors', which most reputable solicitors will be. This should represent a considerable saving in expense for the purchaser, who has to meet both fees, because there is limited duplication of work. The solicitors must remember that they are acting for two conflicting interests, and must not give information to one party and not to the other. If the solicitors feel that they are being asked to act in a conflicting situation, they then must withdraw from the agency of one or both parties immediately. There have been several cases, principally in England, where the solicitors have acted in a conflicting situation, usually with very unhappy results, leading lenders to consider generally instructing their own solicitors from the outset.

Within a firm, different solicitors can act for each party, provided that each party is an 'established client'.

(g) To observe the code of conduct contained in Sch 1 to the Code of Conduct (Scotland) Rules 1992, Admission as a Solicitor with Extended Rights (Scotland) Rules 1992 and Solicitors (Scotland) Order of Preference, Instructions and Representations Rules 1992, which govern general conduct, and particularly in court, by solicitors and solicitor-advocates.

(h) To observe the terms of the Money Laundering Regulations 1993. Briefly these Regulations are intended to prevent the placing of 'dirty' money acquired through drug dealing, terrorism or crime generally into a 'clean' investment, such as a bank account, bonds or house purchase. The investment is then realised and the proceeds emerge as 'clean' or 'laundered' money. The observance of these Rules has become much stricter since the so-called 'war on terrorism' started.

A person may commit five money laundering offences: assistance, concealment, acquisition, failure to disclose or tipping off.

Basically, therefore, if you are approached by a person, whom you have not known for at least two years, with a suitcase full of notes, you are expected to 'verify' that the money has been legally obtained. If you are not certain of this, you will be well advised to contact the National Crime Intelligence Service (tel: 0171 238 8271). It is appreciated that this breaches the rules of client confidentiality, but, where money laundering is concerned, the rule gives way to the duty of non-concealment. It should be noted that a solicitor was jailed in 2002, for six months, for the offence of receiving a sum of money from a client to account of expenses, and then refunding it in a laundered condition.

(i) To maintain complete confidentiality and silence as to a client's affairs, excepting the provisions of the Money Laundering Regulations, outlined above. Solicitors should not reveal details, even names, of their clients, in case someone, in cases where complete secrecy is required, puts two and two together, and perhaps gets four. A major difficulty can arise where solicitors are asked to act against a former client. The rule is that the knowledge they have gained of the former client's affairs should not be used in any way against the interest of the former client. That is a vague enough proposition, and really the only solution is for the solicitor to decline to act for the new client against the former client because suspicions of double dealing are bound to arise. The leading case in this respect concerns an accountancy firm (*Prince Jefri Bolkiah v KPMG [1999] 1 All ER 517*; see also *Koch Shipping Inc v Richards Butler The Times, 21 August 2002*).

(j)   The solicitor will also be subjected to occasional visits from the Law Society, as the profession's regulator, and the tax or VAT inspector none of which are, even remotely, social in character. These people are there to see that you have not done what you ought not to have done, or left undone that which you ought to have done, and should be prepared for and tholed in a spirit of co-operation. Some firms even use retired regulators to do a 'dummy run' before the day, which is undoubtedly useful, as they may spot something that might cause embarrassment.

(k)   It goes without saying, that a group of solicitors, like any other group, should resist the temptation to get together and fix agreed fees. There are various European cases concerning this practice, which all imposed heavy fines on the perpetrators and, sometimes, jail sentences. The Law Society had to abandon its table of fees and the rate for a unit of ten minutes in 2005, because it was anti-competitive after a European Court ruling in the case of 'the Belgian dentists'.

1.12 Having outlined how difficult it is to become a solicitor, and how carefully regulated one's conduct is after that, and perhaps having indicated how expensive this is all going to be for the solicitor, it is now appropriate to consider the benefits of being a solicitor. Quite apart from the intangible benefits of the profession, which are many and depend on the perception of each individual, the most important privilege is the so-called 'solicitors' monopoly' of conveyancing matters. This is contained in the Solicitors (Scotland) Act 1980, s 32, which states:

> 'a person, including a body corporate not being qualified as a solicitor or advocate who draws or prepares a writ relating to heritable or moveable estate shall be guilty of an offence.'

Section 32(3) then continues to to exclude from the definition of a writ: (a) a will or other testamentary writing; (b) a document *in re mercatoria* (in business matters), missive or mandate; (c) a letter or power of attorney; and (d) a transfer of stock containing no trust or limitation thereof.

Thus, of the four major steps of a property transaction: marketing, completing missives, completing title and drafting the deed, and settling up, it is only the third part that is protected by the conveyancing monopoly. A person who is not legally qualified, or employed by a solicitor, may market heritable property, and even complete missives on behalf of a purchaser or seller. When, however, it comes to drawing up the formal deeds (ie those deeds that are not excepted by s 32(3)) this work must be done by a solicitor.

Nothing said above, however, limits the right of non-qualified parties selling or buying houses, to act on their own behalf in the matter. As a rough analogy, if you have a sore tooth, you may pull it out yourself with a doorknob and string, but do not even ask a nondentally qualified person to do the job for you, as that will be an offence. Thus if the Smiths sell a house there is no reason why they should not do all the work themselves—sell the property on the internet or otherwise, complete missives and check the Disposition, prepare a discharge of any security over the property, and present it for registration. A solicitor need not be employed, but a non-solicitor may not be employed, at a fee, to draw up a writ covered by the monopoly. If that person is prepared to act gratuitously that is permitted. The only snag from the Smiths' point of view, is that they cannot grant a valid letter of obligation, which is covered below and is vital to the transaction.

Further it should be noted that advocates are included in the conveyancing monopoly as well, but as a matter of tradition they do not handle conveyancing, except on a personal basis—they have other things to occupy their time.

1.13 Monopolies are, however, currently not at all in favour, and are gradually being dismantled, the ultimate authority being the Treaty of Rome, arts 88 and 89, which set out prohibitions on restriction of trade. These articles are being implemented throughout the European Union, not least in the United Kingdom.

For example, opticians have lost their monopoly on providing spectacle frames, and you can buy simple reading spectacles virtually anywhere, at a modest price. There were regularly prosecutions of opticians who had dared to advertise their services in directories IN BLOCK CAPITALS, although it was pointed out that persons with impaired vision might welcome the use of large type. Referees at rugby matches now, mainly appropriately, wear clothing advertising a firm of opticians, and nobody seems any worse off.

It tends to be the case that other peoples' monopolies are seen as oppressive, while one's own is of course 'in the public interest'. Bearing this in mind, one turns to the Law Reform (Miscellaneous Provisions) (Scotland) Act 1990, which unleashed two new legal and antimonopolistic animals: the solicitor-advocate, who might practise in the higher courts, and the licensed conveyancer and executry practitioner, who might practise conveyancing although not qualified as a solicitor. The former concept has worked quite well, and some solicitor advocates appear in the higher courts, which were previously denied to them, and some have even reached the dignity of QC. Solicitor-advocates have set up their own society, and its website can be found at www.solicitoradvocates.org. Of the latter one cannot claim similar success, as the Board was abolished in 2003 after the expenditure of much money on administrative costs and production of glossy pamphlets and reports, which basically reported nothing. In hindsight the trouble was that the bar was raised too high, and candidates would have been as well to qualify as solicitors. The former Board's responsibilities to the 21 remaining conveyancing practitioners were transferred to the Law Society, which established a Conveyancing and Executory Practitioners' Committee.

A much more realistic concept emerged at about the same time. The Centre for Professional Legal Studies in the University of Strathclyde identified that there was a body of highly-skilled employees of legal firms who did routine conveyancing and other tasks, but had no training of any kind. The training was provided for these 'paralegals' and they became certified paralegals, some even going on to further degrees and qualification as solicitors. The first course in paralegal conveyancing was held in the University of Strathclyde, and soon was extended to other places (Edinburgh, Dundee, and Elgin—by distance learning) and other subjects (executry, court work etc).

The paralegal, in conveyancing, executry, court work, debt collection etc is now a highly-valued part of the legal team, and the Scottish Paralegal Association is recognised by the Law Society (www.scottish-paralegal.org.uk). The SPA grades paralegals according to qualifications and experience:

'The Scottish Paralegal Association

Grade 1

Minimum two years' experience

Formal qualification in an area specific to Scots Law

Working as a fee earner with responsibility for own workload. No secretarial of administration work apart from typing own letters etc

or

Minimum five years' experience

No formal qualification in an area specific to Scots law

Working as a fee earner with responsibility for own workload. No secretarial or administration work apart from typing own letters etc.

Grade 2

Formal qualification in an area specific to Scots law – more than two years' experience but not working as a recognised fee earner with responsibility for own workload and carrying out less than 75% paralegal work – higher or equal proportions secretarial/administration work to paralegal work

or

No formal qualification in an area specific to Scots law, more than five years' experience but not working as a recognised fee earner with responsibility for own workload – carrying out less than 75% paralegal work – higher or equal proportion secretarial work to paralegal work.

Grade 3

Formal qualification in an area specific to Scots law but less than two years' experience.'

The paralegal's immense supporting role was recognised by a suite of articles in the *Journal*, in September 2005.

1.14 Solicitors have long enjoyed being considered as 'men of business', that is to say persons who dealt with a wide variety of affairs—they used to be town clerks of small local government units, banking agents, land and estate agents, company secretaries and any variety of other engagements, as well as looking after what we now think of as legal business. Increased specialisation has closed many opportunities for solicitors, but equally it has opened other doors—employment law, pensions law, family law and many others.

Originally solicitors also used to sell property exclusively, so much so that they were not allowed to use the term 'estate agents' until comparatively recently, because estate agency was considered to be a part of their job description.

Then, in the 1960s, the first commercial estate agency opened and began taking clients from solicitors, simply because they offered a better and more professional service, using, as they did, attractive advertisements, High Street shop windows, attractive block advertising, extended opening hours, helpful staff, and extensive lists of buyers and sellers who were matched up with each other, providing numerous further business opportunities. The first such agency was the Villa Estate Agency in southern Glasgow, set up by a chartered surveyor and two lawyers in the teeth of opposition from their respective professional bodies. They adopted a form of advertisement which pointed out the worst features of each property, a technique which had been originated by the Roy Brooks Estate Agency in London (see his two books of advertisements called *A Brothel in Pimlico* and *Mud, Straw and Insults*).

An example of this genre was Villa's advertisement for a house in Glasgow:

'POLLOKSHIELDS (Ayton Road) Well—what a bargain for anyone who wants to make a home out of of a decrepit mausoleum. The electric bills in this 6/7 apartment Semi greystone Villa are nil, simply because there is no electricity. Yes, dignified Victorian gas lighting sets the Dickensian scene where the grotty dull ancient decoration somehow seems in place. Massive two tractor and car garage (there presently are two tractors and what passed for a car in it now!) Regardless of your fears of 'strange houses' surely £1,850 must tempt a lot of viewers.'

This advertising was a product of the 1960s and would probably cause outrage nowadays, but it certainly worked, as did the modest asking price for a basically very sound house which is probably worth about £250,000 these days. This was in contrast to the service provided by the average solicitors firm, which deputed the selling task to the lowliest member of staff, who did not know what price was expected or even where the house was.

It is questionable whether such an advertisement would run foul of the Property Misdescriptions (Specified Matters) Regulations 1992 if used today—probably not, it is presumably entirely truthful, and possibly too truthful.

It was little wonder then that estate agencies thrived, could charge big fees, multiplied, and then mostly sold out to banks and insurance companies for undreamed of figures. The estate agents retired to enjoy their wealth, and a few years later bought back their businesses from the big company who had found out that estate agency, like law, is a very personal business. For example, the Nationwide Building Society bought a chain of 305 branches for a large sum, and sold it on a few years later at a loss of £200m The Prudential Assurance Company (more of whom later) lost £340m on its 500-branch chain of estate agencies (financial figures courtesy of *Daily Telegraph*, 12 October 1994).

None of these financial triumphs cheered the legal profession, however. They had let a great opportunity slip, and now had business rivals being the all important first contact with the client. The estate agents could sell mortgages (incidentally ignoring the existence of a conflict in acting for the sellers and buyers) and life assurance policies, and even nominate solicitors to act for the sellers.

Solicitors hit back, rather late in the day. The Law Society finally permitted solicitors to describe themselves as 'solicitors and estate agents' and to permit rather more attractive advertising of properties for sale. Solicitors got together and formed Solicitors' Property Centres, which centralised marketing of properties. The most successful were the Aberdeen Solicitors Property Centre (ASPC) and the Edinburgh Solicitors Property Centre (ESPC), which are very powerful, as are many smaller centres. In Glasgow, an alternative course was followed. A company called Solicitors Estate Agency (SEAL) was set up, but it became obvious that it was not so successful as the SPCs. Accordingly SEAL was sold to another estate agency, with no connection with solicitors, and the Glasgow Solicitors Property Centre was set up. This centre has shown remarkable growth, and does a lot of business, although mainly around the lower end of the market. For details of property centres, see the Scottish Solicitors property centre's website www.sspc.co.uk.

The difference between SEAL and GSPC is that SEAL is an estate agency, the owners of which were solicitors firms, which referred house sales to SEAL at the outset, which marketed the property, and then when offers were received, referred the offers back to the instructing solicitors to complete the conveyancing formalities. SEAL would then charge a fee for its services, as would any other estate agency. GSPC on the other hand is merely a display facility for solicitors, holding particulars of all houses being sold by its members, and advertising these in its prominent shop window and spacious premises, and printing details of properties being sold by solicitors in a weekly bulletin, which circulates widely. The solicitor handles the marketing and conveyancing, and pays only a small facility fee to GSPC.

The Solicitors' Property Centres act as a central point which gives out details of properties being sold by their solicitors members, printing a weekly list and maintaining a website of properties being sold which are widely circulated. This caused a furore, when an estate agency in Aberdeen complained that it was not allowed to advertise in the Aberdeen SPC's weekly list, which amounted to a restraint of competition. The matter came to court (*Aberdeen SPC Ltd v Director General for Fair Trading 1996 SLT 523*). The court decided that ASPC were not in restraint of fair trade. The Office of Fair Trading then persuaded the Monopolies and Mergers Commission (MMC) to hold a formal hearing under the Fair Trading Act 1973. The MMC decided that ASPC were not acting unfairly in not allowing estate agents to advertise in its weekly lists, since when estate agents have virtually taken over the property sections in local newspapers, such as the *Herald* and *The Scotsman*.

Looking at the property supplements, estate agents or firms of chartered surveyors seem to sell most of the highly-valuable properties. A relatively new development is the interest of international property firms, who are as likely to be selling property in Dubai as Dundee, have entered at the top end of the market.

In all, this whole saga points out the dangers of being uncompetitive, and how the profession can fight back against rivals by offering quality and service.

1.15 Considering the volume, and complexity, of business transacted by solicitors in Scotland, the number of complaints received is remarkably small, and those sustained even smaller. There is always room for improvement though. Each firm must now nominate a partner who is responsible for dealing with complaints made against the firm. These should be handled attentively and courteously and without delay. The robust handling of complaints is a sign of a firm's strength, not weakness. A claim squarely met can provide lessons for future handling of business. A claim not squarely met can result in an embarrassing confrontation with the Law Society, or maybe the Ombudsman, or— strictly to be avoided if possible—a court action which will tie up the partners of the firm for a considerable time and the slender profit margin will quickly disappear.

However much the profession may pride itself on its handling of complaints, there is a general feeling that the profession looks after itself in these matters. The media does much to foster discontent in this matter, as with others. The nihilistic media love to criticise what they consider as 'the establishment' with which they include solicitors. Perhaps solicitors could have done more to counter this tendency, but one cannot be certain how this could have been done except through the same critical media, and thereby giving them more money to spend on their biased stories.

Some of this mud inevitably sticks, and although most people are grateful to their solicitors, there lurks a feeling that solicitors look only after themselves. Perhaps the story in *The Scotsman*, 28 December 2005, that a well-known QC was paid £357,600 in legal aid in 2004/05 leads to the belief that lawyers are seriously overpaid. The truth is that many firms have had to give up legal aid civil cases, because they simply cannot live on the paltry sums paid out. There is probably also confusion with the apparently limitless sums that lawyers in London are paid; again the truth is that many English firms outwith London, barely make a living. *The Times*, 18 December 2006, reports the agreed settlement on the first day of calling in court, of a libel action by Collins Stewart against the *Financial Times*. The original action was for £230.5m of special damages, but it was settled at £300,000 with the Financial Times paying the Plaintiffs' expenses of £2.2m as well as its own legal bill of £2m. *The Times* quoted a leading libel lawyer as saying 'There's only one winner in all of this, and it's Collins Stewart'. To which the reader might say— 'what about the lawyers?' Solicitors in Scotland should set about saying that they do not charge £2m for their services.

This feeling that lawyers are 'out for themselves' penetrates to the highest circles, and even to government. The Lord Chancellor, Lord Falconer, therefore asked a city grandee Sir David Clementi, chairman of Prudential Assurance to conduct a review of the regulation of the legal profession in England and Wales, which was published on 15 December 2004.

The regulation of the legal profession in Scotland is devolved to the Scottish Parliament, and the Clementi Report does not therefore apply to Scotland. It is realistic, however, that some of the alterations made South of the Border will ultimately impact on the profession and public of Scotland. For a discussion of the Clementi Report from a Scottish viewpoint, see an article by the chief executive of the Law Society of Scotland printed in the *Journal* (February 2005, p 14) and also to be found www.journalonline.co.uk

Put briefly, the Clementi Report recommended: (1) that a Legal Services Board and Office for Complaints be set up for England and Wales. This is being done, and the Law Society of Scotland, by proposing that an independent body for complaints be set up in Scotland, has fallen into line; and (2) that Legal Disciplinary Partnerships be established; these could have non-legal proprietors and members, and would permit, say, banks to own an LDP, or to be major investors; thus the term ' Tescolaw', with certain gloomy individuals predicting that a shopper could obtain legal services in a supermarket, along with the proverbial tin of beans.

This is probably fairly unlikely, although the supermarket groups have not ruled themselves out from providing legal services. Certainly, some supermarkets have made incursions into the solicitors' traditional 'bread and butter' offerings, by making highly professional DIY legal forms and letters available. In addition, some large financial institutions, including the Halifax, have declared an interest, but they are already in the business of providing finance for residential conveyancing. In 2005 Halifax became the first lender to offer a fixed fee conveyancing service on a no sale, no fee basis. The fee is fixed on a scale from £299 depending on the sale price of the property involved. Users of the service will be able to keep track of the progress of their transaction online, or by text messenger, email or letter, with automatic alerts at the key stages such as when documents are received.

There is still a large gap between the services provided by large retail businesses and those provided by small service companies. This the Prudential Assurance (now chaired by Sir David Clementi) discovered (**1.14**) when it entered into the estate agency business some years ago, and lost £200m of its policy holders' money.

Large retail businesses, including assurance and insurance companies, buy or produce a product which they distribute and market at a price sufficient to cover their costs of buying or manufacturing, distribution, marketing and sales, overheads and profits. They then make the product available at the price fixed, and hope that it is sufficiently attractive to tempt customers into buying the product and several others at the same time. The really clever trick is to sell the product before having to pay the suppliers, and to invest the money on deposit. This is even more appropriate for insurance and assurance companies, who—in the case of life assurance—may not have to pay claims for several years or—in the case of insurance—not at all. This helps the big business's cashflow, which is very important.

A small service company, like a lawyer's or estate agent's business, is however chosen at the outset to help a client with a particular problem, usually by recommendation. The fee is now always pre-estimated or negotiated. The service provider then helps the client through the problem, and gets a fee at the end of the work, which may be some time later. The purchase of a house, for example, may be a very major transaction for the purchasers, and very stressful, and they may need a lot of personal attention. The small business is perennially having difficulties with cashflow.

Thus the two business models seem widely disparate, and it is submitted that big business will not generally be interested in undertaking small business, because the product is not neatly bundled and the cashflow is not to big business's requirements.

That having been said, conveyancing is now marginally profitable unless carried out in volume. Some solicitors firms have adopted the 'Ryanair' philosophy in a big way and are making considerable amounts of money in the process. Volume conveyancing is big business and the small rural practice will begin to founder.

Of course, none of us can be sure- perhaps the result will be like 'Big Bang' in the city, when all the small stockbroker's firms were taken over by big banks, and partners who were good at long lunches, and little else, were put out to grass. Stockbroking business, however, fitted neatly in with the requirements of big business in a way that legal business may not, in that they have an excellent cashflow, and what little work there is, can be done quite quickly.

It may be that legal firms disappear in the same way, and lawyers will become the legal arm of massive organisations, as it is suspected that is what Sir David Clementi envisages.

One thing is certain: there will be increased competition, in an already highly competitive field. Nobody doing a good job need feel threatened by competition, if they remember what are called 'the three horsemen' of the competitive society: costs, quality and service.

Costs

1.16 There is no need to be a skinflint, but costs must be carefully watched. Thus, a lawyer should have an attractive office which can be easily accessed by people, and nearby easy parking. Finance and bank charges should be kept to a minimum; never be afraid of shopping around for cheaper rates. You have no loyalty to a particular Bank, unless it is built up over a long period, and is mutually beneficial to both parties. What the lawyer does not need is to be cluttered with old files and papers, which should be carefully indexed and sent to a low rent warehouse in a dreary location. The lawyer will have an adequate staff, but should not be overstaffed with an eye to the wages bill, and there should be regular appraisals of staff to reward effective performers, and to make sure that other, more marginal employees, are not spending their time thinking up daft ideas to justify their position, and keeping others off their work. Personnel should not develop the habit of taking a taxi everywhere—they are very useful in certain cases, but a cheaper alternative should always be considered. Energy costs should be carefully controlled. This does not mean 40 watt bulbs everywhere, but perhaps you should fitting low intensity bulbs in lights which get more powerful when there is someone in the room. Machines, and lighting, should be switched off when not in use.

Quality

1.17 The lawyer should have the latest machinery available, for managing accounts, for word processing and drafting, and for taking messages and keeping in touch with clients. The lawyer, it goes without saying, should keep up with changes in the law and practice by attending more than the minimum required of CPD courses. The lawyer should also have access to a good legal library. The lawyer should use good quality stationery, not cheap letterheads which let down the firm badly.

Service

1.18 Above all lawyers should remember that they are engaged to help vulnerable people through perhaps one of the biggest financial events of their lives, and should give them a service that smoothes out the bumps and, as one client once put it, gives them 'a warm feeling inside' and leads to further recommendations. Accept no interruptions to meetings with clients, even 'very important' telephone calls. The client will think you have other things on your mind, and you should never give that impression. Do not constantly look at your watch. Give your clients the impression that they are the only people that matter, for they are and they think that as well. Telephone messages should be carefully recorded and returned that day. Letters should be speedily and helpfully answered. Days on the golf course are probably contra-indicated, but if the lawyer is so tempted, his absence should be covered, and no one should ever indicate where the lawyer is. The phrase 'on a course' can be used because it is sufficiently ambiguous not to indicate whether the course is academic or sporting, but the answer should never be given indicating the true nature of the engagement. Having said that, lawyers are as entitled as anyone else to take a little recreation or a long leisurely lunch, but a client who wants advice urgently should not be told this, and a message should be taken and promptly attended to on your return. Everything should be explained to a client, who has probably watched a house programme on Channel 4 the night before, with the presenters' anglocentric advice, and is now thoroughly confused.

If you pay attention to these three things, there is no reason why you should have to fear the big, bad wolf, and you should be able to build up, and sustain, a good business as well, by word of mouth which is the best way. Either way, welcome to Tescolaw.

Chapter 2

LETTER WRITING

'Grammatical gaffes, incorrect punctuation, and persistent spelling errors are costing UK businesses £2bn a year in lost contracts, according to a survey by Royal Mail delivery.

Businessmen and women seeking to make their fortune in the new year are advised to make sure they never commit an error in grammar or spelling.

Their prices may be competitive and their staff welcoming and helpful, but if they split infinitives, put apostrophes in the wrong place or use suspicious syntax, the chances are that the recipients will be thrown into such a fit of rage that they will eventually sever all potentially lucrative business links with the offender.

Lack of attention to detail and repeatedly making mistakes with names and addresses were also found to be a source of irritation.'

The Herald, 3 January 2001

'The irony for the Legal Services Ombudsman is that most complaints relate to poor communication skills—something which could be nipped in the bud early on in their training. 'One of the first recommendations I made to the Law Society was that trainee lawyers doing the Diploma ought to be taught how to write in plain English, because lawyers' letters and Law Society letters were just legal jargon. They accepted—but I don't think anything has happened.'

The Scotsman, 26 July 2005

2.01 The conveyancer will start training on letter writing before moving on to more complicated deeds. Letter writing is nevertheless a most important part of legal practice. Trainee conveyancers will be presumed to have a basic knowledge of the art of letter writing, and will build on that experience through writing letters, and then move on to drafting. That, however, may be too big a presumption.

Yet, the writing of letters is most important as the firm's clients assess the firm from the letters it writes, if they are unclear or badly presented, the clients will not be impressed. It is said that in the Disney complex in Florida, the two most important categories of staff are the ticket sellers, and the people who pick up the garbage. The reason for this is that these people form the first impression that the public has of the parks, and first impressions set the public mood for the day. Similarly, if asked the same question, a legal firm's clients might answer (a) the telephonist and (b) the letter writers.

Nothing will put clients off more than a surly, unhelpful, or incompetent telephonist,[1] or, similarly, a badly written letter that the client cannot understand. As a case in point let us consider the following letter, written by a trainee, and thankfully intercepted by a partner:

'Dear Sirs,

Your Court Case

We refer to Mr Hope's appearance in court on your behalf. We had in fact minuted for a decree but before this was granted the sheriff clerk advised us that the defenders had lodged a motion asking the court to allow a late NID.

We lodged a notice of opposition and the diet was fixed for today to hear the motion.

The Defenders' agent was seeking to have the NID allowed, although late, and then to sist the action for legal aid on the basis that the matter was res judicata. We opposed this on the basis that there was no excuse for the late appearance, and their legal argument was misconceived. Alternatively we argued that, instead of a sist, the court should simply fix an Options Hearing immediately.

The Sheriff had to proceed on the basis that the statements of the agents are taken pro veritate, but he was uncertain enough to take the matter to avizandum.

We trust that this clarifies the matter. We shall be in touch once there has been an advising.

Yours faithfully'

This is not, on the face of it, a bad letter, and would be quite acceptable if written by one legal firm to another, but, for a letter to a client, it is disastrous, full of legal jargon—some of it in Latin—and not making things at all clear to the poor client.

What the letter is trying to say is that the firm raised an action, and by the date of calling of the action, the defenders had not lodged a notice of intention to defend (a 'NID'). The lawyer, therefore, went to court intending to ask for a decree ('a judgement') against the defenders.

It turned out that, in the meantime, the defenders' agents had lodged a late NID, and were about to ask the sheriff to allow this NID, although it had been lodged late. This is a routine application, and is usually allowed in the name of justice, on the presentation of any excuse, and expression of remorse. The defenders' agents then wanted to sist the case (ie to continue it indefinitely, without further procedure) to allow an application to be made for legal aid to be considered, which can take some time. The grounds for the application, if substantiated, namely that the case had already been decided and was, therefore, *res judicata.*

The sheriff had decided that the case must be treated on the basis that the defenders must be treated as true (*pro veritate*, until proved otherwise), but the sheriff would take time to think about the proposition (ie take the matter to *avizandum*).

In due course the writer will be told what the sheriff has decided ('an advising') and, in turn, will advise the client.

This was a difficult letter to write, and to read for that matter, but would have been much clearer if legal jargon and Latin words had not been used without any form of explanation. The golden rule is use plain English, and read through the finished letter thinking what, if anything, each phrase will mean to the eventual reader.

Note:

1   For a consumer's perspective, see 'Joe Public' 'Your call is important to us ...' The Journal, October 2005, pp 28, 29 available online

2.02 Each firm will have their own rules and house styles, of course, but the remarks that follow may be of interest:

(1) **Address.** Considerable annoyance and delay can be caused by an incorrectly addressed letter. Always make sure that you have the correct address, and the correct post code, which can be quickly checked by reference to the directory of post codes issued by the Royal Mail. If you use a district name, be sure to name it correctly, otherwise great offence may be caused.

If sending mail overseas, make sure that the town and country are correctly, and currently, named and that there has not been a change. For example, do not send a letter to Bombay, which is now called Mumbai. If you write abroad frequently, it is as well to keep an up-to-date atlas or gazetteer to hand, as well as an up-to-date legal directory—do not rely on old ones, they are positively dangerous, and best thrown out.

Most firms use window envelopes to avoid letters being put in the wrong envelopes, and to avoid duplication of work. In that case, the address should show clearly in the middle of the window. Be sure that you know the line numbers for the address on your word processor to achieve this. The letter should then be folded in no more than three equal portions to provide a neat finish. If a letter is folded unequally, or too many times, the result is unattractive and unprofessional.

(2) **Addressees.** This is something which is barely noticed if done correctly, but can cause great offence if done incorrectly. Use Mr, Mrs, Ms, or Miss as appropriate, but be sure to get the correct title. If not, you will not be forgiven lightly. In these less formal days, it may not be necessary to use a title at all, just simply the name. But be very careful before adopting this informality. It is probably all right for younger addressees, but may not go down well with older people. This will probably be the common usage in a few years time, but being in advance of fashion is not necessarily a good idea.

When addressing a male, the feudal title 'Esquire' or 'Esq' may be used. Again this practice is in decline and will probably disappear eventually—in the meantime, never use it with Mr, it is either one or the other. In the USA it is not widely used, but the American Bar Association, in a recent meeting held in London, referred to all delegates as Esquire, whether they were male or female.

A letter to two unmarried women is conventionally addressed to the 'Misses Margaret and Mary Snokes'. How much longer this practice will continue in this politically correct era, is anyone's guess.

Unincorporated partnerships are correctly addressed as 'Messrs. Snokes'. Partnerships consisting entirely of women should, by the same token, be addressed as 'Mesdames Snokes' but this is a bit pernickety, and the term 'Messrs' may be thought sufficiently androgynous not to cause offence.

Married couples are addressed as 'Mr and Mrs John Snokes', which may be a bit strong if the wife has pronounced feminist views. At least we do not have the German usage of 'Frau General' or 'Frau Professor' for married women.

Limited Companies should be addresses 'Snokes Ltd' or 'Snokes PLC' or 'Snokes LLP' as appropriate, but never as 'Messrs Snokes Ltd'.

Modes of address of various dignitaries, from the Royal Family downwards, can be found in *Debrett's Correct Form*, which is 'an inclusive guide to everything from drafting Wedding Invitations to Addressing an Archbishop'. Correct form is still important.

(3) **Ending the Letter.** Letters to persons you do not know should be started off with 'Dear Sir' or 'Dear Madam'. The use of a first name or any other address is highly presumptuous. The letter should be ended 'Yours faithfully', not 'Yours sincerely' which is reserved for people you

do know. Again house styles should be observed. One major Scottish legal firm uses 'Yours Truly' on all its correspondence, and indeed most word processing packages suggest this wording.

In very formal letters, for example to Royalty and other elevated persons, letters may end with the words 'I have the pleasure to remain your humble and obedient servant'. This usage can occasionally be seen (eg in a letter to the editor of *The Times* by Michael Shrimpton of 14 August 2001), but this usage is definitely on the way out in these egalitarian days.

Invitations written in third party form (eg Mr and Mrs John Snokes request the pleasure of the company of Mr and Mrs William Vole at the wedding of their daughter Julia...) are usually replied to in the same manner. Thus 'Mr and Mrs William Vole thank Mr and Mrs John Snokes for their kind invitation to .... and have great pleasure in accepting'. This may sound very old fashioned, but it has the merit of presenting some uniformity and ease of handling to acceptances, which cards, ordinary letters, emails or texts certainly do not have.

Employees of a firm should not use the firm's letterheads for private correspondence. If they do so, they may face disciplinary charges for theft of the firm's property and impersonisation.

Golden rule: while these conventions may seem antediluvian, it is as well to follow them at least initially until you can be sure that the addressee is ready for a 'Dear Jim' correspondence.

(4) **Punctuation.** This is still a matter of extreme importance, proper punctuation lends style and elegance to a letter, and can often prevent disaster. For example, a tabloid newspaper recently had a badly written headline, which was saved from disaster by a comma: 'My nightmare as X was murdered, by his girlfriend'. The wording, without the comma, would indicate that the girlfriend murdered the unfortunate victim, which was not the case. Lack of proper punctuation makes the letter turgid, and possibly even dangerous, where the reader is left snatching for a meaning, and possibly reaches the wrong conclusion, as so nearly happened in the above example. The reasons for a zero tolerance approach to punctuation, and other rules of punctuation and examples, are given in *Eats, Shoots and Leaves* (Profile Books Ltd, 2003) the best seller by Lynne Truss.

(a) *comma and apostrophe*—These are probably the most misused punctuation marks.

The comma, as we have seen, can help the reader to an easy understanding, but if it is used improperly, it is an irritant, and can completely alter the meaning of a sentence. The Lockheed

Corporation misplaced a comma in a quotation adjusting the price of a Hercules aircraft when inflation changed. The resulting loss was believed to be $70m (*Scotland on Sunday*, 20 June 1999.) Some drafters leave out commas in case they alter the meaning of a sentence, but this is not a correct approach; used carefully, punctuation is there to assist the drafter. The general rule of commas is that they occur where a gentle pause in the sentence is required, or where the person reading the letter aloud might draw breath. An example is given by Lynne Truss: 'A woman, without her man, is nothing' can alternatively be read, without punctuation, as 'A woman: without her, man is nothing'. Punctuation can, indeed, make a vital difference.

The apostrophe is another punctuation mark that is widely misused eg 'lorry's turning' (a sign seen at Glasgow Airport) or 'CD's' (a sign in a supermarket) or the greengrocers' apostrophe-'apple's and pear's'. An apostrophe is properly used to indicate possession (John's book) or to mark a missing letter (it's for it is). None of the lorry, the CD, nor the apples and pears possess anything or are missing anything, and are, thus, complete nonsense.

The rules of the apostrophe are:

(i)   For nouns in the singular ending with an S, the possessive is formed by adding an apostrophe with an S, eg Burns's poems. Otherwise for singular nouns, there is usually added apostrophe S, eg the dog's basket.

(ii)   For nouns in the plural ending with an S, the apostrophe follows the S, eg the dogs' kennels.

(iii)   Names ending in ES usually add an apostrophe at the end, eg Moses' law, or Charles' house.

(iv)   Where the word is used collectively to comprise a number of people, the possessive is formed by adding an apostrophe and an S, eg the people's flag, the company's assets (not the companies' assets).

(b)   *Full stops*—The full stop indicates the end of a sentence, but do not forget that a sentence should include a main clause and a finite verb. Thus writing of the late Duke of Windsor, when he was captain of the Royal and Ancient Golf Club in St. Andrews (nb no apostrophe), a newspaper wrote: 'Talking of golf the Duke of Windsor never uses a tee when driving. Just drops a ball and bangs it away. If he uses a tee he is likely to fluff or make an air shot. As he did with his inaugural drive as captain of St Andrews'. This is a bad example of journalese, which is acceptable in a tabloid, but not in correspondence. The second sentence has two finite verbs, but they have no subject (eg it would be all right if it said 'The Duke just drops a ball and bangs it away'); and the fourth sentence contains no finite verb.

It would have been better grammar had the journalist used a semicolon between the third and fourth sentences, which is a half-way house between a full stop and a comma (see the next paragraph), instead of starting a new sentence.

(c)   *Colons and semicolons*—These devices are used as a half-way house between a comma and a full stop. For example, in the following quotation 'The candidate could not be said to give a very good impression; he looked as if he needed a good wash' the use of a full stop to separate the two sentences would be too jerky. A comma could not be used without a conjunction, eg 'The candidate could not be said to give a very good impression, *since* he looked as if he needed a good wash'.

The colon is a rather more finite stop than the semi-colon. The former is more akin to the full stop; the latter to the comma. The traditional legal deed is one long sentence, broken only by semicolons, and the end signified by the use of a colon.

There was a short discussion on semicolons in *The Times* in the spring of 2001, mainly expressing alarm at the complete misunderstanding that generally exists of this useful punctuation mark. Eric Dehn of Bristol stated:

> 'Examiners are dispassionate , but if you succeed infiltrating one semicolon into an essay, they will be so filled with nostalgic delight that a pass grade is assured.'

A useful tip for students, but Philip Hobsbaum of Glasgow warned:

> 'This may be so, but not because it is a sign of the student's literacy. To an old, experienced and necessarily cynical examiner like myself, a semicolon these days is *prima facie* evidence of plagiarism.'

Hopefully we will not abandon the colon or the semi-colon.

(d)   *Dash*—The dash may be, and is, used as a substitute for a comma or semicolon, eg 'The candidate could not be said to give a very good impression—he looked as if he needed a good wash'. There was a prejudice against using the dash in formal correspondence, but it is now quite acceptable, and really rather useful.

(e)   *Brackets*—These are useful when used, with caution, to isolate certain subsidiary information from the main sentence, but they should not be used as an alternative to commas and semicolons, as they rudely interrupt the flow of the sentence, prolong the length of the sentence, and make it harder to understand. However, the use of bracketed information may, in some cases, be inevitable.

2.03 The question of grammar is rather neglected nowadays, as it is not taught to any extent in schools, to the fury of the elderly who learnt grammar the hard way along with multiplication tables and books of the bible, and other routine information which can be very easily found these days. An examiner wrote:

'My concern is that sometimes the students have such a great deal of difficulty with the language that there is really no way they can possibly become lawyers at any reasonable level.'

While we do not necessarily agree with this gloomy view, the writer has a fair point—a mastery of clear and unambiguous English is an essential for the practice of law, and lawyers must learn to be absolutely precise in their use of the language.

Length has virtually nothing to do with good writing. Brevity and conciseness are actually a great virtue. Consider the following definition of a bed prepared by the National Health Service:

'**Bed.** A device or arrangement that may be used to permit a patient to lie down when the need to do so is a consequence of the patient's condition, such as examination, diagnostic investigation, manipulative treatment, obstetric delivery or transport. Beds, couches, or trolleys are also counted as hospital beds where:

(a)   used regularly to permit a patient to lie down rather than for merely examination or transport (eg in a day surgery ward);

(b)   used while attending for a specific short procedure taking an hour or less such as endoscopy, provided that such devices are used only because of the patient's condition;

(c)   used regularly as a means of support for patients needing a lengthy procedure such as renal dialysis (includes special chairs etc.);

(d)   used regularly to allow patients to lie down after sedation.

Note: a device specifically and solely for the purpose of delivery should not be counted as a bed.'

Unsurprisingly this definition was the winner of the Plain English Campaign Golden Bull Award. It is hardly an improvement on the dictionary definition of a bed as 'a piece of furniture on which to sleep'.

The Law Society of Scotland, who should know better, produced this example of gobbledygook on their website, found by Donald Reid, who, as well as chairing a large legal firm in Glasgow, is also an occasional columnist for the *Scotsman:*

> 'Diversity is about harnessing potential to create a productive environment in which the equally diverse needs of the customer/client can be met in a creative environment.'

Donald Reid comments—'How do you feel when you read a sentence like that? For me it is instant exhaustion'.

Try to avoid claptrap like this, even though it comes from the highest source.

2.04 There are a number of traps in the English language, which can present serious difficulties. These are not made any easier by the onslaught of political correctness, with its zero tolerance of any mistakes. Thus, the English language has no equivalent of the useful gender neutral 'on' of the French language. A possible alternative is to use 'one' which is clearly related to 'on', but the usage is rather affected.

There is no distinction between 'you' in the singular and 'you' in the plural. Writers are urged to avoid the use of the pronoun 'he' when they mean persons of either gender, which is fair enough, but it is difficult in practice. The alternative is to use he/she or (s)he, which are both very clumsy. The better course is to use the plural as much as possible, except when quoting from older writers, and non gender specific words, eg 'firefighter' rather than 'fireman'.

Just when English lost the distinction between 'thee' (singular) and 'you' (exclusively plural) is unclear, but they are certainly used to great effect in the King James Bible ('Whither thou goest, I shall go; and where thou lodgest, I will lodge; thy people shall be my people, and thy God my God' Ruth. Ch 1 v 15–17).

In the Glasgow patois there is a clear difference between 'you' (singular) and 'youse' (plural), but one could hardly expect this to be welcomed in Edinburgh legal circles. In the meantime we must cope with the highly imprecise 'you'—as in 'can you come to dinner next Saturday?'—which can either mean the person who is spoken to, or that person with partner and family. Letter writers must handle 'you' with great care, in order that the reader does not misunderstand.

2.05 Let your letter breathe. Use spaces to break up the heavy impression of type. There is really no excuse for a badly-typed letter these days, for the word processor can do the most wonderful tricks to improve the layout of your letter. Unfortunately, the content is not so easily sorted.

Your letter should not be too cramped. Paragraphs and sentences should not be too long. The Plain English Campaign, which has done much good work in the direction of clear business writing, suggests the following rules:

(a)   sentences should not exceed an average of 15 to 20 words;

(b)   letters should be written in everyday English, ie avoid jargon and Latin tags;

(c)   words like 'we' and 'you' should be used instead of 'the insured', 'the applicant' 'the Society' and so on;

(d)   headings may be used which are clear and helpful. The scope of a word processor should be used to make these headings stand out from the text;

(e)   use a good point size and a clear type face;

(f)   an average line length will be between seven and 12 words.

It is helpful to think about your letter for two or three minutes before writing it, and to plan the order of the contents. Nothing is more depressing and unhelpful than reading a letter which has obviously been dictated by the writer, probably into a machine, without any prior thought, and which is merely a disorganised train of thought.

When your letter has been drafted, you should then read it through and correct it, which is easily done with a word processor. It does not now mean the embarrassment of having to ask someone to destroy a letter they may have taken a long time to type, and retype it.

The use of a spell checker, or a grammar checker, on a computer is to be encouraged, as these may detect many small errors. They should not, however, be left as the final arbiters of what is right and what is wrong—that is the drafter's job, with the aid of a good modern dictionary. Spellcheckers tend to suggest American English spellings, which although they are often more logical than the British version (eg 'catalog' instead of 'catalogue') but are nevertheless wrong in British usage.

There is no harm in introducing a few personal touches, where appropriate. It is not advisable in a serious legal letter, which just may be produced in court at a later date. Furthermore you should bear in mind what is liable to be the reaction of the recipient—if in doubt, keep your letter formal.

The letter should be legibly signed, with your name, as you wish to be addressed, printed beneath. Women, in particular, should indicate how they should be addressed—Mrs/Miss/ or Ms names which are gender neuter, such as Chris, let alone Kris, should specify the title. There is nothing worse than getting a reply addressed to 'Dear Sir or Madam'.

2.06 Latin terms and jargon words. These are to be strictly avoided when writing to lay person. They should also be avoided in correspondence with other members of the profession—with the exception that they are acceptable when there is no clear alternative in standard English. Certain Latin expressions have a set meaning, and may not be easily translatable. Such a phrase is the useful *mutatis mutandis*, which can be roughly translated as 'changing that which has to be changed'. If you are making a will on behalf of a spouse, you might make a will on behalf of the other spouse *mutatis mutandis*, that is changing names and hes and shes, but otherwise leaving the contents of the two wills the same. The Latin term is clearer and more elegant, and may be used in correspondence with other professionals who should understand exactly what is meant, but never to a lay person who will only be confused.

In recent times, the learning of Latin was more or less universal, but is not today, even among lawyers and doctors whose professions use Latin tags as virtually standard. Latin phrases are being slowly eradicated from Scots law by the good work of the Scottish Law Commission. We have already lost such phrases as *rei interventus* and *actio quanti minoris* which always required extensive explanation, and which are now statutorily translated into English.

In England there is similarly a move towards the removal of Latin from legal proceedings. The then Lord Chief Justice Wolff told the American Bar Association (*The Times*, 20 July 2000) that he had already promoted the scrapping of Latin in the civil courts, and hoped that the same would apply in the criminal courts. Simultaneously he announced the abolition of the court order of *certiorari*, which would be known henceforth as a 'quashing order'.

The effect of this announcement was slightly diminished by the report of the cases of *Arthur JS Hall & Co v Simons Barratt* and *Wolff v Seddon*, which were reported in *The Times* 21 July 2000 which referred to the maxims *nemo debit bis vexari pro una et eadem causa* (a person should not be troubled twice for the same reason) and *interest rei publicae ut finis sit litium* (there is a general public interest in the same matter not being litigated over again). Obviously the task is more difficult than Lord Wolff might think.

The main attraction of using Latin is that it is a dead language, and the meanings of words cannot change, and have not changed. In contrast English is a living language, which accepts words and the meaning of words from all sorts of sources. A teenager of Asian origin was quoted as saying, when Leeds United players were charged on racial charges, 'We're crazy for football and Leeds United, they're just wicked'. The use of the word 'wicked' has completely changed in certain usages to an expression of approval, rather than the traditional meaning of 'offensive, unpleasant and troublesome' and usually referring to pantomime characters such as the wicked witch.

Herein lies a dilemma for the legal drafter: words must be given their meaning at the time of writing, rather than at the time of reading. The rule of construction known as—*contemporanea expositio* applies, ie the contemporaneous meaning of the word is the best and strongest in the law. You must know the meaning of the word in question at the time it was written, and not the present meaning of the word. You may require to consult an old dictionary to find out what the word meant when it was written. For example James VII when he first saw St Paul's Cathedral pronounced it 'amusing, awful and artificial'. It would be wrong to assume that James had the same opinion of contemporary architecture, as does the current Prince of Wales; in fact he found the building, in the contemporary meaning of the words pleasing to look at (amusing) deserving of awe (awful) and full of skilled artifice (artificial).

The conveyancer must, therefore, remember the contemporary meaning of the word, and not simply assume that it has a modern meaning which the writer could not have foreseen.

For this reason 'business school' English or 'psychobabble' or slang should not be used by the careful drafter, because people in the future may have a different meaning for the words, or, hopefully, they will be forgotten. These 'key' words are hard enough to understand today, and the situation can only get worse.

As an example of the worst kind of meaningless jargon, we turn to an offering by the Supreme Court. 'When expenses are awarded, the court pronounces two interlocutors, the award of expenses itself and the decerniture for those expenses. The significance of the decerniture is that the interlocutor finally determines part of, or the whole, of a case; that has a consequence that the decree may be extracted'.

What can they mean? Was any thought given to the meaning of these words, if they have any meaning at all? It just goes to show that a little calm thought must go into the words chosen, and the impact that they will have on the reader, lay or professional.

The legal drafter should have a perfect knowledge of the language, which basically only comes from extensive reading of literature, and writing. That is why it is suggested that the drafter learns by writing letters, and reading as much good English as possible. Lawyers should be confidently using English, which is now used worldwide, and not hide behind preposterous tags of a long dead language.

Part Two
The Transaction

Chapter 3

MARKETING THE PROPERTY

'We were very concerned, bearing in mind the Property Misdescriptions Act, that we would be misleading by not telling about a ghost, but also misleading if we did come clean about it and then it didn't appear. We felt that if we knew of a ghost which eventually appeared it would only seem fair to tell the purchasers in case they freaked out later when they saw it.'

(Christopher Calcutt, estate agent in Kent, discussing the problems of haunted houses: The Sunday Times)

3.01 Most sale and purchase transactions start with houseowners deciding to move, and putting their property up for sale, although it is not unknown for the purchaser to initiate the process. It has been suggested that the entire contracting process could be speeded up if the seller issued an offer of sale, rather than the other way around. This idea has yet to be tested thoroughly.

As discussed (para **1.12**) the marketing process is not part of the solicitors' monopoly, and may be done by anyone. The choice between solicitor and estate agent is the houseowners', and to a large extent the answer to this question will depend on the services respectively offered, and the part of the country in which the house is situated.

3.02 For present purposes we shall assume that the houseowners choose to employ a solicitor to market the property, and that the solicitor is a member of a solicitors' property centre (SPC). It should be made quite clear, however, that property marketing has become a separate skill, and if a solicitor is to market property it must be done professionally and properly.

3.03 Some solicitors, particularly in Glasgow, may prefer to pass the marketing of houses to estate agents, and this is usually done on a reciprocal basis of instruction. In the case of a reciprocal arrangement being reached it should be remembered:

(a)   That a solicitor may not share with any unqualified person any profits or fees derived from any business transacted by solicitors in Scotland in the course of, or in connection with, their practice.

(b)   Formerly under Practice Rules, a solicitor might not share an office in conjunction with a person who was not legally qualified. This rule has now been relaxed, provided that there is no question of breach of confidentiality in the sharing of staff, and provided that the accommodation is self-contained, and provided there is no suggestion of business being channelled unfairly to the solicitor by the other party involved. If you contemplate such an arrangement, it would be best to obtain a waiver from the Law Society. Among waivers granted are for small offices in supermarkets, and a solicitor and accountant in a remote area using the same premises on alternate days.

(c)   That the basic philosophy of the Law Society is that the only acceptable form of channelling clients to a solicitor is on the personal recommendation of a satisfied client, although the Society admits that it is not always possible to prevent 'less desirable' forms of enticement (Law Society Annual Report 1981, p 14).

(d)   Any suggestion of unfair enticement of clients should be most scrupulously avoided.

In essence the question of whether or not to use an estate agent is one of circumstances, and the only important criterion is the interest of the clients, which in the long run is also the interest of the solicitor.

3.04 If your clients are going to employ an estate agent, it is as well that the wording of the contract is carefully considered. A contract is only likely to diminish the rights of the client. The estate agents will seek sole selling rights, that is they are entitled to commission if the property is sold during the agreed period, whoever finds the buyer—even if it is the clients themselves. Some agents will try to make the agreed period a long one—six weeks should be sufficient, and not any longer. As to commission, the law is quite clear on the subject: if the estate agent is instrumental in the sale of the house, the agent is entitled to claim commission at the standard rate (*Walker Fraser & Steele v Fraser's Trustees* 1910 SC 222). If the agent is unsuccessful, the agent is then entitled to a reasonable remuneration for work done (*quantum meruit*) and for refunding of outlays incurred.

In particular, the clients should not be panicked into employing two agencies. The dangers of this arrangement were highlighted in an unreported case in Paisley Sheriff Court.

Mr and Mrs A decided to sell their house, and asked estate agents F to handle the sale. F duly advertised the sale, and several parties, including a Mr Q, inspected the property. No sale resulted. Mr and Mrs A then saw a property advertised by estate agents Z, and while negotiating with Z, they decided to entrust the sale of their own house to Z. They signed Z's standard sale contract, which required a commission to be paid on sale, whether they were instrumental in effecting a sale or not.

In the meantime, Mr Q returned from abroad, looked again at Mr and Mrs A's house, and bought it. Agents F claimed a commission as they had introduced Mr Q to the sellers. Agents Z also claimed a commission in terms of their contract, which granted them a sole selling agency. It was held that Mr and Mrs A had to pay both agents. (See also *Lordsgate Properties v Balcombe* [1985] 1 EGLR 20, (1985) 274 EG 493, and an article 'Double Jeopardy' in the *Scottish Law Gazette* December 1985.)

3.05 At whatever stage the solicitor is instructed (and we are assuming here that it is at the outset, although sometimes it is not so simple—the first thing you know about your client's intention to sell is when an offer drops onto your desk) the first thing is to obtain the title deeds of the property. This is important in order that you can ascertain whether or not the title is a registered one, and if there are any unusual conditions of title, such as rights of pre-emption or unusual servitude rights.

If the land certificate or the titles are missing, extracts or quick copies may be obtained from the appropriate Land or Sasine Register. It is also helpful at this stage to obtain a property enquiry certificate from the relevant local authority or from searchers, planning certificates, building warrants, completion certificates, a coal mining report, and guarantees of timber treatment, and double glazing. In the case of a first registration, it is also important to receive a form 10A report, which is equivalent to a Sasine Register search, and form P16 report (paras **12.03** and **12.04**) lest there be any major discrepancy in the boundaries. Many of the searching firms now provide a 'multisearch', consisting of the property enquiry certificate, form 10A and P16 report for a combined fee and also a free form 11A report.

These papers should all be scrutinised carefully to ensure that there is nothing in them which would make a sale difficult, such as a preseved right of pre-emption (see para **8.27**) or in land registration cases, an exclusion of indemnity (see para **11.11**) on the land certificate. Bearing in mind the complexity of offers, and the number of warranties that are now required it is as well to know your title before entering into missives, and if there is a weakness in your title, to compromise it with the purchasers' agents before missives are concluded. Better that than to reveal the weakness after conclusion of missives, when the purchasers may be happy to accept a breach of warranty, given blindly, as an excuse to resile from the transaction.

3.06 Armed with as much knowledge as possible, the solicitors who are marketing the property through their own firm, can then prepare property details and instruct advertising.

It is, therefore, suggested that the solicitor who engages in selling houses should adopt a procedure broadly similar to that outlined here (although practice will obviously vary from office to office).

(a)   **Visit the house in question, and take measurements and details.** Take a photograph for publicity purposes. Measurements should be accurately given in metres, as required by the Units of Measurements Regulations 1994. Because the government has never properly standardised measurements, most people, however, still deal with imperial measurements, and the regulations permit subsidiary measurements in feet and inches, which most people understand. The conversion should, however, be made accurately, as they are replied upon for ordering carpets and working out areas. Arrange the viewing— the easiest arrangement is to have the owners show the property, at times that suit them. If the house is empty, you can arrange to show it, but you may wish to agree extra remuneration for this. It is advisable that, wherever possible, two people conduct the viewings, and a representative of your firm should not be alone in an empty house, especially at night. If the house is empty, make sure that you have the key, and at least one spare in the office. NEVER let the key out of your control.

(b)   **If the clients ask you to advise them on how to make the property more attractive to buyers, there are a few basic rules:** Make the house and garden appear attractive from the street; attend to essential repairs; don't spend money on expensive redecoration which may not be to potential buyers' tastes, and is thus a waste of money; keep the house clean and tidy and well lit and as attractive as possible from the outside— so-called 'kerb appeal'; avoid cooking and other smells—even freshly ground coffee, which, contrary to legend, some viewers may not like; make sure that there is a parking space for buyers' cars; be ready to show the house at short notice. While furnishing, decor and personal items are usually insignificant compared to structure and location, it is nevertheless important to make a good impression on potential buyers, so declutter.

(c) **Form a reasoned evaluation and advise the client.** Consult a website to find out prices recently obtained for similar houses, eg www.scotlandshouseprices.gov.uk or www.nethouseprices.com. If in doubt, consult a chartered surveyor for a valuation. The question of the surveyor's fee should, however, be discussed with the client before the surveyor is instructed.

(d) **Instruct a 'For Sale' board and prepare an attractive, concise and truthful advertisement, giving rough details and a telephone number for further details and viewing.** If the house is not constantly occupied, do not indicate this by saying, for example 'viewing after 6pm'. You might as well put a notice in the *Crooks Gazette* intimating that the house will be unoccupied all day. Do not waste your clients' money on wasteful and over-elaborate advertisements. Eschew the temptation to advertise your firm more than the property. Outline your advertising proposals to your client, and provide a rough guide to the cost. When writing the advertisement, stick to the facts—try to avoid 'estate agentese'; some actual examples:

'Situated at a desirable crossroads';

'Designed by the celebrated Scottish architect, Ronnie Mackintosh';

'set in a child-safe cul-de-sac within this sought-after developing area';

'with a field for the possible horse';

'suitable for the disearning (*sic*) purchaser';

'with an Adam TV den';

'positively oozing with olde worlde charm';

'with a 9ft high widow, overlooking the garden';

'with a glazed door in vestibule leading to hell'

'property situated in a beautiful curved cresent'.

Such language is a casualty of the Property Misdescriptions Act 1991 (PMA 1991), which insists on property being accurately described. Prosecutions under this Act and its associated Regulations are relatively rare in Scotland, as breaches of the law are usually dealt with by compensation. There are, however, recorded instances in England of prosecutions where a house was described as 'south facing' when in fact it faced north, and did not accordingly enjoy the same amount of sun. Another case was where a farm building was described as having a three-phase power supply, which was not the case.

Travel agents have had this problem for years and have evolved a new form of language which describes the property in an attractive way but cannot be held as untruthful. Thus 'rapidly developing resort' means tower cranes and 'ideal for sun worshippers' means there's nothing else to do. Resorts described as 'lively' should generally be avoided by the elderly. Estate agents are following suit.

(e) **Similarly, prepare a schedule of particulars to be handed out to reasonably interested enquirers, giving truthful and accurate particulars of the house, preferably with a photograph and location plan (if available) attached.** Moveable items included in the sale should be clearly specified. Bear in mind PMA 1991 which makes it a criminal offence for an agent to misdescribe a property, or to 'touch up' a photograph to give a false impression. A semi-detached house can be photographed in such a way as to make it appear detached, but this is not allowed. The Property Misdescriptions (Specified Matters) Order 1992 gives a list of specified matters that must be correctly stated in particulars of the property.

Oddly enough PMA 1991 ignores a misdescription by a person who sells the house personally.

(f) **Set a sensible asking price in consultation with the client.** If this is set too low, people will wonder what is wrong with the property. If it is set too high, they will be scared off. Estate agents have a practice of setting a low price, and expecting offers at least 15–20% above. The asking price is thus equivalent to the upset price in an auction, and potential purchasers are left in the dark as to what price is acceptable. This is contrary to English practice, where the asking price is fairly accurate, and buyers can sometimes negotiate a price lower than that asked. The Scottish practice was referred to the Office of Fair Trading, as a possible example of a property misdescription, but the objection was not sustained. It is difficult to see why Scottish practice should differ from the English, and indeed largely universal practice, and it is encouraging to note the number of sales that are now advertised at a 'fixed price' (see **5.04**).

(g) **Register the house with the local solicitors' property centre,** if that is the chosen method of sale, which will help with the marketing by providing a 'high street' display facility for all properties, and will publish an advertisement in its regular property list. The centres charge a one-off fee, and will hold the property until it is sold. If the sale is slow after a period of months the SPC may seek a re-insertion fee. The solicitor will supply the SPC with details of the property and a supply of property schedules. Bear in mind that the SPC will not arrange for sale boards. These are the responsibility of the solicitor. The SPC will put the details on the internet, display them in its centre, and publish them in its weekly newspaper. It will also make available to prospective purchasers copies of the property schedule.

(h) **Obtain as much information as you can, as soon as you can.** The sellers' solicitor should at this stage obtain the property enquiry certificate, matrimonial and any necessary matrimonial and family homes affidavits required in terms of the Matrimonial Homes (Family Protection) (Scotland) Act 1981 and the Civil Partnership Act 2004 (see **App I**). The reason for this is to avoid unfortunate delays by others at a future date, when the pressure is on you.

(i) **Keep main details (e g price, entry, moveables included, rateable value etc) preferably on computer or a card index.** Keep a list of all serious enquiries for future reference. Note in particular all formal notifications of interest, preferably on the back of the card.

(j) **Fix a closing date and advise all parties who have notified interest when it becomes clear that there is going to be competition**. The rule of thumb used to be that a closing date should be set once two surveyors had valued the property. In the property hotspots that emerged in recent years, the practice has been either to 'buy' the survey from the firm of surveyors who have already valued the property or to instruct an offer subject to survey. A good agent should have a feel of when there is sufficient serious interest to merit a closing date. Collect all offers, and arrange to discuss these with the sellers, giving them your advice. Accept the offer most attractive to your clients (see para **5.01**) and advise all unsuccessful offerors.

(k) **When missives are concluded, inform the property centre, cancel all advertisements and remove all boards etc.** Nothing so much infuriates the general public as applying for details of an advertised house and being informed that it's under offer.

3.07 The big London broadsheets are rapidly catching on to the concept that, with the internet, the expensive services of estate agents may not be necessary, and that the main expense of selling a house is not that of legal expenses. Take a house, valued at £400,000, the estate agent charges 2% say, which is £8,000, while the lawyer charges a few hundred pounds for the better part of the work involved. The machinery now exists, through the property centres, for property to be advertised on the internet, while solicitors have hopefully got better at marketing and have staff dedicated to sales, who are not necessarily lawyers. Solicitors should therefore be able to offer a better 'one stop' service.

Chapter 4

THE PURCHASER MAKES OVERTURES

Carpe diem, quam minimum credula postero. (Seize the day, place as little trust as possible in tomorrow.)

4.01 A Purchase file might look like this, with comments in italics:

Purchase of 3 Miller Drive, Newton Mearns, Renfrewhire (Glasgow G77 10EU)

File note by Henry Pink, partner of Brown, Jarvie & Walker dated 06.02.06.

Attendance at meeting with Stuart and Henrietta James. I met them through mutual friends recently, who had recommended the firm to them. Noting that Mr and Mrs James were interested in purchasing a house at 3 Miller Drive, Newton Mearns, and wanted a lawyer to act on their behalf. Saying that we would be pleased to act on their behalf, and roughly explaining what we would charge, and what other expenses there would be, with special reference to Stamp Duty Land Tax, which if they bought at £250,000 would be £2,500. When they expressed surprise at the extent of this outlay, explaining that it was something we had no control over, it was simply another tax from which there was no escape. Similarly the land register charges and VAT are on a fixed scale, over which we have no control.

Noting that they were selling their house in the Lake District, and were obtaining a loan from their bank to cover bridging finance and any shortfall. Perusing the details of the house they were interested in (details attached), noting that the price was fixed, and that we would have to offer quickly. Noting that they were having the property surveyed, by their own surveyor, and would decide if they were to offer when the survey report was received. Explaining that we were required to establish their identity in conformity with the Money Laundering Regulations, and that, ridiculous as it might seem, I would have to see some evidence of their identity, such as passports or driving licences. Further explaining that although they were consulting the firm as a married couple, we would have to treat them as separate individuals with separate interests to protect which might lead to our having separate consultations with only one or the other being present. Saying that we would write a letter setting out the terms of our engagement and what would be likely to be the charges we would make.

Engaged 1 hour.

Note: A promising start. The partner dealing with the matter has explained to the clients the terms on which he proposes to act, and has outlined the main parts of the Money Laundering Regulations which are binding on all parties. The formalities must be observed, however irksome this may be. He has explained in advance the liability for SDLT, which the lay public have the unfortunate belief is another lawyers' fee, and not that the lawyer is merely an unpaid collector on behalf of HM Revenue and Customs. The SDLT position could be a lot worse—it is payable at 1% on the whole consideration between £125,000 and £250,000 (2006/07 figures); at 3% on the whole consideration between £250,000 (the price of a good flat in Edinburgh) and £500,000; and at 4% on the whole consideration over £500,000 (the price of a good house in London).

It is unlikely that the James will be engaged in money laundering, but one never knows, and the Regulations require that the conveyancer be satisfied, and that there is evidence on the file to that effect, to satisfy the Law Society, as regulator. This is the same law that requires you to produce evidence of identity even when you are opening a small bank account. It is surprising just how many people are unable to identify themselves in particular by not having a passport or driving licence.

The price is fixed, which means that the first acceptable offer of the price asked will be accepted. This may mean that the house has proved difficult to sell, but there is no reason to hang about—it's first come, first served, so speed is of the essence in such matters. The clients are waiting for a survey report, and will decide whether to offer or not. They will take note of the seller's survey and questionnaire, but prefer to seek the advice of a surveyor who is acting on behalf of them, the purchasers.

4.02 Particulars of 3 Miller Drive, Newton Mearns, Renfrewshire

This is a delightful and spacious detached villa quietly situated in the residential suburb of Newton Mearns. Close to Whitecraigs railway station, with regular trains to Glasgow Central station, and to the motorway network, providing easy access to extensive shopping, cultural and sporting facilities. Nearby sporting facilities include Whitecraigs Tennis, Bowling and Golf Clubs. For enthusiastic dog walkers, nearby Rouken Glen provides ample exercise areas. For those with an artistic inclination, the nearby Burrell Collection provides an outlet. Good local shopping area, and several excellent schools.

The district is also a few miles from Glasgow and Prestwick Airports, with their frequent domestic and international flights.

The villa has been extended and upgraded to provide adaptable and well-maintained accommodation and is presented in good decorative order. It comprises a hall, sitting/dining room, four bedrooms, two bathrooms, utility area, and a rear porch. The property also benefits from full gas central heating and double glazing throughout. It was recently rewired.

The property is set back off the main access road and has a long gravel driveway to one side which leads to the attached double garage and provides extensive off-road parking. A most attractive feature of the property is the lovely garden with high walls. The front of the property catches the sun throughout the afternoon and into the late evening and there is a charming patio area with colourful flowers and dappled shade from the established trees.

Beyond this there is a large, easily maintained area of lawn enclosed by hedging and fencing. At the rear the garden features a gravel patio area with access to both the garage and the sun porch, an area of lawn and colourful herbaceous borders and herb garden. The back garden is sheltered and receives the sun in the morning, and through much of the afternoon. A timber shed provides useful external storage.

In detail the accommodation comprises:

Fully glazed entrance door opens into the Hall.

HALL

Laminate flooring. Radiator. Small built-in meter cupboard. Two pendant lights. Door to Bedroom 1 and Bathroom. Opening to Dining Kitchen. Fifteen-pane glazed door to Sitting/Dining Room.

SITTING/DINING ROOM: 24'7' × 12'9' (7.23m × 3.89m)

Double window to front. French windows to Rear Porch. Two radiators. Television aerial point. Telephone point. Open fireplace with Scandinavian multi-fuel stove in stone surround. Natural wood flooring. Recessed alcove with open shelving. Wiring for stereo speakers. Recessed alcove with exposed stone wall. Four wall lights. Door to Rear Porch.

DINING KITCHEN: 19'9' × 11'.0' (6.02m × 3.35m)

Window to side. Natural pine open staircase to upper floor. Natural wood flooring. Pine ceiling. Fitted wall and base units with co-ordinated worktop. Coloured circular sink and drainer. Bosch dishwasher. Slot in electric cooker with filter hood cover. Tiled splash back. Telephone point. Radiator. Extractor fan. Built-in storage cupboard with shelving. Built-in bookcases under staircase. Opening to Utility Area.

UTILITY AREA: 8'3' × 5'3' (2.51m × 1.58m)

Window with patterned glass to bathroom. Stainless steel sink and drainer. Plumbing for washing machine. Space for tumble drier. Wall-mounted gas central heating boiler. Tile splash back. Radiator. Spotlight. Natural wood floor. Fifteen-pane glazed door to Rear Porch. Opening to Dining Kitchen.

REAR PORCH: 12'9' × 6'3' (3.90m × 1.90m)

Glazed on three sides with French windows to garden. Radiator. Two wall lights. Natural wood flooring. Fifteen-pane glazed door to Utility Area with adjoining side screen with patterned glass. French windows to Sitting/Dining Room.

BEDROOM 1: 12'1' × 10'5' (3.69m × 3.18')

Window to front. Telephone point. Radiator. Pendant light. Door to Hall.

BATHROOM 1: 7'8' × 5'10' (2.35m × 1.78m)

Window with patterned glass to rear. Coloured three-piece suite with wash hand basin set in vanity unit. Tiling around bath area. Electric shower over bath. Shower screen. Radiator. Pine ceiling. Extractor fan. Two downlighters. Door to Hall.

FIRST FLOOR LANDING

Lit by roof light. Doors to Bedrooms 2, 3, and 4 and Bathroom. Storage cupboard with hanging rail and shelf above.

BEDROOM 2: 16'5' × 7'9' (4.95m × 2.36m)

Window to rear. Two windows to the side. Under eaves access for storage. Coombed ceilings. Radiator. Natural wood floor. Pendant light.

BEDROOM 3: 11'9' × 10'2' (3.56m × 3.06m) Window to front. Two storage cupboards in eaves. Telephone point. Radiator. Pendant light. Coombed ceilings.

BEDROOM 4: 14'10'× 7'11' (4.53m x 2.41m)

Window to front. Coombed ceilings. Radiator. Pendant light.

BATHROOM 2: 6'9' × 5'9' (2.05m × 1.75m)

Window to side. White three piece suite with tiling around bath area. Radiator. Extractor fan. Natural wood floor. Recessed alcove with shallow open shelves. Pendant light.

OUTSIDE

Gardens as previously described. Double garage with windows and door to rear garden. Timber shed. Storage area for bins.

FIXTURES AND FITTINGS

Included within the sale are the integrated oven, hob and extractor fan, all the fitted floor coverings and the custom-made kitchen blind.

COUNCIL TAX BAND 'E'

VIEWING

By appointment with Messrs O'Neill Middleton, Solicitors, Glasgow.

ENTRY

By arrangement, but not earlier than 15 April 2006.

PRICE

Fixed Price £250,000. Offers should be made in writing to O'Neill Middleton, 999 Lally Street, Glasgow G2 4XX.

While every effort is made to ensure the accuracy of these particulars, no warranty is given and prospective purchasers should satisfy themselves to their accuracy. In particular, the measurements given, while believed to be accurate, should not be used for ordering floor coverings or kitchen appliances.

Authorised to conduct investment business under the Financial Services Act 1986 by the Law Society of Scotland.

4.03 Email

From: Henry Pink <hpink@bjw.co.uk>

Sent: 6 February 2006 11:03

To: Property Department <property@bjw.co.uk>

CC: Veronica Vanbrugh <vvanbrugh@bjw.co.uk>

Subject: Mr & Mrs James—purchase of 3 Miller Drive.

Please look at the particulars of the house at 3 Miller Drive, Newton Mearns on the GSPC website and let me have your comments about (1) please ask the surveyor if the property is fully double glazed, as stated (2) can you please check from an Ordnance Survey map that it is feasible to enjoy as much sun as is stated (3) can you check that the metric measurements are accurately transferred to the imperial measurements (4) any other comments. HP

4.04 Email

From: Property Department <property@bjw.co.uk>

Sent: 6 February 2006 14:17

To: Henry Pink <hpink@bjw.co.uk>

CC: Veronica Vanbrugh vvanbrugh@bjw.co.uk Subject: Re: Mr & Mrs James—purchase of 3 Miller Drive.

We have checked the particulars, as requested. The surveyor says that not all of the windows are double glazed, as stated. We looked at the map, and find that the property faces Eastwards and can benefit from the sun as stated. The measurements correspond to each other. The house was advertised at 'offers over £275,000' but obviously did not sell at that price, probably because of the SDLT implications—sounds like a good buy at £250,000.

Note: It was sensible of Mr Pink to take the advice of his specialist property department, who have provided some useful information. The fact that the windows are not all double glazed is possibly an offence under the Property Misdescription Regulations, entitling the James to compensation. The point about SDLT is a valid one—at £275,000 the SDLT payable at 3% is no less than £8,250 which might put people off. Obviously the sellers are looking for a quick sale at £250,000, on which the SDLT payable by the purchaser is 'only' £2,500, making it a far more attractive purchase. It is quite in order to check the measurements; the surveyor measures accurately in metric measure, which is then transferred into imperial measure to make it understandable to the general public. This is frequently wrongly done, and should not be relied upon when ordering carpets etc.

4.05 (a) Letter of engagement from Brown Jarvie & Walker to Mr and Mrs James

Brown Jarvie & Walker
Solicitors and Estate Agents
42 Registration Row
GLASGOW G1 3XX

Mr and Mrs Stuart James
The Ritz Hotel
Buchanan Street
GLASGOW G1 2ZZ

7 February 2006

HP/VV/ Jame 323

Dear Mr and Mrs James

3 Miller Drive, Newton Mearns

We refer to your recent meeting today with Mr Pink of this firm.

We are pleased to confirm that Messrs. Brown, Jarvie & Walker will be acting on your behalf in connection with the purchase of 3 Miller Drive, Newton Mearns.

The partner in charge of your transaction is Mr Pink, who will be assisted by Veronica Vanbrugh, paralegal, and Wendy Robertson, trainee solicitor.

We will advise you at regular intervals regarding the progress of your work, and will keep you informed of all significant developments. If you, or either of you, are uncertain about what is happening at any time, please ask.

We enclose an estimate of our fees and outlays for this transaction. If the work turns out to be more complex than normal, we may require to increase our estimate to take account of this. We shall inform you as soon as possible about any such increase.

The Money Laundering Regulations require us to be satisfied as to the identity of our clients and as to the source of any funds passing through our hands. In order to comply with these Regulations, we may need to ask you both for proof of identity and other information in relation to these matters. We reserve the right to withdraw from acting for you, or either of you, if either of you fail to provide us with the information requested of you in connection with our money laundering procedures.

Finally our aim is to provide a service which is satisfactory in every respect. However, if you, or either of you, have any concerns about the manner in which work is carried out on your behalf, please contact our client relations partner, Mr Brown, who will be happy to discuss your concerns.

Yours faithfully

Note: Under the Solicitors (Scotland) (Client Communications) Rules 2005, it may be an inadequate professional service not to send a letter to cover these points.

(b) Fee quotation to accompany above letter

Foo for doing all work in connection with the purchase of the house a 3 Miller Drive, Newton Mearns at £250,000.

Fee	£450.00
VAT thereon at 17.5%	£ 78.75
Outlays on your behalf	
Land Registration fee	£500.00
Stamp Duty Land Tax @ 1%	£2,500.00
	£3,528.75

The proposed fee is for a normal transaction involving the normal amount of work. In the event of the work required involving more than normal time or being of an unusually complex nature, the proposed fee may require to be increased. You will be advised of any such development in the course of the transaction. Outlays are estimated at current rates.

Note: It is as well to allow an increase if something horrible is found in the title, and the matter requires to be sorted after much work. The outlays are stated to be at current values. The Chancellor might, and did in this example, for instance, change SDLT in his Budget which occurred prior to settlement, but not to any material extent—he only raised the tax threshold from £120,000 to £125,000.

4.06 Minute of meeting—Mr Pink, Veronica Vanbrugh, and Mr and Mrs James

MEETING WITH Mr and Mrs James. Going through the identity checklist-see below.

8 February 2006

Discussing with them the surveyor's report, which said that the house was fairly valued at the fixed asking price, required some routine maintenance, but nothing too serious. The surveyors pointed out that not all the windows were double glazed, despite what the particulars say, and advising that this is a property misdescription. Noting that the James were content to let matters rest at this stage, and instructing us not to do anything about it.

Checking their finances, and noting that they were getting the price from their sale of their house in the Lake District at £500,000, which was sold at auction, and that they would not therefore require a loan at this time. They produced a letter from their bank stating that they would make funds available, if the sale was not completed in time for settlement.

Explaining Scottish procedure to them, and that we would sign a contract on their behalf, which would be binding on them and that there was no 'subject to contract' as in England, which would enable them to walk out of the contract. Emphasising this point and asking them to be sure that they wished us to proceed. They said that they were very keen to proceed.

Stating that we would send an offer by courier and wishing them luck.

Veronica Vanbrugh

Engaged ½ hour.

4.07 Verification of identity of clients checklist

Name: Stuart James and Henrietta James

Evidence obtained to verify name and address: I saw Full UK Passports in both cases. These gave the address in Kendal, but they are presently staying in the Ritz Hotel in Buchanan Street, to facilitate their moving arrangements, where we have been writing to them.

I confirm that

a.   I have seen the originals of the documents indicated above and have identified the above clients.

(*Signed*) Henry Pink, Solicitor. (*Date*) 8 February 2006.

Note: This may seem unduly fussy, but is required by the Money Laundering Regulations, even if you are opening a Post Office account with £5 that your uncle gave you. You will need to keep this certificate on file, in case the Law Society ask for it. It is good practice to keep copies of the evidence as to identity and address on the file, for future reference.

The minute of meeting with the clients is also good practice. In six months' time, the parties will have forgotten what was said, and it is useful to have a minute. The advice given, and the instructions taken, were all quite clear. It is also useful if you have to justify your fee. It is particularly important to outline differences between the English and Scottish procedures for clients coming from England. In particular they should be told that the missives are a binding contract, and are not 'subject to contract' as is the preliminary contract. That means that either party can, for any reason or no reason, walk out of the contract without financial penalty. The exception to this rule is that if a property is sold at an auction in England, the parties are then bound to complete the contract, as in the case with the James's house.

The clients could have made something of the property misdescription, but chose not to. Probably a wise move, if they want a quick contract.

4.08 (a) Email

From: Veronica Vanburgh <vvanburgh@bjw.co.uk>

Sent: 6 February 2006 15:27.

To: O'Neill Middleton <sales@oneillmiddleton.com>

Subject: 3 Miller Drive, Newton Mearns.

Please note that our clients, Mr and Mrs James, have seen the house being sold at 3 Miller Drive, Newton Mearns, and have asked us to intimate that they have asked us to lodge an offer. Please therefore note their interest. BJ&W

Note: It is virtually standard practice to note an interest with the sellers' agent, although it is not obligatory. It is a first step in the negotiating process. It means that a sellers' agent should not ethically accept another offer without giving other interested parties a chance to bid. In this particular case, it could be argued that it is not strictly necessary to intimate interest—because this is a fixed price sale, where the first acceptable offer of the asking price will be accepted regardless of any other interest. On balance it is probably just as well to intimate the interest, just in case the sellers decide to change their minds, as is their privilege, and change the basis of the sale.

4.9 (b) Letter from O'Neill Middleton

O'Neill Middleton
Solicitors and Estate Agents
999 Lally Street
GLASGOW
G2 4XX

Messrs Brown Jarvie & Walker
Solicitors and Estate Agents
42 Registration Row
GLASGOW

G1 3XX

7 February 2006

Dear Sirs

Mr and Mrs James

Mr and Mrs McDuff

3 Miller Drive, Newton Mearns

Thank you for your email today. We confirm that we have noted your client's interest. We enclose our clients' Property Sales Questionnaire and Single Survey, and trust that you will find this of assistance in preparing your clients' offer, if so instructed.

Yours faithfully

(c) Property sale questionnaire and single survey.

See Appendix IV.

Note: These documents are required by the terms of the Housing (Scotland) Act 2005. They represent a watering down on the original clamour for 'a sellers' pack' which was particularly advocated by the consumer lobby. The questionnaire will be seen as fairly sensible, but the single sellers' survey is more controversial. It will probably be a type (b) survey. It is designed to get round the situation that there may be ten offerors for the property, who will each commission a survey report at huge expense, and only one offer will be accepted. Nine offerors will thus have to pay for a useless survey. This may happen to offerors several times, thus costing them a fortune. If there is a lender involved, they will certainly not be content to accept the sellers' valuation and will commission their own survey.

A survey may be of three types: (a) a simple valuation- relatively cheap; (b) a full structural survey, with detailed report on the property-very expensive: (c) a half-way house between (a) and (c)—moderately expensive. With these surveys the person instructing obtains a possible claim for a negligent survey—the chances of success depend on the wording of the survey and the kind of survey—the claimer has the best chance with a full structural survey. In this field, as others, you get what you pay for.

It is hard to predict what will happen in practice. Purchasers will probably obtain a type (b) survey, notwithstanding the seller' survey, and possibly make their offer subject to obtaining a satisfactory survey within a short time. See notes on suspensive clauses at para **4.49**. Lenders will still require a satisfactory valuation—probably indicating a survey type (c) for both purposes.

4.10 Offer by Brown Jarvie & Walker

Note: The offer is made by the Purchasers' solicitor to the selling agents. The offer is made in the form of the Glasgow Standard Offer' prepared by a working party from of the Royal Faculty of Procurators in Glasgow.

The working party state in its introduction that offers in the 1970s consisted of only five clauses, which were readily acceptable, and meant that missives were concluded speedily, so that both parties were tied into a legally enforceable contract, and could sue or be sued if any breach occurred. Therefore both parties knew exactly where they stood. This was the greatest advantage of the Scottish system.

Then offers got progressively longer and more complex, with each firm having its 'own' offer, and sometimes each partner in the firm having their own style. This means that each offer had to be carefully studied, and a bespoke qualified acceptance prepared. The parties would spend considerable time negotiating the contract, and sometimes would only agree on the day of settlement. Or, even worse, they would not agree at all. Thus in Scotland, we had managed to reach a system which was the worst of both worlds and, as was pointed out in a letter to the

Journal recently, actually worse than the English system, where at least contracts are exchanged a week before completion.

The Law Society tried to introduce a standard Scottish contract, but this was not acceptable to the profession at large due to the lack of flexibility. We now have standard offers for Highland, Aberdeen and Aberdeenshire, Tayside, Edinburgh and Glasgow. Details of each can be found at the 'Conveyancing Essentials'page on the Law Society website. Each have regional variations, and hopefully are in terms which most practitioners can accept, and issue a de plano acceptance (ie an unqualified acceptance of the offer in a short time). Thus there will be concluded missives and either party can sue the other party to carry out the bargain.

You should use the regional variation most appropriate to the property for which you are offering.

To date, the standard offer has proved successful and it is hoped that it will be adopted universally. If it is not, at least a study of its terms will prove more than useful, as it contains the standard elements of most forms of missives.

BROWN JARVIE & WALKER
Solicitors and Estate Agents
42 Registration Row
GLASGOW G1 3XX

Messrs O'Neill Middleton
Solicitors and Estate Agents
999 Lally Street
GLASGOW G2 4XX

BY COURIER

8 February 2006

HP/VV/ Jame 323

Dear Sirs

For the purposes of this offer and the Glasgow Standard Conditions (2005 Edition) aftermentioned.

The Purchaser means Stuart and Henrietta James residing at Wordsworth Cottege, 19 Daffodil Road, Kendal.

The Property means 3 Miller Drive, Newton Mearns, G77 10EU.

Together with any garage, carport, parking space, garden ground and outbuildings pertaining thereto; all necessary rights of access and all rights exclusive, common, mutual and others pertaining thereto and the parts privileges and pertinents thereof.

The Price means Two Hundred and Fifty Thousand Pounds Sterling (£250,000).

The Date of Entry means the day when vacant possession of the Property will be given in exchange for the Price and will be 1 April 2006 or such other date as may be mutually agreed in writing.

The Purchaser hereby offers to purchase from your client (hereinafter referred to as 'the Seller') the Property at the Price and upon the conditions contained in the Glasgow Standard Clauses (2005 Edition) specified in the Deed of Declaration by Marie Elizabeth Brown and Others dated Eighth and registered in the Books of Council and Session for preservation on Ninth, both days of November Two Thousand and Five, and upon the following further conditions:

(One) The Price will include the following additional items:

The integrated oven, hob and extractor fan, all fitted floor coverings, the custom made kitchen blind and the oak dining room table and matching chairs.

(Two) This offer, unless previously withdrawn, is open for verbal acceptance by midday on 9. February 2006 with a written acceptance reaching us no later than 5.00 pm on the fifth working day following the date of this offer, and if it is not so accepted will be deemed to be withdrawn.

Yours faithfully

(*signed*) Brown Jarvie & Walker

Witness Wendy Robertson
Legal Trainee
42 Registration Row
Glasgow G1 3XX

Note: The purchase price of £250,000 attracts stamp duty at 1%. A price of £250,000.01 as would attract stamp duty at 3%. The purchaser can elect to apportion the price between heritable and moveables, which should save some money, but keep a note on file with relative values endorsed

by the client in case HM Revenue and Customs come knocking on your
door.

4.11 The Glasgow Standard Clauses (2005 Edition)

This is the Schedule referred to in the foregoing Declaration by Marie
Elizabeth Brown and others dated Eighth and registered in the Books of
Council and Session for preservation on Ninth both days of November
Two Thousand and Five.

Note: The Books of Council and Session are one of the Registers of
Scotland, kept at Meadowbank House, Edinburgh EH8 7AU. Probative
writs are registered here, mainly for safe keeping, but also, less
commonly, for execution. Examples of deeds to be registered here are
leases, wills of persons who have died, and lengthy schedules to deeds
such as the form of offer, or conditions of a standard security. Extracts are
then obtained, which are as effective as the original deed, which now
never leaves Register House. Marie Elizabeth Brown is a member of the
working party that drew up the standard clauses.

These are the Glasgow Standard Clauses (2005 edn) in the deed of
declaration by Marie Elizabeth Brown and others dated 8 November
2005.

4.12 Fixtures, fittings & contents

The Property is sold with:

(a)   all heritable fittings and fixtures;

(b)   all items of whatever nature fixed or fitted to the Property the
        removal of which would damage the fabric or decoration of the
        Property; and

(c)   the following in so far as any were in the Property when viewed
        by the Purchaser; all types of blinds, pelmets, curtain rails and
        runners, curtain poles and rings thereon; all carpets and floor
        coverings (but excluding loose rugs), stair carpet fixings; fixed
        bedroom furniture, all bathroom and cloakroom mirrors,
        bathroom and toilet fittings and accessories; kitchen units, any
        cooker, hob, oven, washing machine, dishwasher, fridge and/or
        freezer if integral to or encased within matching units, extractor
        hood and extractor fan; electric storage heaters, electric fires,
        electric light fittings (including all fluorescent lighting, wall
        lights, dimmer switches and bulbs and bulb holders but not
        shades); television aerials and associated cables and sockets,
        satellite dishes; burglar alarm, other security systems and

associated equipment; secondary glazing; shelving fireplace surround units, fire grates, fenders and associated ironmongery; all growing plants shrubs, trees (except those in plant pots), external lighting, rotary clothes driers, garden shed or hut, greenhouse, summerhouse.

Note: The rule is all property that is heritable is included in the sale, and that moveable property is excluded. More and more the distinction between the two becomes blurred, and it is not unknown for sellers to strip the house, especially of bulbs—both light bulbs, which are moveable, and garden bulbs, which are heritable. This clause sets out that all heritable property is included in the purchase, but also items which might be either heritable or moveable, to avoid tiresome disputes. The dining room furniture, which is clearly moveable, is included in the main offer.

4.13 Specialist reports

(a) Any Guarantees in force at the Date of Entry in respect of (i) treatments which have been carried out to the Property (or to the larger subjects of which the Property forms part) for the eradication of timber infestation, dry rot, wet rot, rising damp or other such defects, and/or (ii) insulation and double glazing, together with all supporting estimates, survey reports and other papers relating thereto ('the Guarantees') will be exhibited on conclusion of Missives and delivered at settlement.

(b) The Seller confirms that he is not aware of anything having been done or omitted to be done which might invalidate the Guarantees.

(c) If requested, and insofar as necessary and competent, the Guarantees will be assigned to the Purchaser at the Purchaser's expense.

Note: This clause is largely self-explanatory. The guarantees should be examined, in case of recurrence of the problem, and should be checked as to what area is affected by the guarantee, and the status of the guarantor—is the guarantee worth the paper it is written on? Most of these guarantees do not require a formal assignation to the purchaser and transfer automatically, but it is as well to check.

4.14 Central heating etc

(a) The Seller undertakes that any systems or appliances of a working nature (including central heating, water, drainage, electric and gas) forming part of the Property will be in working order commensurate with age as at the Date of Entry.

Note: It is easy to forget that these pipes wear out, and are often lethal.

(b) The Seller will make good any defect which prevents any system or appliance being in such order provided said defect is intimated in writing within five working days of Settlement. Failing such intimation, the Purchaser will be deemed to be satisfied as to the position.

Note: The Purchaser should get these systems checked by a qualified person at the date of entry, and submit any claim timeously.

(c) The Seller will only be responsible for carrying out any necessary repairs to put any system or appliance into such order and will have no liability for any element of upgrading (except to the extent such upgrading is required to put any such system or appliance into that order).

(d) The lack of any regular service or maintenance of any system or appliance or the fact that it may no longer comply with current installation regulations will not, of itself, be deemed to be a defect.

(e) The Purchaser will be entitled to execute any necessary repairs at the expense of the Seller without reference to the Seller or the Seller's tradesmen (i) in the event of an emergency; (ii) in the event that the Seller's tradesmen do not inspect the alleged defects within five working days of intimation; or (iii) in the event that any necessary repairs are not carried out within five working days of inspection.

(f) The Seller confirms that he has received no notice or intimation from any third party that any system or appliance (or any part thereof) is in an unsafe or dangerous condition.

4.15 Development

The Seller warrants that he has not been served with, nor received any, neighbour notification notice issued in terms of any planning legislation by any third party. In the event of any such notice being served on or received by the Seller prior to the Date of Settlement the seller will forward such notice to the Purchaser within five working days of receipt of such notice.

Note: This can be verified by the planning department of the local council.

4.16 Statutory notices etc

(a) Any Local Authority (or other public body) notices or orders calling for repairs or other works to the Property issued prior to or on the Date of Entry (or any other work affecting the Property agreed to or authorised by the Seller outstanding as at the Date of Entry) will be the responsibility of the Seller outstanding as at the Date of Entry) will be the responsibility of the Seller. Liability under this condition will subsist until met and will not be avoided by the issue of a fresh notice or order.

Note: This covers notices or orders issued prior to the date of entry, and thus complies to the common law rule of res perit domino (things perish at the risk of the owner). The seller should receive, and exhibit to the purchaser, a letter from the local council stating what notices there are, if any.

(b) The Seller warrants that he has not received written notification of, approved, entered into or authorised any scheme of common repairs or improvement affecting any larger building of which the Property forms part. Where the Seller approves, enters into or authorises any such scheme or where any such scheme is instructed, the Seller will remain liable for his share of the cost of such scheme. Details of any such scheme will be discloses to the Purchaser prior to Settlement.

Note: This provision applies only to flats in a tenement.

(c) When any work in terms of clauses (a) or (b) above is incomplete or unpaid for at the Date of Settlement the Purchaser will be entitled to retain from the Price a sum equivalent to the estimated cost of the Seller's share of such works (which estimate will be augmented by 25%). Such retention will be held in an interest bearing account opened by the Purchaser's solicitor, pending discharge of the Seller's liability. The retention will not be released or intromitted without the written authority of the solicitors for both parties. Any shortfall will remain the liability of the Seller.

(d) On issue of invoices for such works in terms of (a) and (b) above by the Local Authority or other authorised party the retention will be released to make payment of such invoices as soon as reasonably practical.

(e) Notwithstanding any other term within the Missives this condition will remain in full force and effect without limit of time and may be founded on until implemented.

(f)   Without prejudice to the above the Purchaser may retain from the Price such sum as is reasonably required to meet any costs for which he may be contingently liable under section 10(2) of the Title Conditions (Scotland) Act 2003 or section 12(2) of the Tenements (Scotland) Act 2004.

(g)   Prior to the Date of Entry the Seller will provide full details of any common repairs in respect of which a notice if potential liability for costs has been or is to be registered.

Note: This condition provides an equitable agreed mechanism for retention of a sum to deal with notices served on the property, a situation which in the past has provided many problems through the default of sellers.

4.17 Common repairs and charges

Where the Property is part of a larger building or of a development, it is a condition that:

(a)   the common charges will be apportioned between the Seller and the Purchaser as at the Date of Entry on the basis that (i) the Seller will be responsible for all common repairs and improvements instructed or authorised on or prior to the Date of Entry and (ii) there are no common repairs or improvements instructed or authorised but not yet paid for;

(b)   there are no repairs authorised or instructed nor outstanding work undertaken but not yet completed (or completed, but not yet paid for) in respect of the Property or the larger building or development of which it forms part; and

(c)   evidence in respect of any block insurance policy will be exhibited prior to the Date of Entry.

Note: This applies an equitable scheme of division between seller and purchaser of accounts for maintenance and repair of parts of a building which is in multiple ownership. If there is a factor, he will carry out an apportionment between the parties. It is up to the seller's solicitor, and obviously desirable, to inform the factor of the change in ownership so that the seller's responsibility for such accounts shall cease. Please note that the seller will remain liable for repairs authorised or instructed, or work undertaken but not yet completed, or completed but not yet paid for.

4.18 Alterations

(a)   It is an essential condition that all Consents, Planning Permissions, Listed Building Consents, Building Warrants and

Completion certificates have been obtained from the Local Authority or any other relevant authority or from any other person whose consent may be required in terms of the title deeds for the erection of or conversion to form the Property and for any alterations, improvements or extensions made thereto, and that any conditions imposed thereby have been fully complied with. All relevant Plans, Permissions, Warrants, Certificates and Consents will be exhibited prior to and delivered at settlement.

Note: The importance of this provision cannot be overstated. It is stated to be an essential condition of contract—that is, any breach entitles the innocent party to withdraw from the contract without legal consequences. Any building work, with only very minor exception; (1) must have planning permission from the local Council that certifies that it meets the requirements of planning legislation; (2) listed building consent—applies only to buildings that are listed. The consent is again from the planning committee, and is strictly monitored; (3) building warrant—available from a different committee of the local council. Plans of the building work contemplated are examined to ensure that the increasingly tight Building Regulations are complied with; (4) completion certificate—when the work is complete the building will be inspected, to ensure that the approved plans have been faithfully followed; if so, a certificate will be issued; if not, it is an offence to occupy the building; (5) consents from any party who may have a right to object to the work proposed. All of these consents must be obtained. The possession of one does not pre-suppose the granting of any other. Failure to obtain or comply with, planning or building certificates can, at worst, entitle the local council to require that the property be restored to its original condition, even if this involves demolition. It is vital that the purchaser is satisfied of these consents, and form part of the purchaser's marketable title, and any lender will insist on these being obtained. Planning and building certificates will not be available for alterations predating local government reorganisation in 1975.

(b)   As at the date of conclusion of the Missives the Seller warrants (i) that any building work carried out to the Property has been in a state of substantial completion for a period of not less than twelve weeks prior to the date of conclusion of Missives and (ii) that no valid objection to the work was made at any time by a person with title and interest to do so under a real burden.

Note: This provision is to ensure that there are not any botched repairs, either by enthusiastic DIYers or cowboy tradesmen. Twelve weeks is the period in which neighbouring proprietors have the right to object to any work; after that the right is lost.

4.19 Family Law Act/litigation

The Seller warrants that neither the Property nor the Seller's title are effected by or under consideration in any court proceedings or other litigation or are the subject of any dispute.

Note: The Family Law (Scotland) Act 1985, s 8(1)(aa), enables either party in an action of divorce to apply to the court for an order transferring property to him or her by the other party to the marriage. Such an order has to be registered but the purchaser's solicitor should be satisfied that no such order has been granted and not yet registered.

4.20 Title warranty

There are no current disputes with neighbouring proprietors or occupiers or any other parties relating to access, title and common property.

Note: This provision is more or less self-explanatory—the last thing the purchaser will expect is to walk into a dispute with a neighbour, which can be very bitter, insoluble, and expensive.

4.21 Utilities

Prior to settlement the Seller will confirm the present suppliers of utility services (gas, electricity and telephone as applicable) to the Property. The Seller will act reasonably in ensuring that such services are not terminated prior to the Date of Settlement and will co-operate reasonably the Purchaser in ensuring the transfer of such services.

Note: This provision is largely self-explanatory—the seller should inform the suppliers of the change of ownership and should clear up all arrears of accounts.

4.22 Breach of contract by seller

If at the Date of Entry the Seller does not give vacant possession or otherwise fails to implement any material obligations due by him in terms of the Missives then the Purchaser will be entitled (provided the Purchaser is in a position to settle the transaction on the Date of Entry) to claim damages for any reasonable loss incurred by him arising from such failure. In the event that the Seller's breach of contract continues for fourteen days after the date the Date of Entry the Purchaser will be entitled to treat that breach as repudiation and to rescind the Missives on giving the Seller notice to that effect. The condition will apply without prejudice to any other rights or remedies available to the Purchaser.

Note: It is more common for the purchaser to fail to honour the contract, through financial or personal difficulties, but it does occasionally happen that the seller has a change of mind and refuse to honour the contract. The remedy of the purchasers lies in the case of *Mackay v Campbell* (1967 SC (HL) 53).

The purchaser can ask the court: (1) for declarator that the seller has failed to implement missives; (2) for decree ordaining the seller to implement the missives and deliver a valid title; and (3) failing such implement for the payment of a sum in damages.

This clause in missives entitles the purchaser merely to repudiate the contract and claim damages for loss thus caused ie cost of alternative accommodation, storage of furniture, kennelling of pets etc.

If the seller refuses, or is unable, to sign a valid disposition the court may order the Deputy Principal Clerk of Session or the sheriff clerk to sign a disposition on the seller's behalf (see *Pennell's Trustee* 1928 SC 605).

4.23 Breach of contract by purchaser

(a)   It will be an essential condition of the Missives that the price is paid in full by 2.30 pm on the Date of Entry.

Note: This underlines the essential condition of contract that the price must be paid in full on the date of entry, otherwise the purchaser is in breach of contract. Payment should be made by 2.30 pm to allow the money to be banked in the purchaser's solicitors', account for clients. Failure to do so is thought to be the most common reason for breach of contract.

(b)   The Seller will not be obliged to offer vacant possession except against payment of the Price and any interest or damages due aftermentioned. Failure to pay will entitle the Seller to rescind the Missives on the expiry of fourteen days from the Date of Entry on giving written notice to that effect and without prejudice to any other rights or remedies available to the Seller. In the event of failure to pay the Price as aforesaid then notwithstanding consignation nor the fact that the Purchaser may have obtained entry interest will accrue in favour of the Seller at the rate of 4% above the Royal Bank of Scotland plc base rate from time to time in force from the Date of Entry until full payment of the price is made or, in the event of the Seller exercising his right to rescind the Missives, until the contractual date of entry on the first resale of the Property by the Seller (or for a period of twelve months from the Date of Entry whichever is shorter).

(c)   If the Seller exercises his right to rescind then he will be entitled to (i) proceed to resell the Property and (ii) the continuing payment of interest as aforesaid but that without prejudice to the Seller's right to claim additional damages from the Purchaser for any proper and reasonable costs incurred by the Seller arising from the Purchaser's failure to settle.

(d)   The provisions of this clause will not have any effect in any period during which the delay in settlement is attributable to the Seller or his Solicitors.

(e)   This condition will continue to be enforceable notwithstanding rescission.

Note: If the purchasers do not settle on the due date, the sellers will probably be caught in a very difficult situation through no fault of their own. The common law provides a cumbersome, and frankly unreliable, remedy. Over the years therefore a more foolproof contractual remedy has evolved. This allows the sellers to rescind the contract, to re-sell the property and to claim interest from the date of entry originally agreed until the date of settlement of any subsequent sale. See *Lloyds Bank v Bamberger* 1993 SCLR 727. Interest runs at a rate to be agreed, but generally at 4% over bank minimum lending rate, which is at time of writing (September 2006) 4.75%, plus 4%. This is intended to compensate for the overdraft interest incurred by the disappointed sellers.

The common law remedy is to raise an action of implement of missives, which merely adds delay to the process.

It should be noted that the provisions of this clause do not apply when the fault is that of the sellers or their solicitors.

Entry should, except in the most exceptional circumstances or where a retention has been agreed, never be given without payment of the price in full.

These clauses may sound very severe on the purchasers, but are in fact a fair solution to a difficult problem brought about the failure of the purchasers to meet their obligations. The purchasers should accept these conditions, and be careful to meet their part of the bargain.

4.24 New home warranty schemes

If the Property was constructed within a ten year period prior to the Date of Entry there will be delivered at Settlement a Local Authority Completion Certificate in respect of the Property and

Either:

(a)   the appropriate documentation to vouch that the Property is fully covered under the new home warranty schemes by NHBC, Zurich Insurance Company, Premier Guarantee or other provider acceptable in terms of the then current edition of the CML Lenders' Handbook for Scotland ('CML'). In this event, the Seller warrants that no claims have been made or ought to have been reported or are pending under the relevant scheme; or

(b)   In the event that the Property was not constructed under the said new home warranty schemes, a Professional Consultant's Certificate (the 'PCC') in terms of the current edition of the CML. If the Purchaser, acting reasonably, is dissatisfied with the terms of the PCC, the Purchaser will be entitled to resile from the Missives without penalty to either party but only provided that the Purchaser exercises this right within five working days of the receipt of the PCC.

Note: A house is treated as being 'new' for ten years from its building, in that it is covered for most defects for two years, and for major defects for up to ten years. The cover is provided either by the National House Builders Council ('NHBC') or by a company approved by the Council of Mortgage Lenders ('CML') the organisation representing most mortgage lenders.

Not all builders are covered by these schemes, in which case they will produce a PCC certifying that they have supervised the building and that they are satisfied that the work is satisfactory. The granter of the PCC should, of course, have professional indemnity insurance, and anyone relying on the PCC should see that this is so. This is asked for in the PCC, (see Chs 8 and 21).

4.25 Title conditions

(a)   Where the Property forms part of a larger building the Property will have the benefit of and be subject to the usual common law rights applicable to flatted or divided dwellinghouses including a right in common to the *solum* on which the building of which the Property forms part is erected, the foundations; the roof and roof systems; rhones, downpipes and drains and boundary walls, fences or divisions and the liability for the share of maintenance, renewal and upkeep of the foregoing will be shared by the respective proprietors on an equitable basis.

Note: This paragraph refers only to flats in a tenement or to houses which are divided. In either case, the maintenance of the common parts should be a shared responsibility among the various owners, and not be the responsibility of one owner who might be unable or unwilling to pay for the repairs (see Ch 16).

(b)   Any reservation of minerals will be subject to conditions as to adequate compensation and will not include any right to enter the Property or lower its surface. The minerals are included so far as the Seller has the right to same.

Note: This refers to the situation where the original sellers of the property have sold it, but have reserved the minerals in their own ownership. This is quite common, and the mineral owner will also reserve the right to enter the property, and work the minerals. They should also pay compensation to the house owner. It is unlikely that an oil gusher will be found in Newton Mearns, or elsewhere, workable in profitable quantities, but nevertheless this clause must go in. Failure to mention the exclusion of the minerals from the sale can mean that there is not a proper contract, as there is no consensus in idem ('agreement to the same thing'). See *Campbell v McCutcheon* (1963 SLT 290).

(c)   The existing use of the Property is in conformity with the title deeds. There are no unduly onerous or restrictive burdens, conditions, servitudes or overriding interests (within the meaning of Section 28 (1) of the Land Registration (Scotland) Act 1979 affecting the property.

Note: Section 28 of the LR(S)A 1979 sets out a number of restrictions to the free ownership of land, as do burdens, conditions, and servitudes. The impact of the latter has been lessened by the terms of AFT(S)A 2000 and the TC(S)A 2003, but they may still exist. Normal burdens are acceptable, but if they are unduly onerous and restrictive, the purchaser may withdraw from the purchase. This is part of the task of examining title, and satisfying the purchaser that the title is valid and marketable (ie readily resaleable).

(d)   There is no outstanding liability for any part of the cost of constructing or maintaining walls, fences, roadways, footpaths or sewers adjoining or serving the property.

Note: This paragraph is largely self-explanatory, but some mention must be made of roadways, footpaths and sewers. As a general rule these are taken over and maintained by the council, and this can be certified by the council. But, particularly in rural areas or certain urban areas where the roads have never been made up to council standards, the ownership remains in the adjoining proprietors and they maintain the roadway at their own expense in accordance with their respective frontages. They should also insure the public against injury through falling into potholes etc. There are certain advantages in having the roadway private, in that access can be restricted and there is no danger of the council painting yellow lines and restricting parking. Nevertheless most homeowners opt for public ownership of these features. It is obviously important to find out the status of any roads, footpaths and sewers, and to be sure that there is no inherited debt from the previous owner.

(e)   The Property has the benefit of all necessary servitudes and wayleaves required for its proper enjoyment (including vehicular access rights).

Note: This is to ensure that the owner has free rights of access and egress from the property for self and cars without recourse to a helicopter. This is a fairly safe assumption in urban areas, but must always be carefully checked in rural and semi-rural areas.

If the title deeds disclose a position other than as stated above the Purchaser will be entitled to resile from the Missives without penalty to either party but only provided the Purchaser exercises the right within five working days of receipt of the Seller's titles. The Purchaser's right to resile will be the sole option in terms of the Missives.

Note: This condition is essential to the rapid conclusion of missives. If something nasty is found in the title exhibited, the Purchaser may resile (ie withdraw) from the Missives, but has only five days to do so. This is therefore a case of carpe diem (seize the day) because if the opportunity is missed then the purchaser is stuck with it. There is no other right open to the purchaser. In practice, the title deeds are usually sent with the sellers' solicitors' qualified acceptance, so the purchasers' solicitors can satisfy themselves as to the title before missives are concluded.

4.26 Settlement

The Price will be payable on the Date of Entry, in exchange for (i) delivery of a validly executed Disposition in the favour of the Purchaser or his nominee; (ii) vacant possession of the Property; and (iii) the keys for the Property; together with:

(a)   If the provisions of the Land Registration (Scotland) Act 1979 ('the Act') relating to a **first registration** under the Act apply, a valid marketable title together with: (i) a form 10 report brought down to a date not more than three working days prior to the Date of Entry and showing no entries adverse to the Seller's interest in the Property (the cost of the said report being the Seller's liability); and (ii) such documents and evidence including a plan as the Keeper may require to enable the Keeper to issue a Land Certificate in the name of the Purchaser as the registered proprietor of the Property without exclusion of indemnity in terms of section 12(2) of the Act. Such documents will include (unless the Property comprises only part of a tenement or flatted building and does not include an area of ground specifically included in the title to that part) a plan or bounding description sufficient to enable the whole Property to be identified on the Ordnance Survey map and evidence (such as a form P16 report) that the description of the whole Property as contained in the title deeds is *habile* to include the whole of the occupied extent.

(b)   If the title to the Property is **already registered** in terms of the Act a valid marketable Land Certificate containing no exclusion of indemnity in terms of section 12(2) with all necessary links in title evidencing the Seller's exclusive ownership of the Property together with (i) a form 12 report brought down to a date not more than three working days prior to the Date of Entry and showing no adverse to the Seller (the cost of the said report being the Seller's liability); and (ii) such documents and evidence as the Keeper may require to enable the interests of the Purchaser to be registered in the Land Register as registered proprietor of the Property without exclusion of indemnity under section 12(2).

(c)   Where (a) or (b) apply the Land Certificate will disclose no entry, deed or diligence prejudicial to the Purchaser's interest other than such as have been created by or against the Purchaser or have been disclosed to and accepted by the Purchaser prior to the Date of Settlement.

(d)   If the application for First Registration of the title to the Property is still being processed by the Keeper, the Seller warrants (i) that no requisitions have been made by the Keeper but not implemented; (ii) the Keeper has not indicated any concern with the Application such as might result in any restriction of indemnity or refusal to register, and (iii) any copy documentation provided to the Purchaser are true copies of the originals.

(e)   Without prejudice to the above, the Seller warrants that the Property is not affected by any entry in the Register of Community Interests in Land.

(f)   Notwithstanding any other term within the Missives this condition will remain in full force and effect without limit of time and may be founded upon until implemented.

Note: This clause sets out the obligations of the seller which are: (i) to deliver a valid disposition (ii) to give vacant possession and (iii) to hand over the keys of the property. If it is a first registration the seller will show the purchaser a clear form 10A report and, nearer settlement, a clear form 11A report which continues the searching process almost up to the date of entry. It is thought that to leave the form 10A report until, possibly three days before settlement is dangerous, as it leaves no time to sort out matters disclosed in the form 10A report, such as an Inhibition against the seller. Similarly, the seller should exhibit to the purchaser a form P16 report (a comparison of boundaries) in such good time as shall allow for any corrective action.

In a sale of land that is already registered, forms 12 and 13 take the places of, respectively, forms 10 and 11, and a form P16 is not required as the boundaries are clearly delineated on the land certificate.

For greater detail on the conveyancing process, see Ch 8.

4.27 Incorporated bodies

(a) If the Seller is a limited company then prior to the Date of Entry the Seller will exhibit searches in the Register of Charges and company file of the Seller brought down to a date not more than three working days prior to the Date of Entry which Search will confirm that there is no notice regarding the appointment of a receiver administrator or liquidator, winding up, striking off or a change of name affecting the Seller and the full names of the present directors and secretary of the Seller. In the event of such searches disclosing any floating charge affecting the Property at the Date of Entry, there will be delivered a certificate of non-crystallisation of such floating charge granted by the chargeholder, dated not more than seven working days before entry prior to the Date of Entry confirming that no steps have been taken to crystallise such Floating Charge and undertaking upon delivery of the Disposition by the Seller to the Purchaser the Property will cease to form any part of the assets which are subject to the Floating Charge. Within three months after the Date of Settlement such searches against the Seller will be exhibited or delivered or exhibited brought down to a date 22 days after the date of registration of the Disposition in favour of the Purchaser or his nominees or 43 days after the Date of Entry whichever is the earlier disclosing no entries prejudicial to the registration of the said Disposition;

(b) The Seller will exhibit or deliver clear searches in the Register of Charges and company files of all companies disclosed as owner or former owner of the Property, in the Land Certificate or

Forms 10, 11, 12 or 13 reports, brought down in each case to a date 22 days after registration in the Land Register of the deed divesting the relevant company of its interest, disclosing no entries prejudicial to the registration of the said deed.

Note: This clause deals with the possibility that the seller is a limited company, and the additional searches that should be made in the Register of Charges and in the company's file. For greater detail, see para **8.32**.

4.28 Risk

(a)   The seller will maintain the Property in its present condition, fair wear and tear excepted, until the Deed of Settlement.

Note: Paradoxical as it may seem, the risk of destruction of, or damage to, the property passes on the completion of missives according to the case of *Sloan's Dairies Ltd v Glasgow Corporation* (1979 SLT 17). This is an obvious nonsense in practical terms, and it has long been the custom of the profession to provide that the risk shall stay with the sellers until they give vacant possession. In any event, it is always advisable that the purchasers take out building insurance—it is better to be over insured.

(b)   The risk of damage to or destruction of the Property howsoever caused will remain with the Seller until the date of settlement.

(c)   In the event of the Property being destroyed or materially damaged prior to the Date of Settlement either the Purchaser or the Seller will have the right to resile from the Missives without penalty to the other.

Note: Although the eventuality of damage or destruction will presumably be covered by insurance, the purchaser may not want a burnt out shell, and may withdraw. Equally, the seller—may not want the trouble that is entailed.

4.29 Property enquiry certificates

(a)   A Property Enquiry Certificate ('PEC') complying with the current edition of the CML dated not earlier than three months prior to the Date of Entry will be exhibited by the Seller to the Purchaser's Solicitors prior to the Date of Entry.

(b)   If the PEC discloses any matter which is materially prejudicial to the Purchaser or the Property, the Purchaser will be entitled to resile from the Missives and that without penalty to either party but only provided that the Purchaser exercises his right to resile within five working days of receipt of the PEC. The Purchaser's right to resile will be his sole option in terms of the Missives.

(c)   For the avoidance of doubt the PEC (i) will not be materially prejudicial if the Property or any part thereof is shown to be subject to an Article 4 direction, to be situated in a conservation area, to be affected by a Tree Preservation Order or to be listed as a building of architectural or historic interest and (ii) will be materially prejudicial if the roadway, footpath, and sewer *ex adverso* or the Property are not maintained by the Local Authority or the Property is not served by a public water supply.

Note: PECs can be obtained from the local council or from specialist agencies, on payment of a fee. This should be obtained as early as possible by the seller, in case it presents any difficulty, preferably before missives are concluded, but it should be borne in mind that the information contained is out of date. The PEC gives details of any notices served upon the property owners, such as a repairs notice, which obviously must be dealt with. Rather more benevolent notices are excluded, such as a notice that the property lies within a conservation area, but this should be declared to the purchaser at the earliest opportunity, preferably before missives are concluded, as the purchasers may not find the notice to his liking. For instance, a scheme to knock the building down and rebuild may exist.

4.30 Coal mining report

If the Coal Authority or similar statutory body recommends that a coal mining report is obtained for the Property then such report will be exhibited prior to the Date of Entry. In the event that such report discloses a position materially prejudicial to the Property or the Purchaser's proposed use of the same then the Purchaser will be entitled to resile from the Missives and that without penalty to either party provided the Purchaser exercises the right in writing within five working days of receipt of said report.

Note: It may appear unnecessary to obtain a coal mining report for a newish suburb like Newton Mearns, but there has been coal mining in the most unlikely places, as disclosed in the Coal Authority Handbook (available from the Coal Authority 200 Lichfield Lane, Berry Hill, Mansefield NE18 4RG). Coal mining can cause subsidence—the last thing that the purchaser wants. Again the position must be 'materially prejudicial' to the purchaser, and not something that is quite minor.

4.31 Occupancy rights

At Settlement the Property will not be affected by any occupancy rights as defined in the Matrimonial Homes (Family Protection) (Scotland) Act 1981 as amended or the Civil Partnership Act 2004.

Note: All rights under the two Acts mentioned must be discharged, in order that the purchaser shall obtain a land certificate without exclusion of indemnity.

4.32 Supersession of Missives

The Missives will cease to be enforceable after a period of two years from the Date of Entry except in so far as (i) they are founded upon in any court proceedings which have commenced within the said period or (ii) this provision is excluded in terms of any other condition of the Missives.

Note: This clause brings back unhappy memories of the terrible string of cases resulting from *Winston v Patrick* (1981 SLT 41). Rather than rake over the coals of past controversy, we would simply refer to the Handbook of Scottish Conveyancing (4th ed, para 3.29), where the matter is discussed. The Contract (Scotland) Act 1997 brought relief by stating that a prior contract (ie missives) would not be superseded by a subsequent contract (ie disposition) but allowed parties to agree a date when the prior contract would no longer be enforceable. In this case the time agreed is two years, unless the dispute arises under cl 5 and 16. In the latter case, the missives never go out of force.

4.33 Seller's address

The Seller irrevocably authorises his Solicitors to disclose his address after settlement to the Purchaser if requested by the Purchaser in the event of any claim arising after settlement under the Missives.

Note: This is in case the seller has to raise a court action against the purchaser for any reason.

4.34 Limitation of claims

Section 3 of the Contract (Scotland) Act 1997 will be qualified to the extent that any competent claim thereunder will not be available in respect of (i) matters disclosed to and accepted by the Purchaser prior to the Date of Entry or (ii) any item of claim amounting in value to less than £100.

Note: Section 3 of the 1997 Act provided that the rule of Scots law that the Purchaser could not claim damages for defective performance of a contract, but must reject the property and rescind the contract, would no longer be applicable. This rule should be contrasted with the Roman law where the purchaser who purchased cattle which subsequently proved damaged could keep the cattle and claim damages. That was the equitable rule of actio quanti minoris which, for some reason, was not adopted by Scots law.

Under this clause the purchaser, who finds that the house is not what he thought may, since 1997, claim damages and not have to reject the house. This position is slightly modified by the wording of this clause, and does not cover disputes valued at less than £100. (*De minimis non curat lex*: 'the law is not concerned by small matters').

4.35 Entire agreement

The Missives will constitute the entire agreement and understanding between the Purchaser and the Seller with respect to all matters to which they refer and supersede and invalidate all other undertakings, representations and warranties relating to the subject matter thereof which may have been made by the parties either orally or in writing prior to the date of conclusion of the Missives. Either party warrants to the other that he has not relied on any such undertaking, representation or warranty in entering into the Missives.

Note: The old rule was that missives supersede all prior communings, but the Requirements of Writing (Scotland) Act 1995, with its general relaxation of the standards of writing, allowed the possibility of prior communings between the parties or their solicitors being taken into account. Thus, for example, a verbal agreement of sale might be made, and be considered. This clause restores the primacy of missives over prior communings.

4.36 Interpretation

(a) In these Clauses (i) the masculine includes the feminine and (ii) words in the singular include the plural and vice versa.

(b) In these Clauses the word 'Settlement' or words 'Date of Settlement' mean the date on which settlement is actually effected whether that is the Date of Entry or not.

(c) In these Clauses 'the Missives' means the contract of purchase and sale concluded between the Purchaser and the Seller and constituted *inter alia*_by the Offer or other document incorporating reference to these Clauses.

(d) In these Clauses 'the Purchaser', 'the Seller', 'the Property', 'the Price' and 'the Date of Entry' have the meaning set out in the

Offer or other document incorporating reference to these Clauses.

(e)   Where, in these Clauses, there is a requirement to exhibit or deliver anything, it will be sufficient compliance if exhibition or delivery is effected on the solicitors acting for the Purchaser or the Seller as appropriate.

(f)   Any intimation will be in writing, and where any intimation must be given within a specified period, time will be of the essence.

Note: These clauses are thought to be self-explanatory, and similar clauses are to be found in most contracts.

4.37 Covering letter

BROWN JARVIE & WALKER
Solicitors and Estate Agents
Registration Row
GLASGOW
G1 3XX

Messrs O' Neill Middleton
Solicitors and EstateAgents
999 Lally Street
GLASGOW
G2 4XX

HP/VV/Jame 323

8 February 2006

Dear Sirs

Stuart and Henrietta James
3 Miller Drive, Newton Mearns

We enclose an offer for the above property, at the fixed price.

We shall be pleased to have your acceptance, within the time limit imposed, if so instructed.

Yours faithfully

(*signed*) Brown Jarvie & Walker

4.38 Email to clients

To: Stuart and Henrietta James <jamesfamily26@tiscali.co.uk>

From: Veronica Vanbrugh on behalf of Heny Pink <vvanbrugh@bjw.co.uk>

Subject: 3 Miller Drive, Newton Mearns

Attachment: jame323offer.doc

We enclose a copy of an offer lodged by us today for 3 Miller Drive. We shall inform you of the reply. Please read it through and telephone any queries to me. Good luck!

Henry Pink

Notes on Suspensive Clauses

4.39 Properly completed Missives disclosing *consensus in idem* ('complete agreement to the same thing') constitute a legally-binding contract. It is, however, possible to complete Missives with a suspensive condition— that is a condition that suspends the effect of missives until the terms of the suspensive condition are met. For example:

(a)   You buy a big, run-down house which you intend to turn into a superior hotel. You offer £200,000 instead of the market value of £100,000 on the suspensive condition that you will get planning and building permission for the alterations you intend to make and that you will get a licence to serve drinks. If none of these conditions are met to your full satisfaction, the missives will become inoperative and the deal is off, with no damages payable by either party.

(b)   You buy a field which can accommodate 50 grazing sheep or for building 20 houses. The price you pay is the building value rather than the agricultural value. You make the missives subject to planning permission and a change of use from agricultural use to residential use.

(c)   You buy a house for your own use, and put a suspensive condition in the missives that the deal is subject to your getting a survey report that is to your own satisfaction.

A prudent seller will want to put a time limit on the operation of the condition, otherwise you will keep trying till kingdom comes, and the seller will be bound to the contract (see *Imry Property Holdings Ltd v Glasgow Young Men's Christian Association* 1979 SLT 261, and an article on the subject by RB Wood 1980 SLT 129).

A condition that a condition is met 'to the purchaser's complete satisfaction' will be construed as excluding capriciousness and arbitary actings and will imply a condition of reasonableness (*Gordon District Council v Wimpey Homes Holdings Ltd* 1989 SLT 141).

Most suspensive clauses are drawn to allow the purchaser absolute discretion, to avoid arguments, and to allow purchasers to withdraw a suspensive condition even though the condition has not yet been met (see *Manheath v H & J Banks Ltd* 1966 SLT 42).

Chapter 5

THE SELLERS ACCEPT

'When acting for an elderly lady, I was instructed to accept a far lower offer for her house than had been made by someone else. In enquiring the reason for this, the lady explained that the higher offeror owned an Alsatian, and the cat next door would not like that.'

(Clydebank conveyancer, as told to the authors)

'Scotland will not have the English equivalent of a "seller's pack". Instead, I understand that each house for sale will require to come with a report which is somewhere between a basic valuation and a full structural survey and a completed questionaire. With the cost of the survey being met by the seller, this could put people off placing their properties on the market.'

(Keith Oliver WS quoted in The Scotsman)

5.01 The sellers' agents receive all offers and submit them to the sellers for instruction together with such advice as they may feel necessary.

Thus a slightly lower offer may actually be preferable to a higher offer, if there is a significant difference in the dates of entry and the lower offeror is prepared to name a date of entry suitable to the sellers, while the higher offeror is not. If the sellers want to sell in a month's time, a slightly lower offer with this date of entry may well be preferable to a higher offer with a date of entry in two months. You should consider the interest the sellers may lose by accepting the second offer.

That apart, the highest offer should in normal circumstances be preferred although in law the sellers are not bound to accept the highest offer, or indeed any offer. However, there have doubtless been many occasions on which a lower offer has been accepted for extraneous reasons, eg 'they were such a nice young couple' is a very common syndrome. Sellers can also take a violent dislike to viewers who criticise the house too volubly.

This pleasure of accepting a poorer offer from someone you like is not, however, open to persons acting in a fiduciary capacity, such as trustees, heritable creditors etc. Please note that it would very possibly be illegal to discriminate against potential purchasers on grounds of race, gender, sexuality, age or disability.

5.02 What is important is that there must be fair dealing by the sellers' agents, and that everyone should get a fair chance. Our selling system of closed bidding is a fertile breeding ground if not for malpractices, then for suspicion and accusation of malpractice, which are in many cases misplaced, but not all.

The rule is that the terms of no one's offer should ever, under any circumstances, be made known to another offeror. This is an ethical rule, not enforceable at law, but solicitors break it at the peril of their good reputation. You may, by bending the rule, have some cheap triumph at the start, but sooner or later your reputation will overtake you. If you are tempted, as with all ethical considerations, think 'Would I like someone to do that to me?'.

5.03 The following practices are extremely dubious.

(a) Dutch auction. Anybody who has been at a flower auction in Holland will tell you that a 'Dutch auction' is simply a sale in which the auctioneer offers the goods at gradually decreasing prices, the first bidder to accept being the purchaser. This is just as legitimate as a system of starting with a low bid and moving progressively higher.

The words 'Dutch auction' have, however, acquired a slightly sinister meaning (compare the British habit of blaming the Dutch and the French for everything as in Dutch courage, Dutch treat, Dutch talent, Dutch uncle etc) of an underhand sale, where the sellers take advantage of our system of closed bidding by revealing genuine offers to other bidders in an attempt to force up the price. You should not get involved in this, especially as a seller, but also as a lawyer. If the purchasers are suspicious that a Dutch auction may develop, they should put an offer in with a very short time limit. Quite apart from moral considerations, if someone says to you 'We have an offer of £X, can you beat it?' you have not the slightest idea whether they are telling the truth or not, and if you accept their word then you may be the laughing stock.

(b) Referential bid. Similarly any such arrangement as an offer of '£5 more than the highest offer received by you' should be avoided, because it makes reference to another offer and it is unfair to put the highest offeror to expense and trouble of survey and putting in an offer without giving this offer a fair chance. Further, if two or more such offers are received the whole thing is a nonsense. (On this topic generally see 1967 JLSS 2, and see the case of *Harvela Investments Ltd v Canada Royal Trust Co Ltd* [1985] 2 All ER 966, [1985] 1 All ER 261, where a referential bid was briefly approved by the court, but the decision was reversed by the House of Lords.)

(c) Progressive bid. Here a bidder frames a number of offers that are identical except that the price in each is progressively higher than the last. They are then put in numbered envelopes, and the sellers are told to open them in sequence, until a satisfactory price is reached. The snag from the bidders' point of view is that the sellers must be tempted to open only the envelope last in the sequence.

(d) eBay™. No discussion of actions would be complete without the internet phenomenom that is eBay™. Originally conceived as an electronic noticeboard for pedlars of junk in the San Fransisco Bay Area, it has grown to become a central part of our way of life. Although intended for unwanted items and collectibles it also has a section for residential property (29 properties at the time of writing). eBay™ works like any other auction—the highest bid at the close secures—but a seller may wish to treat eBay™ as a form of advertising since there would have to be doubts about how legally binding such an action would be.

5.04 Other perfectly legitimate ways around the problem have been tried, and may commend themselves:

(a) Raffle. There seems to be nothing to prevent you from copying Mr Barney Curley of Dublin, who raffled his country house and made a profit of £1m in the process, except that a public raffle on this scale in Scotland is probably illegal in terms of the Betting, Gaming and Lotteries Act 1963, s 45, in that 9,000 tickets were sold at £175 each, which exceeds the permitted ticket price and the value of the offerable prize. What you can do, however, is have a 'test of skill', requiring entrants to answer questions and complete a tie-breaker. This form of enterprise was last heard of in use in the sale of the Royal Hotel in Anstruther.

(b) 'Fixed price offer'. This is basically an acceptable idea, in that the first offer of the price fixed by the seller is accepted. It is abused, however, when the price fixed is too high. Sellers who adopt this method really should inform their solicitors, otherwise embarrassing situations may arise. Two examples:

(i) Prospective purchasers saw a house being sold on a fixed price basis, and informed their solicitors, who intimated the clients' interest and instructed a building society valuation. When the valuation was received, the solicitors were instructed to lodge an offer which was posted by first class mail. The following day, having received no reply, the solicitors telephoned the sellers' solicitors and were told that the house had been sold to an offer received earlier on the previous day. The solicitors concerned were, to say the least, extremely unhappy (see 1985 JLSS 346).

(ii)   A house was advertised personally by the sellers at a fixed price of £X. Offerors had a valuation made and instructed their solicitors to offer for the property at the fixed price. The solicitors hand-delivered the offer because there was word of another party being interested. The sellers' solicitors informed the offerors' solicitors that although their offer was the first received, it would not be accepted and that a closing date had been fixed. The selling solicitors had not apparently been informed of the method of sale. In due course the offerors' solicitors received a letter stating that a higher offer had been accepted. Furious exchanges followed, but the offeror had no grounds for action. (*Reason*: see *Pharmaceutical Society of Great Britain Boots Cash Chemists (Southern) Ltd* [1983] 1 QB 401, CA, the advertisement is only an offer to treat, and the bargain must be concluded by written offer and acceptance, as is the rule with heritable property generally.)

(c) Auction. There is no reason why the property should not be sold by auction, or to use the old Scots word, 'roup'. This was the method by which many sales were formerly made, and sales under bonds had to be made in this manner. The modern law of securities now, however, allows sales under securities to be made by private bargain, provided that the best price is obtained. There is a fairly brisk market in auctions of unusual properties, such as railway and telecom property, and a legal firm in Edinburgh specialises in such auctions. Auction sales of heritable property generally are making a modest revival. There is a body of opinion that says that sale by auction, being open and fair, and producing a fair market price, should be used universally.

When there is a sellers' market, as there—with occasional slips—from 1950 to the present time, the sellers of property can choose the method of sale, and will usually prefer a sale by closed offer. The reason for this is that this method will probably produce not so much a fair market price, as a much higher 'shutout' bid, that will easily top all the other offers. For that reason a return to full-scale sale by roup is not foreseeable.

The process of a sale by roup is: (i) the sellers prepare articles of roup, which is effectively an open offer to sell; (ii) the auction takes place, and when the hammer falls, the highest bidder is preferred; (iii) the successful bidder and the auctioneer then sign a minute of enactment and preference, which has the effect of an acceptance of the offer, yielding a binding contract, similar in effect to missives.

Sales may also be made by auction on the internet. Details of the property are given on the sellers' website, and bids are requested. The size of bids are publicised on the website, and interested parties are given a certain time to raise the bid. If this is not done, the highest bid received is the succesful one. The difficulty here is that a signature to the documents must be given, which is not, at present, possible electronically. The necessary framework for electronic signatures is, however, contained in the Electronic Communications Act 2000 and the Electronic Signatures Regulations 2002. The Law Society has appointed consultants to advise it, and will, no doubt, issue regulations for the guidance of solicitors in this direction.

5.05 When one offer has been identified as being better than the rest, the offeror should be told, and the disappointed bidders should also be told. They will want to know how much they missed out by, and a vague indication may be given. Do not, under any circumstances, tell people that they missed by only a few pounds, for the immediate reaction will be to increase the bid, and under the Law Society Guidelines on Closing Dates 1993, you are not allowed to negotiate with anyone other than the chosen offeror.

There may be allegations of shady dealings made, and allegations of Dutch auctions. You only have your own clear conscience to defend you against these allegations. The practice followed in Aberdeen is worth noting: all parties who have bid are invited to the opening of the offers, and can thus see that there is no shady dealing. The prices are not, however, revealed.

5.06 When a successful purchaser has been selected by any method other than roup, the sellers' agents then send a formal acceptance, which again is in the form of a letter (see para **8.16**). Technically it should be sufficient to simply say 'On behalf of A, I hereby accept your offer of yesterday's date for the property at ...'. Unfortunately, life is not so simple, and more complex offers produce more complex acceptances.

What must always be uppermost in your mind is that there must be a complete agreement as to details (*consensus in idem*) before a binding contract exists.

5.07 If a complex offer is followed by a complex acceptance, there is still no consensus in idem, and the purchasers' agents will have to write again formally, accepting the qualifications made by the seller before a binding contract can exist. Theoretically this process can go on indefinitely. It should not be allowed to do so. A 'three letter contract' is ample. The more letters that are exchanged, the more complex the contract becomes, and the longer the missives remain unconcluded, thereby yielding uncertainty and the possibility of the whole deal collapsing.

It is suggested that, rather than exchanging letters like tennis lobs, you have a meeting with the other solicitors, thrash out the differences, and then the purchasers should produce a new offer, reflecting the agreement, to be accepted *de plano* (i e unconditionally) by the sellers. If a meeting is not possible or desirable, the offer could be treated as a draft until consensus is reached, whereupon a revised version of the offer is sent and *de plano* accepted received. The dire consequences of having too many letters can be seen in the case of *Rutterford Ltd v Allied Breweries Ltd* 1990 SLT 249.

If the other solicitors are far away, the same result can be achieved by the sensible use of fax or email, which can greatly speed up a transaction. Thus you can have points clarified by return, and have an offer in another solicitors' hands immediately, thus enabling them to take instructions right away. It should however be remembered that faxes are not self-proving or formally valid, as they are not signed, and it is, therefore, recommended that the original of the fax be sent to the addressee forthwith. Again you are reminded that an electronic signature cannot be added, and a faxed contract is not binding on the parties (see para **5.04**).

It should also be remembered that we have a very good document exchange post service (DX) and legal post services (LP) guaranteeing next day delivery, unless the weather is very bad, and also an excellent postal service. Non-urgent mail should be sent by these methods, and not fax or email. Writing in the *Journal of the Law Society of Scotland* (1994 JLSS 197) Graeme Pagan says: 'In an uncomplicated non-urgent conveyancing transaction, I received by fax, twenty minutes before the office closed, a seventeen page draft feu charter, the principal of which reached me at 7.45 am the following morning'. This is a wasteful practice which should be avoided. The recipients of such junk mail can feel aggrieved, because it is their paper that is used for printing the document, and their machine is tied up for a few minutes, when somebody might be trying to send an important document—known in the jargon as 'opportunity costs'. It is, for this reason, that the form of 'acceptable' offer (see ch 5) is welcome. Anything that cuts down these bulky missives—sometimes running to 14 letters—where sight of the parties' intentions are completely lost in a welter of adjustments (see *Rutherford Ltd*) and it often emerges that there is no completed agreement despite the mass of paperwork.

5.08 As mentioned in the previous chapter, from 2007 onwards the seller of a house will be required to produce to potential buyers, a property sale questionnaire and form of single survey prepared at the seller's expense (see Appendix IV). This fulfils partially the dream of consumer groups that the purchasers should not have to obtain a survey report every time they are interested in a property, often at great expense. It does, however, fall short of the consumerist lobby's dream of a seller's pack which is being introduced in England, mainly to shorten the time the sale is 'subject to contract', ie of little worth. A pilot scheme was tried in Scotland, mainly with inconclusive results. We shall just have to wait and see what transpires. It will mean, however, that some of the information now supplied after missives have been completed, will have to be provided by the seller at the start of the sale process.

5.09 We shall now refer again to the purchase of 3 Miller Drive, Newton, Mearns:

Note of telephone conservation between Mr Pink and Mr Blue dated 14.02.06.

Attendance with Mr Blue of O'Neill Middleton, who said that he would be sending an acceptance of our offer for 3 Miller Drive, Newton Mearns. He noted that our offer was in the form of the Glasgow Standard Offer, and accordingly he would send a *de plano* acceptance subject to one condition—his client also owned the adjoining house at 1 Miller Drive, and he would like to impose a real burden on Number Three stopping the use of the ground for parking caravans and motor homes, as this would spoil the outlook of Number One. Mr Blue was rather apologetic at raising this matter at this late stage—it should have been mentioned in the particulars of the house. Telling Mr Blue that this would probably prove acceptable, but to write it down in the acceptance, and I would take instructions.

Engaged 10 minutes.

Note: This fulfils the first obligation on the seller in the offer—which is to accept the offer verbally within the time limit. There is, however, no agreement to accept by condition 24 of the offer which requires all conditions of contract to be in writing.

5.10 Email Henry Pink to Veronica Vanbrugh, paralegal and Wendy Robertson, trainee solicitor.

From: Henry Pink <hpink@bjw.co.uk>

Sent: 14 February 2006 15:33

To: Veronica Vanbrugh <vvanbrugh@bjw.co.uk.;
Wendy Robertson<wrobertson@bjw.co.uk>

Subject: 3 Miller Drive, NM

Attached: jame323phonenote.doc

Please see my note of telephone conversation with Bobby Blue of O'Neill Middleton. I am a bit unsure of all this modern stuff, but you have had the benefit of classes on feudal reform. Are they entitled to do this? I hope the James will accept this condition Bobby Blue has sprung on us.

Note: Pink is a crafty old bird. He knows perfectly well that an adjoining property owner has a perfect right to impose this condition, but he is keeping the younger members of the staff on their toes.

5.11 Veronica's reply:

From: Veronica Vanbrugh <vvanbrugh@bjw.co.uk>

Sent: 14 February 15:45

To: Henry Pink <hpink@bjw.co.uk>;
Wendy Robertson <wrobertson@bjw.co.uk>

Subject: Re: 3 Miller Drive, NM

That's the second potential misdescription!

Yes, this is quite in order by the Abolition of Feudal Tenure etc (Scotland) Act 2000, which allows neighbouring proprietors who have a real interest in the use of neighbouring land, as opposed to feudal superiors who had no real interest in the property other than financial, to enforce such amenity burdens. Good luck with the James. No doubt we shall get the titles soon!

5.12 Acceptance of Offer by O'Neill Middleton dated 15.02.06.

O'NEILL MIDDLETON
Solicitors and Estate Agents
999 Lally Street
GLASGOW
G2 4XX

Messers Brown Jarvie & Walker
Solicitors & Estate Agents
42 Registration Row
GLASGOW
G1 4XX

15 February 2006

Our Ref: RB/C.120

Your Ref: HP/VV/jame323

Dear Sirs

Mr and Mrs Angus McDuff

Mr and Mrs Stuart James

3 Miller Drive, Newton Mearns

On behalf of our clients Mr Angus and Mrs Williamina McDuff, we hereby accept your offer, made on 8 February 2006 on behalf of Mr Stuart and Mrs Henrietta James, to purchase the property at 3 Millar Drive, Newton Mearns, and that at the price of TWO HUNDRED AND FIFTY THOUSAND POUNDS (£250,000) and on the terms and conditions stated in the Glasgow Standard Offer.

This acceptance is, however, conditional on your clients' acceptance of the following condition:

Mr and Mrs McDuff, as the owners of the adjoining house at 1 Miller Drive, will insert a clause in the Disposition to be granted by them preventing the parking of any caravan or motor home on the land at 3 Miller Drive, which shall be a valid real burden.

We shall be pleased to receive your acceptance of this condition, on behalf of your clients. And conclusion of the Missives by mid-day on 18 February 2006, failing which this acceptance shall not be valid.

Yours faithfully

(*signed*) 'O'Neill Middleton'

Signed by Robert Blue, Partner of O'Neill Middleton on this Fifteenth day of February 2006 before the witness subscribing.

(*signed*) Rory Redknapp

Trainee Solicitor, Lally Street, Glasgow G2 4XX.

5.13 Email Henry Pink to clients:

From: Henry Pink <hpink@bjw.co.uk>

Sent: 15 February 2006 10:06

To: Stuart and Henrietta James <jamesfamily26@tiscali.co.uk>

CC: Veronica Vanbrugh <vvanbrugh@bjw.co.uk>

Subject: 3 Miller Drive, Newton Mearns, Glasgow

Attachement: jame323QA.pdf

Here is the acceptance of your offer. Congratulations. There is, however, one extra condition—that you don't use the ground for parking a caravan and motor home. I'm sorry that this matter should be raised at this late stage. Although it is late in the day to raise this, this is quite a usual stipulation and is 100% within the law, as the sellers own the house next door and seek to protect their amenity. Can you accept this? If so, please let me know as soon as possible, and I will conclude Missives on your behalf. HP

5.14 Stuart and Henrietta James reply.

From: Stuart and Henrietta James <jamesfamily26@tiscali.co.uk>

Sent: 16 February 2006 08:32

To: Henry Pink <hpink@bjw.co.uk>

Subject: Re 3 Miller Drive, Newton Mearns, Glasgow

Hi Henry

Delighted with your news! We don't own a caravan or a motor home, so this is quite acceptable to us. Please complete Missives.

Stuart and Henrietta.

Note: A quite serious situation is thus avoided. It might have been that the James are keen caravaneers, and would have been offended by the McDuff's lack of frankness and would have withdrawn their offer. This would have probably led to a claim against the McDuffs for misrepresenting their property, and misleading the James into bidding for a property without a restriction like this. The James at the very least would have a claim for survey and solicitors fees, and probably their costs of travelling to view the property.

5.15 Letter concluding Missives

BROWN JARVIE & WALKER
Solicitors & Estate Agents
42 Registration Row
GLASGOW
G1 4XX

Messrs O'Neill Middleton
Solicitors and Estate Agents
999 Lally Street
GLASGOW
G2 4XX

20 February 2006

Our Ref: HP/VV/jam 323

Your Ref: RB/C.120

Dear Sirs

Mr and Mrs James

Mr and Mrs McDuff

3 Miller Drive, Newton Mearns

Thank you for your letter dated 15 February 2006, enclosing a qualified acceptance on behalf of your client.

The time limit in your acceptance is hereby deleted. Please let us have your conclusion of the agreement.

We shall be pleased to receive the title deeds and other drafts as soon as possible.

Yours faithfully

(*signed*) 'Brown Jarvie & Walker'

The firm's signature is appended by Henry Pink, a partner of the firm, on 20 February 2006 in presence of Wendy Robertson, legal trainee, of 42 Registration Row, Glasgow.

(*signed*) Wendy Robertson

Notes: 1. That's that: Missives are now complete, and the partners are in a legally binding contract from which they cannot unilaterally withdraw.

2. Wendy had three settlements on Friday, 17 February, two of which turned out to be last minute rushes, despite her preparation, so unfortunately she did not attend to the conclusion of Missives until Monday, 20 February 2006, technically exposing her clients to risk if the deal collapsed for any reason over the weekend. Because she had not met the time limit specified in the Acceptance of Offer (6.12), while substantially agreed, are not in full consensus in idem. Therefore the time limit must be deleted and the deletion accepted by O'Neill Middleton.

5.16 Letter concluding Missives

O'NEILL MIDDLETON
Solicitors and Estate Agents
999 Lally Street
GLASGOW
G2 4XX

Messrs Brown Jarvie & Walker
Solicitors
42 Registration Row
GLASGOW
G1 4XX

22 February 2006

Dear Sirs

Mr and Mrs Angus McDuff
Mr and Mrs Stuart James
3 Miller Drive, Newton Mearns

On behalf of our clients, Mr and Mrs Angus McDuff, we hereby accept the deletion of our time limit specified in our letter of 15 February 2006, and we confirm that we are holding the Missives concluded on the basis of:

1. Your offer of 12 February 2006;

2. Our qualified acceptance of 15 February;

3. Your letter of 20 February;

4. This letter.

Yours faithfully

O'Neill Middleton

(Signed by a partner and witnessed)

Chapter 6

THE PURCHASERS CONCLUDE

'A verbal contract isn't worth the paper it's written on.'

(Samuel Goldwyn)

6.01 The bargaining process has already been discussed in chs 5 and 6. As contract lawyers say 'these remarks are held to be herein repeated *brevitatis causa*' (for the sake of brevity).

6.02 Similarly, the topic of risk was covered at para **4.28**. It is important, however, to underline that the risk passes to the purchasers on completion of the missives unless that risk is shifted back to the sellers in missives (see para **4.28**). It is unusual for the sellers not to accept the insurance risk until entry. If the risk is not so shifted back, it should be insured again immediately on completing missives by instructing cover in the name of the purchasers 'as purchaser, price unpaid'.

At this stage, as always, the insurance cover should be for full reinstatement value, and not for market value. In a modern house there may not be much difference between the two values but in an older house, built of traditional materials, the cost of repairing the house to the same standard may well be considerably in excess of what the house cost to buy.

6.03 The solicitors then tell the purchasers of their good fortune and advise them to get their finances and the removal van ready.

6.04 The purchasers might also be reminded that they have entered into a formal binding contract, and the consequences of failing to meet the commitment are severe. They should have been kept informed at all stages of formation of the contract.

6.05 Brown Jarvie & Walker might write to Mr and Mrs James as follows:

Dear Mr and Mrs James

Congratulations, we have now concluded a binding contract for your purchase of 3 Miller Drive, Newton Mearns.

Points to note are:

(a)   This contract is legally binding upon both sellers and purchasers. There is no concept in Scotland of a deal 'subject to contract', and if one party does not wish to complete, there is no question of withdrawing from the agreement on a unilateral basis.

(b)   Entry is on 1 April 2006 and we shall request the price and our fees and outlays, as quoted, in enough time to clear the cheque and settle.

Yours faithfully

To which they might receive a reply:

To: Henry Pink <hpink@bjw.co.uk>

Sent: 21 February 085:24

From: Stuart and Henrietta James <jamesfamily26@tiscali.co.uk>

Subject: purchase of 3 Miller Drive

Hi Henry

Thanks for the good news—all the details in your letter are understood by us.

Just one thing—April 1 is a Saturday! Could we not bring the entry date forward by a couple of days?

Stuart

Note: April fool! Does no one look at their diaries? Weekends are a non starter for house transactions, because it is impossible to arrange removal vans, and completely impossible to make financial transfers at weekends. This has escaped the notice of two professional firms, and their clients, who nevertheless were relying on the solicitors. Well, mistakes do happen, although they shouldn't, and the important thing is to apologise and to put the mistake right quickly, and to devise a system which prevents the same thing happening again. The mistake is corrected by a simple amendment to the contract, and a system of diary entries will be instituted—better late than never.

6.06 Note of telephone call with Messrs O'Neill Middleton 21.02.06

Speaking on the telephone with Mr Blue of O'NM and explaining the difficulty that had arisen with the date of entry. Mr Blue said that the new date of entry of 31 March was fine by him, but he would take instructions from his clients. He telephoned me back to say that the new date was acceptable to his clients, and I said we would let him have the appropriate letter.

HP

Engaged ¼ hour.

6.07 Letter to Mr and Mrs James from Henry Pink dated 21.02.06

Dear Mr and Mrs James

I very much regret the mistake with the date of entry and offer my apologies.

Messrs O'Neill Middleton have agreed, on behalf of their clients, to the date being changed to 31 March and we are exchanging formal letters to that effect.

With regards to you both.

Henry Pink

6.08 Letter from Brown Jarvie & Walker to O'Neill Middleton dated 21.02.06

Note: From this point on, all addresses, references and headings on letters will not be printed, to save endless repetition.

Dear Sirs

With reference to the missives concluded between our respective clients for the sale and purchase of 3 Miller Drive, Newton Mearns we now make it a condition of purchase that the date of entry shall be 31 March 2006.

In all other respects we confirm the terms of the missives entered into between us, and shall be pleased to have your acceptance of this amendment.

Yours faithfully

'Brown, Jarvie & Walker 'Wendy Robertson Witness'

Signed by Messrs Brown Jarvie & Walker at Glasgow on Twenty-first February Two Thousand and Six, the firms signature being adhibited by Henry Pink, a partner of the said firm in presence of the witness Wendy Robertson, Legal Trainee of 42 Registration Row, Glasgow.

6.09 Letter by O'Neill Middleton to Brown Jarvie & Walker

We acknowledge your letter of 21 February 2006, and accept your proposed change of the date of entry. We are therefore holding the Missives concluded between us for the sale and purchase of 3 Miller Drive, Newton Mearns as amended to the extent that the date of entry is 31 March 2006, but otherwise unchanged.

Yours faithfully

'O'Neill Middleton' 'Rory Redknapp, Witness'

Signed by O'Neill Middleton at Glasgow on 22 February 2006, the firm's signature being adhibited by Robert Blue, a partner of the said firm in presence of Rory Redknapp, Legal Trainee of 999 Lally Street, Glasgow.

Note the amendment should be made, and accepted, formally as with the original missives. This has been done and the amendment is therefore legally binding on both sets of parties.

6.10 A regrettable feature of modern conveyancing is the long delay in conclusion of missives, sometimes until the date of settlement. This is very bad practice and it equates to the English system of the contract only being complete when contracts are exchanged. This allows the English features of gazumping, gazundering and contract chains to enter Scottish conveyancing. In Scotland, we have long prided ourselves on the superiority of our binding missives, and we should not let it be eroded. The principal culprits are the lending institutions, which are taking longer and longer to issue loan papers (see 'Lenders offer late service' by Graeme Pagan in 2002 JLSS 15). Let us also be honest and admit that the pressure of business is also often to blame. I suspect also that some solicitors, faced by increasingly complex contracts, are quite happy not to conclude them. The Law Society has issued a Practice Note urging conveyancers to conclude contracts at an early stage, and I can only agree with them. See Appendix I.

Chapter 7

THE SELLERS SHOW THEIR HAND

'You ought to take the bull between the teeth'
(Sam Goldwyn)

The saga of 3 Miller Drive might continue as follows:

7.01 Letter from O'Neill Middleton

O'Neill Middleton
Solicitors and Estate Agents
999 Lally Street
GLASGOW
G2 4XX

Messrs Brown Jarvie & Walker
Solicitors and Estate Agents
42 Registration Row
GLASGOW
G1 4XX

OUR REF: RB/C120
YOUR REF: HP/VV/Jame 323

22 February 2006

Dear Sirs

Mr and Mrs McDuff

Mr, and Mrs James

3 Miller Drive, Newton Mearns

Thank you for your letter of 20 February amending the agreement to purchase the above property.

We now enclose the following documents:

1. Disposition by Angus McDuff in favour of Stuart James recorded GRS (Renfrew) 28 June 1978.

2. Disposition by Robert McRobert in favour of Angus McDuff recorded GRS (Renfrew) 12 August 1975. This will be a first

registration of title. You will note that the title stands in Mr McDuff's name only, and a consent by Mrs McDuff will be given in terms of the Matrimonial Homes (Family Protection) (Scotland) Act 1981.

3. Coal Authority Report dated 30 January 2006 disclosing no coal workings in the vicinity of the subjects.

4. Feu Disposition by Walter John MacFarlane to James Mearns Davidson recorded 25 September 1919 and Feu Disposition by Mickle & Muckle Ltd to Robert McRobert recorded 11 November 1936, being the writs referred to for burdens.

5. Draft forms 10 and P16 for your approval.

6. Planning Enquiry Certificate by East Renfrewshire Council dated 10 February 2006.

7. Standard Security by Angus McDuff in favour of Black County Building Society recorded GRS (Renfrew) 12 August 1975.

8. Draft Discharge of Standard Security by Black Country PLC (formerly Black Country Building Society).

9. Draft Letter of Obligation.

10. On letter concluding the bargain in the amended terms.

We shall be pleased to hear from you, and in the meantime, please acknowledge receipt.

Yours faithfully

(*signed*) O'Neill Middleton

Note: These are the commonest things to be sent with the first post-missive letter. Good practice dictates that they are assembled at the earliest opportunity, to speed the transaction on. The form 10P 16 report may already have been issued. The property enquiry certificate should not, however, be more than three months old as things may have changed in the interim. Although the non-entitled spouse's consent will be in grant of the disposition, the Keeper will still need to see an affidavit for family homes under the Civil Partnership Act 2004, to issue a land certificate with exclusion of indemnity. The Writs referred to for burdens are pretty standard feudal deeds full of obsolete burdens. The purchaser's solicitor must, however, be sure to check that these have not been kept alive by recording a notice. After that the Keeper will simply omit them from the Land Certificate, and that means they will be gone for ever. The Disposition in favour of the McDuffs is however important, as it forms the basis of the registered title.

7.02 Memo note Henry Pink to Wendy Robertson dated 23.02.06

Here are the titles to 3 Miller Drive. Please deal with them. Also please remember that we have five working days to accept the position stated by the PEC and Coal Report. I have had a quick look at them—there doesn't appear to be anything untoward, but please check carefully and confirm. I have asked Veronica to look after the case management here and make appropriate diary entries etc. and shall be obliged if you look after the conveyancing formalities.

Copy: VV

HP

Note: After the fiasco of the entry date, Henry Pink wisely delegates his functions to his capable team, and outlines their respective responsibilities. He should have thought of this much earlier, as diary entries are a sign of a well-run firm. Better late than never.

7.03 Email Brown Jarvie & Walker to O'Neill Middleton

To: Rory Redknapp <rory.redknapp@oneillmiddleton.com>

Sent: 24 February 2006 16:31

From: Wendy Robertson <wrobertson@bjw.co.uk>

Subject: 3 Miller Drive, NM

Hi Rory

Thank you for your letter of 22 February with its enclosures. I will write to you again within five working days in terms of the missives.

Have a good weekend!

Wendy.

7.04 Disposition in favour of Angus McDuff—the last Sasine title deed

I, ROBERT McROBERT, residing at Four Taeping Road, Glasgow IN CONSIDERATION of the sum of Fifty Thousand pounds (£50,000) paid to me by ANGUS McDUFF residing at Forty Three Ariel Drive, Edinburgh DO HEREBY DISPONE to and in favour of the said Angus McDuff and his executors and assignees heritably and irredeemably ALL and WHOLE that area or plot of ground with the dwellinghouse known as and forming Three Miller Drive, Newton Mearns and being the subjects more particularly described in, disponed by and delineated in black and coloured pink on the plan annexed and executed as relative to the Division of the Feu Disposition by Mickle & Muckle Limited in my favour dated Sixth May and recorded in the Division of the General Register of Sasines applicable to the County of Renfrew Eleventh day of May both months in the year Nineteen Hundred and Thirty Six TOGETHER WITH (One) the whole rights common, mutual or sole effeiring thereto; (Two) the whole parts, privileges and pertinents thereof: (Three) the whole fittings and fixtures therein and thereon and (Four) my whole right, title and interest present and future in and to the said subjects; BUT ALWAYS WITH AND UNDER in so far as still valid, subsisting and applicable the burdens, conditions and others specified and contained in (First) Feu Disposition by Walter John MacFarlane in favour of James Mearns Davidson dated Fourteenth and recorded in the said Division of the General Register of Sasines Twenty Fifth both days of September Nineteen Hundred and Nineteen; (Second) the said Feu Disposition by Mickle & Muckle Limited in my favour dated and recorded as aforesaid; WITH ENTRY as at the Tenth day of August Nineteen Hundred and Seventy Five; and I grant warrandice: IN WITNESS WHEREOF Signed by the said Robert McRobert at Glasgow on the Fifth day of August Nineteen Hundred and Seventy Five in presence of these witnesses Charles Spence, Solicitor, and Mary Griffiths, Typist, both of Thirty Three Cornwallis Street, Glasgow.

REGISTER on behalf of the within named Angus McDuff in the Register for the County of Renfrew.

'Spence & Spence'

Solicitors, Glasgow, Agents

Note: A fairly typical disposition of its time, with a lot of irrelevant detail that will require to be cut down. Please note that it is incompetent to refer to this disposition for a description of the plot of ground, because it makes reference to an earlier description in the deed by Mickle & Muckle in favour of Robert McRobert, which is the one that must be used.

7.05 Draft disposition on first registration, drafted by Wendy Robertson along the lines of the previous disposition

I, ANGUS McDUFF, residing at Three Miller Drive, Newton Mearns, Renfrewshire, (1) heritable proprietor of the subjects hereinafter disponed IN CONSIDERATION of the sum of TWO HUNDRED AND FORTY NINE POUNDS (£249,000) (2) paid to me by STUART

JAMES and HENRIETTA JAMES, both residing at Daffodil Cottage, Wordsworth Lane, Kendal in equal proportions HAVE SOLD and DO HEREBY DISPONE with the consent and concurrence of my wife MRS. WILLIAMINA McDUFF, residing with me, for all her rights in the property whether under the Matrimonial Homes (Family Protection) (Scotland) Act 1981 or otherwise, to the said STUART JAMES and the said MRS. HENRIETTA JAMES equally and to the survivor (3) of them and to their, his or her Executors and assignees whomsoever heritably and irredeemably ALL and WHOLE that plot or area of ground in the County of Renfrew known as and forming Three Miller Drive, Newton Mearns described in, and shown outlined in black and coloured pink on the plan annexed to Disposition by Mickle & Muckle Limited recorded in the Division of the General Register of Sasines for the County of Renfrew Eleventh May Nineteen Hundred and Thirty Six (4); Together with all rights of servitude pertaining to the subjects, all rights of common property, the parts, privileges and pertinents thereof, all fittings and fixtures therein and thereon, and my and the said consenter's whole right, title and interest in the said subjects (5); BUT THE PROPERTY HEREIN DISPONED is so disponed always subject to the following burdens and servitudes, in so far as still valid, subsisting and applicable thereto (6) contained in: (One) Feu Disposition by Walter John McFarlane in favour of James Mearns Davidson recorded in the said Register Twenty Fifth September Nineteen Hundred and Nineteen; and (Two) Feu Disposition by Mickle & Muckle Limited recorded in the said Register Eleventh May Nineteen hundred and Thirty Six; AND THE SAID PROPERTY at Three Miller Drive aforesaid (hereinafter referred to as 'the Burdened Property') is disponed with and under the following real burden (7) created in my favour as the owner of One Miller Drive, Newton Mearns (hereinafter referred to as 'the Benefited Property') namely that the owner or occupier of the Burdened Property shall not use, or permit to be used, the Burdened Property for the parking of any caravan or mobile home; This burden will be enforced by me and my successors as owners of the Benefited Property in terms of the Title Conditions (Scotland) Act 2003; with entry at the Thirty-first day of March Two Thousand and Six, notwithstanding the date thereof; AND I the said ANGUS McDUFF with consent foresaid notwithstanding that I have sold the said subjects to the said Stuart James and Mrs Henrietta James and have received payment of the price in exchange for delivery of the Disposition, do hereby declare that until the title of Stuart James and Mrs Henrietta James has been registered in the Land Register in pursuance of these presents I shall hold the said subjects as trustee of the said Stuart James and Mrs Henrietta James (8); AND I with consent foresaid grant warrandice: IN WITNESS WHEREOF

Notes: The following remarks are made about the draft disposition, following the numbering in the deed:

(1) The Sellers' solicitors have mistakenly concluded missives on the assumption that the title is in the names of both spouses, whereas it is in the name of Mr McDuff alone. This mistake is easily rectified by Mrs McDuff giving consent to the disposition. Under the MH(FP)(S)A 1985, the non-entitled spouse or non-entitled civil partner must consent to any deed of the property (see App I). This can be given in a separate Affidavit, but it is usually more convenient to incorporate the consent in the recorded disposition and thus having only one deed to think about, although the Keeper may require an affidavit to be sworn that there is no civil partner non-entitled spouse.

(2) The price is reduced by a deduction for the oak table and chairs, which are moveable for the purposes of SDLT. Ideally, this apportionment should have been provided for in the missives. The effect on the duty paid is virtually negligible, but the value of moveables deducted has to be reported to HM Revenue and Customs, who may challenge the value. This is quite understandable, as a method of tax evasion was to make a huge deduction for a few valueless moveables when the price paid was just over the threshold for a tax change. In this case, it is probably all in order.

(3) Wendy has drafted this deed on the assumption that, because Mr and Mrs James are in a settled marriage, they would wish a survivorship destination. This would automatically pass the half share of the property to the survivor on the first death. On this topic see generally an article by Ken Swinton Scottish Law Gazette, February 2006, p 12, 'And to the survivor of them?'. This sets out why it may not be advisable to use this clause. It is probably what most settled spouses would want, as it passes title to the survivor without any difficulty, but it can be terribly complicated if a marriage is in difficulties. Another good reason for not using this clause is that of inheritance tax planning. This clause makes it very difficult to pass on death one spouse's share to, say, the children of the marriage, to take advantage of an inheritance tax concession. In any

event, the parties should have been advised on this point, and have given their instructions. There is still time …

(4) There is no need to put in the dates of a deed referred to, so long as the date of recording is given (see C(S)A 1874, s 32 and Sch H and the C(S)A 1924, s 9 and Sch E. Similarly it is not necessary to specify the Register, other than as above.

(5) This clause is a lot of flim flam, and much of it is not necessary.

(6) As immediately above.

(7) The whole matter of real burdens requires a knowledge of the Title Conditions (Scotland) Act 2003, which broadly put the whole complicated business on a more sensible and modern footing. Details of the old law can be found in Professor McDonald's *Conveyancing Manual*, (7 ed, LexisNexis, 2004). The rules are: (1) title conditions can only be created in a registered deed of any kind; (2) the expression 'real burden' must be used in the constitutive deed; (3) the deed must identify the burdened and benefited proprietors; and (4) the deed must be registered against both properties. Thus everyone knows where they stand and there are no unexpected nasty surprise burdens.

(8) Although the price is paid and the disposition is delivered the property is not safe from the Sellers' creditors until the title of the purchasers is registered, see the unfortunate case of *Burnett's Trustee v Grainger* (2004 SC (HL) 19) which is fully digested in *Conveyancing 2004* by Professors Reid and Gretton, (Avizandum 2005). To prevent a recurrence of the unfortunate circumstances it is vital to register the title as soon as possible, but to guard the purchaser until the title is recorded, it is necessary to insert this clause, known as 'the trust clause'. Please note that Wendy has used the wording suggested by Professors Reid and Gretton, which should amply suffice.

7.06 Notes on title of 3 Miller Drive, Newton Mearns.

(a) Feu Disposition by Walter John MacFarlane in favour of James Mearns Davidson recorded GRS (Renfrew) 25 September 1919.

The following feudal burdens were created in favour of MacFarlane whose address is given as Stirlingshire.

1. Liability on the feuar to form and maintain the road and water supply pipe (now maintained by East Renfrewshire Council and Scottish Water).

2. Feuar to build a detached dwellinghouse with relative offices. Building to be of stone or brick roughcast and to maintain and uphold said house. It shall be built to plans approved by the seller. (Done.)

3. The purchaser shall build fences and walls round the property and shall recompense the adjoining property owner for any wall or fence already built and used by the purchaser. (Done.)

4. Not to make or burn bricks or other similar nuisances . (Not enforceable.)

5. Irritancy clause in the event of the purchaser being in breach of any of these conditions. (Irritancies no longer competent.)

Note: The house was built in the first half of the last century, thus the building conditions are badly out of date. Now, thanks to the FT(S)A 2000 and TC(S)A 2003, they can be safely ignored.

(b) Feu Disposition by Mickle & Muckle Ltd. In favour of Robert McRobert recorded GRS (Renfrew) recorded 11 May 1936.

This disposition describes the property and carries a plan which is photocopied and annexed.

(c) PEC from East Renfrewshire Council dated 1 February 2006.

This discloses no outstanding notices. The roads and sewers are publicly owned and maintained. The house is not in a Conservation Area. There is, however, a tree preservation order.

(d) Coal Authority letter dated 2 February 2006.

This does not disclose that any coal mining has ever taken place in the vicinity of this house.

(e) Draft discharge of standard security by Black Country PLC.

WE, BLACK COUNTRY PLC incorporated under the Companies Acts and having our Registered Office at Arnold Street, Stoke-on-Trent, in the County of Derby in consideration of the sum of THIRTY THOUSAND POUNDS (£30,000) being the whole amount secured by the Standard Security by ANGUS McDUFF residing at Three Miller Drive, Newton Mearns, Renfrewshire HEREBY DISCHARGE a Standard Security by the said ANGUS McDUFF in favour of Black Country Building Society registered in the County of Renfrew on Twelfth August Nineteen hundred and Seventy

Five; which Standard Security was last vested in Black Country Building Society as aforesaid and from whom Black Country PLC acquired right on Fourth December Two Thousand by (one) a Transfer Agreement pursuant to section 97 of the Building Societies Act 1986 between Black Country Building Society and the said Black Country PLC dated Ninth May Two Thousand and (two) Confirmation of the transfer by the Building Societies Commission pursuant to section 98 of the Building Societies Act 1986 dated Twenty Eighth September Two Thousand: IN WITNESS WHEREOF

Draft approved.

WR.

Note: The Black Country Building Society was one of the original great societies which did so much to spread homeownership. It was built on a basis of mutual ownership, that is to say it was owned as joint property by its members who did not get a share of the assets until the Society was dissolved. In 2000 its members voted overwhelmingly to reject mutual ownership, and to turn the Society into a limited company. This was done, and each member, including borrowers, received 500 shares in the company. The discharge has to be granted by the PLC, which must deduce its title to do so. The drafter of the discharge has done this. Incidentally, if the members had kept their shares and did not sell them for a quick profit, they have been rewarded by a steady increase in the value of the share.

(f) Draft form 1 in relation to disposition.

REGISTERS OF SCOTLAND
Executive Agency
Information about Scotland's land & property

FORM1

e **FORMS ONLINE**

(Land Registration (Scotland) Rules 1980 Rule 9(1)(a))

No covering letter is required

APPLICATION FOR FIRST REGISTRATION

VERSION 28/11/2004

1. **Presenting Agent (see Note 1)**

   Brown Jarvie & Walker
   LP34
   Glasgow -2

   Keeper of the Registers of Scotland
   Meadowbank House
   153 London Road
   Edinburgh EH8 7AU
   Telephone: 0131 659 6111

Part A

2. **FAS No.** (see Note 2)   3. **Agent's Tel No.** (include STD Code)   4. **Agent's Reference**

   | 0975 | 0141 221 4343 | HP/VV/WR/JAME323 |

3. **FAS No.** (see Note 2)   3. **Agent's Tel No.** (include STD Code)   4. **Agent's Reference**

   | 0975 | 0141 221 4343 | HP/VV/WR/JAME323 |

5. **Name of Deed in respect of which registration is required**   6. **County** (see Note 3)   If more than one county, click here to mark X in box and select further counties.

   | Disposition | RENFREW | |

7. **Subjects**   (see Note 4)

   Street No. **3**   Street Name **Miller Drive**

   Town **Newton Mearns, Glasgow**   Post Code **G77 10EU**

   Other

8. **Name and Address of Applicant** (see Note 5)

   1. Surname   Forename(s)

   | James | Stuart |

   Address

   Daffodil Cottage, Wordsworth Lane, Kendal

2. Surname

| James |

Forename(s)

| Henrietta |

Address

| Daffodil Cottage, Wordsworth Lane, Kendal |

and/ or company/ firm or council etc

If more than 2 applicants, click here to mark X in box and add further applicant details.

Address

9. **Granter/Last recorded title holder** (see Note 6)

1. Surname

| McDuff |

Forename(s)

| Angus |

2. Surname

Forename(s)

and/or company/firm or council etc

If more than 2 granters, click here to mark X in box and add further granter details.

10. | Consideration (see Note 7) | Value (see Note 8) | Fee (see Note 9) | Method of Payment | Date of Entry |
| --- | --- | --- | --- | --- |
| 249,000 | | 500 | Cheque | 31/03/2006 |

11. **If a Form 10 Report has been issued in connection with this Application, please quote Report Number**

12. **I/ We apply for registration in respect of Deed(s) No 6   in the inventory of Writs (Form 4). I/ We certify that the information supplied in this application is correct to the best of my/ our knowledge and belief.**

FOR OFFICIAL USE

Signature   Date

Notes 1-9 referred to are contained in Notes and Directions for completion of Applications for First Registration EFORMS09752006050110:06:44

PART B

Delete **YES** or **NO** as appropriate
N.B. If more space is required for any section of this form, a separate sheet, or separate sheets, may be added.

1. Do the deeds submitted in support of this application include a plan illustrating the extent of the subjects to be registered?   ☒ Yes   ☐ No
    If **YES**, please specify the deed and its Form 4 Inventory number:

Item 2 on form 4

    If **NO**, have you submitted a deed containing a full bounding description with measurements?   ☐ Yes   ☒ No
    If **YES**, please specify the deed and its Form 4 Inventory number:

    N.B. If the answer to both the above questions is **NO** then, unless the property is part of a tenement or flatted building, you must submit a plan of the subjects properly drawn to a stated scale and showing sufficient surrounding features to enable it to be located on the Ordnance Map. The plan should bear a docquet, signed by the person signing the Application Form, to the effect that it is a plan of the subjects sought to be registered under the attached application.

2. Is a Form P16 Report issued by the Keeper confirming that the boundaries of the subjects coincide with the Ordnance Map being submitted in support of this Application?   ☒ Yes   ☐ No

    If **NO**, does the legal extent depicted in the plans or descriptions in the deeds submitted in support of the Application cohere with the occupational extent?   ☐ Yes   ☐ No

    If **NO**, please advise:-

    (a) the approximate age and nature of the occupational boundaries, or

    (b) whether, if the extent of the subjects as defined in the deeds is larger than the occupational extent, the applicant is prepared to accept the occupational extent as viewed, or   ☐ Yes   ☐ No

    (c) whether, if the extent of the subjects as defined in the deeds is smaller than the occupational extent, any remedial action has been taken   ☐ Yes   ☐ No

3. Is there any person in possession or occupation of the subjects or any part of them adversely to the interest of the applicant?   ☐ Yes   ☒ No
    If **YES**, please give details:

4. If the subjects were acquired by the applicant under any statutory provision, does the statutory provision restrict the applicant's power of disposal of the subjects?   ☐ Yes   ☐ No   ☒ N/A
    If **YES**, please indicate the statute:

5. (a) Are there any charges affecting the subjects or any part of them, except as stated in the Schedule of Heritable Securities etc. on page 4 of this application?
If **YES**, please give details: ☐ Yes   ☑ No

 _____

 (b) Apart from overriding interests are there any burdens affecting the subjects or any part of them, except as stated in the Schedule of Burdens on page 4 of this application?
If **YES**, please give details: ☐ Yes   ☑ No

 _____

 (c) Are there any overriding interests affecting the subjects or any part of them which you wish noted on the Title Sheet?
If **YES**, please give details: ☐ Yes   ☑ No

 _____

 (d) Are there any recurrent monetary payments (e.g. leasehold casualties) exigible from the subjects or any part of them?
If **YES**, please give details   ☐ Yes   ☑ No

 _____

6. Where any party to the deed inducing registration is a company registered under the Companies Acts

 Has a receiver or liquidator been appointed?
If **YES**, please give details: ☐ Yes   ☐ No   ☑ N/A

 _____

 If **NO**, has any resolution been passed or court order made for the winding up of the Company or petition presented for its liquidation?
If **YES**, please give details: ☐ Yes   ☐ No

 _____

7. Where any party to the deed inducing registration is a company registered under the Companies Acts can you confirm

 (a) that is it not a charity as defined in section 112 of the Companies Acts 1989 and   ☐ Yes   ☐ No   ☑ N/A

 (b) that the transaction to which the deed gives effect is not one to which section 322A of the Companies Act 1985 (as inserted by section 109 of the Companies Act 1989) applies?   ☐ Yes   ☐ No   ☑ N/A

 Where the answer to either part of the question is **NO**, please give details:

 _____

8. Where any party to the deed inducing registration is a corporate body other than a company registered under the Companies Acts

   (a) Is it acting intra vires?
      If **NO**, please give details: ☐ Yes   ☐ No   ☑ N/A

       [   ]

   (b) Has any arrangement been put in hand for the dissolution of any such corporate body?
      If **YES**, please give details   ☐ Yes   ☐ No   ☑ N/A

       [   ]

9. Are all the necessary consents, renunciations or affidavits in terms of section 6 of the Matrimonial Homes (Family Protection)(Scotland) Act 1981 being submitted in connection with this application?   ☑ Yes   ☐ No   ☐ N/A

N.B. if sufficient evidence to satisfy the Keeper that there are no subsisting occupancy rights in the subjects of this application is not submitted with the application then the

statement by the Keeper in terms of rule 5(j) of the Land Registration (Scotland) Rules 1980 will not be inserted in the Title Sheet or will be qualified as appropriate without further enquiry by the Keeper.

10. Where the deed inducing registration is in implement of the exercise of a power of sale under a heritable security

       Have the statutory procedures necessary for the proper exercise of such power been complied with?   ☐ Yes   ☐ No   ☑ N/A

11. Where the deed inducing registration is pursuant on a Compulsory Purchase Order

       Have the necessary statutory procedures been complied with?   ☐ Yes   ☐ No   ☑ N/A

12. Is any party to the deed inducing registration subject to any legal incapacity or disability?   ☐ Yes   ☑ No

    If **YES**, please give details:

    [   ]

13. Are the deeds and documents detailed in the Inventory (Form 4) all the deeds and documents relevant to the title?   ☑ Yes   ☐ No

    If **NO**, please give details:

    [   ]

14. Are there any facts and circumstances material to the right or title of the applicant which have not already been disclosed in this application or its accompanying documents?   ☐ Yes   ☑ No

If **YES**, please give details:

| |
| |

SCHEDULE OF HERITABLE SECURITIES ETC.

N.B. New Charges granted by the applicant should not be included.

| item 3 on form 4 |
| |

SCHEDULE OF BURDENS

| items 1, 2 and 6 on form 4 |
| |

REGISTERS OF SCOTLAND EXECUTIVE

Draft approved.

These forms relate to the registration of the discharge.

 FORM 4

(Land Registration (Scotland) Rules 1980 Rule 9(2))

INVENTORY OF WRITS RELEVANT TO APPLICATION FOR REGISTRATION (see Note 1)

(to be completed in duplicate)

Title Number(s)

(to be completed for a dealing with registered interests in land.)

Brown Walker & Jarvie

LP34

GLASGOW

Subjects (see Note 3)   3 Miller Drive, Newton Mearns, Glasgow G77 10EU

Registration County   RENFREW

Applicants Reference   HP/WR/VV/JAMR323

Please complete Inventory below as in this specimen

Particulars of Writs (see Note 4)

Item No	Please mark "S" against documents submitted	Document	Grantee	Date of Recording
☐	☐	Land Certificate*		
☐	☐	Charge Certificate*		
1	-	Feu Charter*	Upright Builders	
☐	☐			

*delete if inapplicable

Notes 1-4 referred to are contained in Notes and Directions for Completion of Inventory Writs Relevant to Application for Registration.

FOR OFFICIAL USE
ONLY

APPLICATION NUMBER	DATE OF RECEIPT	TITLE NUMBER

The Writs marked "S" on this inventory were received on the Date of Receipt stamped on this page.

INVENTORY

Particulars of Writs (see Note 4)

Item No	Please Mark "S" against documents submitted	Document	Grantee	Date of Recording
☐	S	Land Certificate		
☐	S	Charge Certificate		
1	S	Feu Disposition	James Mearns Davidson	25/09/1919

130

2	S	Feu Disposition	Robert McRobert	11/11/1936
3	S	Standard Security	Black County BS	12/08/1975
4	S	Disposition	Angus McDuff	12/08/1975
5	S	TPO	by East Renfrewshire Council	13/07/1986
6	S	Disposition	Stuart James & Spouse	TBR
7	S	Standard Security	Cumbrian Bank plc	TBR
8	S	Family Homes Affidavit	Angus McDuff	
9	S	SDLT Certificate		

FORM2

(Land Registration (Scotland) Rules 1980 Rule 9(1)(b))

No covering letter is required

APPLICATION FOR REGISTRATION OF A DEALING

VERSION 28/11/2004

1. Presenting Agent (see Note 1)

O'NEILL MIDDLETON
LP353
GLASGOW -2

Keeper of the Registers of Scotland
Meadowbank House
153 London Road
Edinburgh EH8 7AU
Telephone: 0131 659 6111

Part A

2. FAS No. (see Note 2) 3. **Agent's Tel No.** (include STD Code) 4. **Agent's Reference**

| 1024 | 0141 221 3456 | BTB/RXR/FAC/@DUF43.2 |

5. **Name of Deed** in respect of which registration is required   6. **County** (see Note 3)   Mark X in box if more than one county.

| Discharge | RENFREW | |

7. **Title No(s) of registered interest(s) affected by this application** (see note 5)   Mark X in box if more than one Title Number

8. **Subjects**   (see Note 5)

Street No. **3**   Street Name **Miller Drive**

Town **Newton Mearns, Glasgow**   Post Code **G77 10EU**

Other

9. **Name and Address of Applicant** (see Note 7)

1. Surname   Forename(s)

| McDuff | Angus |

Address

> **3 Miller Drive, Newton Mearns, Glasgow G77 10EU**

2. Surname   Forename(s)

Address

and/ or company/ firm or council etc   Mark X in box if more than 2
                                                   applicants.

Address

10.	Consideration (see Note 7)	Value (see Note 8)	Fee (see Note 9)	Method of Payment	Date of Entry
	15,000		22.00	Direct Debit	

11.

I/ We apply for registration in respect of Deed(s) No ☐ 1 in the inventory of Writs (Form 4). I/ We certify that the information supplied in this application is correct to the best of my/ our knowledge and belief.

FOR OFFICIAL USE

Signature   Date

Notes 1-10 referred to are contained in Notes and Directions for completion of Applications for a Dealing
EFORMS10242006050110:13:08

PART B

Delete **YES** or **NO** as appropriate

N.B. If more space is required for any section of this form, a separate sheet may be added.

1. Where the dealing in respect of which registration si sought transfers the interest specified in the Property Section of the Title Sheet

   (a) Is there any person in psssession or occupation of the subjects or any part of them adversely of the interest of the applicant?
   If **YES**, please give details: ☐ Yes   ☐ No   ☒ N/A

   (b) If the subjects were acquired by the applicant under any statutory provision, does the statutory provision restrict the applicant's power of disposal of the subjects?
   If **YES**, please indicate the statute: ☐ Yes   ☐ No   ☒ N/A

(c) Apart from overriding interests are there any burdens affecting the subjects or any part of them, except as already disclosed in the Land Certificate and in the documents produced with this application?
If **YES**, please give details:

☐ Yes ☑ No

```
[                                          ]
```

(d) Are there any overriding interests affecting the subjects or any part of them which you wish noted on the Title Sheet?
If **YES**, please give details:

☐ Yes ☑ No

```
[                                          ]
```

(e) Are there any recurrent monetary payments (e.g. leasehold casualties) exigible from the subjects or any part of them?
If **YES**, please give details:

☐ Yes ☑ No

```
[                                          ]
```

2. Where any party to the dealing is a company registered under the Companies Acts

Has a receiver or liquidator be appointed?
If **YES**, please give details:

☐ Yes ☐ No ☑ N/A

```
[                                          ]
```

If **NO**, has any resolution been passed or court order made for the winding up of the Company or petition presented for its liquidation?
If **YES**, please give details:

☐ Yes ☐ No

```
[                                          ]
```

3. Where any party to the dealing is a company under the Companies Acts can you confirm

(a) that it is not a charity as defined in section 112 of the Companies Act 1989 and

☐ Yes ☐ No ☑ N/A

(b) that the transaction to which the deed gives effect is not one to which section 322A of the Companies Act 1985 (as inserted by section 109 of the Companies Act 1989) applies?

☐ Yes ☐ No

Where the answer to either of the questions is **NO**, please give details:

```
[                                          ]
```

4. Where any party to the dealing is a coroprate body other than a company registered under the Companies Act

(a) Is it acting *intra vires*?
If **NO**, please give details:

☐ Yes ☐ No ☑ N/A

```
[                                          ]
```

(b) Has any arrangement been put in hand for the
dissolution of any such corporate body? ☐ Yes ☐ No
If **YES**, please give details:

[ ]

---

5. Are all the necessary consents, renunciations or
affidavits in terms of section 6 of the Matrimonial Homes ☐ Yes ☐ No ☑ N/A
(Family Protection)(Scotland) Act 1981 being submitted
in connection with this application?

---

6. Where the dealing is in implement of the exercise of a
power of sale under a heritable security

Have the statutory procedures necessary for the
proper exercise of such power been complied with? ☐ Yes ☐ No ☑ N/A

---

7. Where the dealing is pursuant on a Compulsory
Purchase Order

Have the necessary statutory procedures been
complied with? ☐ Yes ☐ No ☑ N/A

---

8. In all cases

(a) Is any part to the dealing subject to any legal
incapacity not already disclosed on the Land ☐ Yes ☑ No
Certificate?
If **YES**, please give details:

[ ]

(b) Are the deeds and documents detailed in the
inventory (Form 4) all the deeds and documents ☑ Yes ☐ No
relevant to the application?
If **NO**, please give details:

[ ]

(c) Are there any facts and circumstances material to
the right or title of the applicant which have not ☐ Yes ☑ No
already been disclosed in this application or its
accompanying documents?
If **YES**, please give details:

[ ]

 **FORM 4**

(Land Registration (Scotland) Rules 1980 Rule 9(2))

INVENTORY OF WRITS RELEVANT TO APPLICATION FOR REGISTRATION (see Note 1)

(to be completed in duplicate)

Title Number(s)

(to be completed for a dealing with registered interests in land.)

O'NEILL MIDDLETON

LP53

GLASGOW -2

Subjects (see Note 3)

3 Miller Drive,
Newton Mearns,
Glasgow G77 10EU

Registration County   RENFREW

Applicants Reference   BTB/RXR/FAC/@DUF4

Please complete Inventory below as in this specimen

Particulars of Writs (see Note 4)

Item No	Please mark "S" against documents submitted	Document	Grantee	Date of Recording
☐	☐	Land Certificate*		
☐	☐	Charge		

136

| 1 | - | Feu Charter* | Upright Builders | |
| | | | | |

*delete if inapplicable

Notes 1-4 referred to are contained in Notes and Directions for Completion of Inventory Writs Relevant to Application for Registration.

FOR OFFICIAL USE ONLY

| APPLICATION NUMBER | DATE OF RECEIPT | TITLE NUMBER |

The Writs marked "S" on this inventory were received on the Date of Receipt stamped on this page.

INVENTORY

Particulars of Writs (see Note 4)

Item No	Please Mark "S" against documents submitted	Document	Grantee	Date of Recording
		Land Certificate		
		Charge Certificate		
1		Discharge	McDuff	TBR

(h) Draft form 10

(Form 10)

(Land Registration (Scotland) Rules 1980 Rule 24(1))

APPLICATION FOR A REPORT PRIOR TO REGISTRATION OF THE SUBJECTS DESCRIBED BELOW

Note:No covering letter is required and an existing Search should not be submitted.

VAT Reg No. GD 410 GB 888 8410 64

Please complete in DUPLICATE and in BLACK TYPE

From   FOR OFFICIAL USE

Name	**O'NEILL MIDDLETON**	Report Number	
Address	**LP53**	Date of Receipt	
	GLASGOW -2	Search Sheet Nos.	
		Fee	
County	**RENFREW**	FAS No.	**1024**
Applicant's Reference	**BTB/RXR/FAC/@DUF43.2**	FAX No.	**0141 221 4567**
Telephone No.	**0141 221 3456**	FAX Response Required	✓

POSTAL ADDRESS OF SUBJECTS

Street No.	**3**	House Name	**Miller**	Street Name	**Drive**
Town	**Newton Mearns**		Postcode	*G77 10EU*	

The above subjects being **edged red and the subjects described in**

feu disposition by Mickle & Muckle Limited in favour of Robert McRobert recorded GRS (Renfrew) 11 November 1936

I/We apply for a report

(1) on the subjects described above, for which an application for registration in the Land Register is to be made, from
(a) the REGISTER OF SASINES and
(b) the LAND REGISTER stating whether or not registration of the said subjects has been effected [3]

138

1. A plan need not be attached if a verbal description will sufficiently identify the subjects.

2. Describe by reference to a writ recorded in the Register of Sasines.

3. If the subjects have been registered, the Keeper will supply an Office Copy of the Title Sheet only on a specific request

and (2) from the Registers of Inhibitions and Adjudications for 5 years prior to the date of Certificate against in the
Register of Inhibitions and Adjudications, viz.

1. Surname(s)	McDuff	Forename(s)	Angus

Address(es)	3 Miller Drive, Newton Mearns, Glasgow G77 10EU

2. Surname(s)	James	Forename(s)	Stuart

Address(es)	Daffodil Cottage, Wordsworth Lane, Kendal

3. Surname(s)	James	Forename(s)	Henrietta

Address(es)	Daffodil Cottage, Wordsworth Lane, Kendal

4. Surname(s)		Forename(s)	

Address(es)	

5. Company/ Firm/ Corporate body	

Address(es)	

6. Company/ Firm/ Corporate body	

Address(es)	

Approved.

WR.

(i)   Draft form P16.

(Form 16)
APPLICATION TO COMPARE A BOUNDING DESCRIPTION1 WITH O.S. MAP

Applicant's Reference	**BTB/RXR/FAC/@DUF43.2**	County	As above
From		Postcode	**G77 10EU**
Name	**O'NEILL MIDDLETON**	Telephone No.	**0141 221 3456**
Address	**LP53**	FAS No.	**1024**
Address	**GLASGOW -2**	FAX No.	**0141 221 4567**

OS Map Grid
reference (if
known)

I/We apply for the boundaries of the subjects

POSTAL ADDRESS

Street No.	**3**	House Name		Street Name	**Miller Drive**
Town	**Newton Mearns**			Postcode	**G77 10 EU**

(1) Described below to be compared with the OS Map.2

(2) Deliniated on the plan annexed to be compared with the OS Map. 2

see copy annexed.

[1] *The bounding description must sufficiently define the extent of the subjects to enable the keeper to identify them on the O.S. Map by supplying:*

(a) a plan with boundaries of stated lineal dimensions or boundaries which can be measured from an adequate scale appearing on the face of the plan, the position of the property being tied by stated measurements to road junctions or other features which are depicted on the O.S. Map, or

(b) such a plan, together with a postal address, but without the position of the property being so tied to features which are depicted on the O.S. Map, or

(c) a written description which includes measurements and refers to adjoining subjects by name and not by the name of the owner, together with a postal address

2Delete (1) or (2) as applicable

Please state the Date and   Date
Time you require report

| 24 FEB 06 |

Time

| 12:00 |

Registers of Scotland

Approved.

WR.

(j)   Draft letter of obligation by O'Neill Middleton

Messrs. Brown Jarvis & Walker.

(to be dated)

Dear Sirs

3 Miller Drive, Newton Mearns

With reference to the settlement of this transaction today, we hereby:

1.   Undertake to clear the records of any deed, decree or diligence (other than such as may be created by or against your clients) which may be recorded in the Personal Register or to which effect may be given in the Land Register in the period from.............. to 21 days from the date hereof inclusive which would cause the Keeper to make an entry on, or qualify his indemnity in, the Land Certificate to be issued in respect of that interest; and

2.   Confirm that, to the best of knowledge and belief, the answers to the questions numbered 1 to 14 in the draft form 1 adjusted with you (in so far as these answers relate to our client or to our clients' interest in the above subjects) are still correct.

3.   We also undertake to deliver to you within 21 days of this date the duly executed Discharge of the existing Standard Security granted by our client with our forms 2 and 4 thereanent and our cheque made payable to the Keeper for the registration dues thereof.

Yours faithfully

Approved

WR.

7.07 Email

To: Henry Pink <hpink@bjw.co.uk>

Sent: 27 February 2006 11:03

From: Wendy Robertson<wrobertson@bjw.co.uk>

Subject: 3 Miller Drive, NM

Attached: notesontitlejame323.doc

Here are my Notes on the Title of 3 Miller Drive, as requested. There seems to be nothing particularly strange about the title, and I think we can accept the PEC and Coal certificates, as we are still within the five working days period. There is a tree preservation order, which the James's may or may not like and we would need to see a copy of this. I have also drafted a Disposition in favour of Mr and Mrs James and the survivor of them. I am now having doubts about the survivorship destination. Do you think it is the right thing to do? Should we maybe consult them?

Wendy

Note: Wendy has been busy researching an access problem for another client and has only noted the title today. BJW have until Wednesday to be satisfied, or resile to protect their clients' position.

7.08 Email

To: Wendy Robertson<wrobertson@bjw.co.uk>

Sent: 27 February 2006 12:22

From: Henry Pink <hpink@bjw.co.uk>

Subject: RE: 3 Miller Drive, NM

! Message was sent with high importance

Thanks for noting the title of 3 Miller Drive. I will call clients to discuss the TPO and the survivorship destination.

In the meantime I suggest that you get hold of a copy of the TPO asap. HP.

7.09 Minute of telephone communication held on 27.02.06

JAME323.1—Mr and Mrs James Purchase of 3 Miller Drive, Newton Mearns.

Attendance at telephone with clients.

Mr Pink explained that we (*note: 'royal we'*) had noted the title, which was very much in order. There was, however, a tree preservation order on the property which restricted the option of felling any trees, without the consent of the Council which would only be given if the trees were dangerous, and would be subject to replanting. Mr James said that there were some fine trees at the front, and they had no intention of cutting them down.

HP then explaining that, when a married couple were buying together, they had two options (a) to take title in their joint names and their executors, which meant that when one of them died, that person's executors would admister their half according to the will and (2) to take the title in their joint names and the survivor of them, which meant that when one died, their half share would pass automatically to the survivor of them. This latter destination, while sounding suitable, could lead to difficulties, because it could not be overridden by a will. Thus if the James decided to leave a half share of the house to their children in their Wills, and thus reduce the liability for Inheritance Tax of the survivor, they could not do so. They could, however, obtain this valuable tax concession if they used method (a). Clients decided to follow option (a). HP saying that we would draw up the Disposition and Wills accordingly *(again note the royal we!).*

Engaged ½ hour.

Note: With a half share of the house being worth £125,000 it is sensible to pass it on the first death, and thus escape inheritance tax to that extent. The other option is to pass the half share to the survivor, who will then have an estate which will probably attract inheritance tax, the threshold for this tax being perilously near, and possibly exceeded if pensions, life insurance etc are taken into account.

7.10 Email

To: Rory Redknapp <rory.redknapp@oneillmiddleton.com>

Sent: 27 February 2006 13:09

From: Wendy Robertson<wrobertson@bjw.co.uk>

Subject: 3 Miller Drive, Newton Mearns

! This message was sent with high importance

Rory

Help! I need a copy of the TPO for this urgently, before Pinkers blows his top!

Wendy

Note: The legal profession is still very fraternal, especially in adversity.

To: Wendy Robertson<wrobertson@bjw.co.uk>

Sent: 27 February 2006 15:45

From: Henry Pink <hpink@bjw.co.uk>

Subject: 3 Miller Drive, NM

I think we got away with that one! *(note the royal we again—it was Henry Pink's duty to explain the destination question to the James at an earlier meeting.)* Please do the necessary with the draft. Have you got the TPO yet?

Note: Henry Pink is losing confidence in Wendy's ability to deliver, which makes life harder for Wendy.

7.11 Letter to O'Neill Middleton 27.02.06

On behalf of our Clients, we accept the terms of the Coal Authority letter and the PEC.

BJ&W

Note: Acceptance of these certificates would be deemed to have happened if Brown Jarvie & Walker did not respond within five working days, but it is good practice to clarify the position.

IN WITNESS WHEREOF

7.12 REDRAFTED DISPOSITION IN FAVOUR OF MR and MRS JAMES WITHOUT A SURVIVORSHIP DESTINATION

I, ANGUS McDUFF, residing at Three Miller Drive, Newton Mearns, Renfrewshire heritable proprietor of the subjects hereinafter disponed IN CONSIDERATION of the sum of TWO HUNDRED AND FORTY NINE THOUSAND POUNDS (£249,000) paid to me by STUART JAMES and HENRIETTA JAMES, both residing at Daffodil Cottage, Wordsworth Lane, Kendal, in equal proportions HAVE SOLD and DO HEREBY DISPONE with the consent and concurrence of my wife MRS WILLIAMINA McDUFF, residing with me, for all her rights in the property whether under the Matrimonial Homes (Family Protection) (Scotland) Act 1981 or otherwise, to the said STUART JAMES and to the said MRS HENRIETTA JAMES equally and their respective Executors and assignees heritably and irredeemably ALL AND WHOLE that plot or area of ground in the County of Renfrew known as and forming Three Miller Drive, Newton Mearns described in, and shown outlined in black and coloured pink on the plan annexed to Disposition by Mickle & Muckle Limited recorded in the Register for the County of Renfrew Eleventh May Nineteen hundred and Thirty Six; Together with all rights of servitude pertaining to the subjects, all rights of common property, the parts privileges and pertinents thereof, all fittings and fixtures therein and thereon, and my and the said consenter's whole right, title and interest in the said subjects; BUT THE PROPERTY HEREIN DISPONED is disponed always subject to the following burdens and servitudes, in so far as still valid, subsisting and applicable thereto, contained in: (One) Feu Disposition by Walter John McFarlane in favour of James Mearns Davidson recorded in the said Register Twenty Fifth September Nineteen Hundred and Nineteen; and (Two) Feu Disposition by Mickle & Muckle Limited recorded in the said Register Eleventh May Nineteen hundred and Thirty Six; AND THE SAID PROPERTY at Three Miller Drive aforesaid (hereinafter referred to as 'the Burdened Property') is disponed with and under the following real burden created in my favour, as the owner of One Miller Drive, Newton Mearns (hereinafter referred to as 'the Benefited Property') namely that the owner or occupier of the Burdened Property shall not use, or permit to be used, the Burdened Property for the parking of any caravan or mobile home; This burden will be enforced by me and my successors as owners of the Benefited Property in terms of the Title Conditions (Scotland) Act 2003; WITH ENTRY at the Thirty-first day of March Two Thousand and Six, notwithstanding the date hereof; And I the said Angus McDuff, with consent foresaid, notwithstanding that I have sold the said subjects to the said Stuart James and Mrs Henrietta James and have received payment of the price in exchange for the delivery of the Disposition, do hereby declare that until the title of the said Stuart James and Mrs Henrietta James has been registered in the Land Register in pursuance of these presents I and the said consentor shall hold the said subjects as trustee of the said Stuart James and Mrs Henrietta James; And I and the said consentor grant warrandice: IN WITNESS WHEREOF

To: Wendy Robertson<wrobertson@bjw.co.uk>

Sent: 27 February 2006 18:42

From: Rory Redknapp <rory.redknapp@oneillmiddleton.com>

Subject: RE: 3 Miller Drive, Newton Mearns

Attachment: TPO.pdf

! This message was sent with high importance.

Wendy

Here is a scanned copy of the TPO.

How is it going? Sounds like Pinkers is working you hard. I've got 4 settlements this week! Are you going out on Friday night?

Cheers Rory

Note: The trainee social scene is fairly active.

7.13 Letter by Brown Jarvie & Walker to O'Neill Middleton dated 28.02.06

Dear Sirs

We refer to our previous correspondence in this matter and now return the title deeds together with your various drafts (forms 10, P16, letter of obligation, and discharge) and enclose the draft Disposition in favour of our clients. We look forward to hearing further from you.

Yours faithfully

'Brown Jarvie & Walker'

Note: Just in time! The ball is now in O'Neill Middleton's hands and there are less than four weeks until settlement. Everything is going smoothly.

7.14 Letter by O'Neill Middleton to Brown Jarvie & Walker dated 03.03.06

Dear Sirs

We now enclose form 10A report and form P.16 report. The latter document appears to confirm the boundaries on the title plan.

Please note that the form 10A report discloses and Inhibition against an Angus McDuff, residing in Inverness. We have spoken to our Mr McDuff, who says that it is nothing to do with him, and he has never lived in Inverness. He is prepared to swear an Affidavit to that effect. We shall be pleased to hear from you.

Yours faithfully

'O'Neill Middleton'

Note: This is an example of why it is good to get the form 10A report as early as possible. The matter of the inhibition must be cleared up well before settlement. An inhibition means that the person or persons named are not allowed to alienate their heritable property until the matter is settled, one way or another. In this case the person named is clearly not the seller, but he needs some sort of proof that this is the case. An affidavit should suffice.

7.15 Letter by Brown Jarvie & Walker to Mr and Mrs James dated 06.03.06

Dear Mr and Mrs James

Purchase of 3 Miller Drive, Newton Mearns.

We have examined the title to the property at 3 Miller Drive, Newton Mearns and confirm that it is in order, subject to the following points:

1.   There is a prohibition against parking caravans and motor homes. We have already mentioned this, and you have agreed that it is in order.

2.   There is an Inhibition against 'Angus McDuff, residing at 23 Torgorm Street, Inverness'. This means that Mr McDuff is not allowed to grant deeds of property. Mr McDuff's solicitors assure us that Mr McDuff is not the person named. This matter must, however, be cleared up, and we propose to ask Mr McDuff to grant a sworn Affidavit, which will serve the purpose.

How is your sale in England coming along? May we remind you that we should receive the funds in our Bank by 23 March to allow us to complete your purchase.

Yours faithfully

'Brown Jarvie & Walker'

7.16 Letter by Henrietta James to Henry Pink dated 9 March 2006

Dear Henry

Many thanks for your letter of 6 March. We are due to exchange contracts next week and our solicitor here will wire the money to you. Our solicitor is Tom Johnstone at Didley and Squat, 10 Market Street, Kendal. Can you contact him direct with your bank details etc?

Yours sincerely,

Henrietta

7.17 Letter by Brown Jarvie & Walker to O'Neill Middleton dated 10.03.06

Dear Sirs

We refer to previous correspondence, and would confirm that we have heard from our clients that they will require a sworn Affidavit from Mr McDuff that he is not the Mr McDuff named in the form 10A report. We enclose a suitable Affidavit which we hope that you will find acceptable, and be able to have signed and sworn before a Notary Public.

Yours faithfully.

Brown Jarvie & Walker

7.18 Affidavit by Angus McDuff

I, ANGUS McDUFF, residing at Three Miller Drive, Newton Mearns, East Renfrewshire being solemnly sworn and examined, hereby depone:

That I am not the person known as 'Angus McDuff, residing at Twenty Three Torgorm Street, Inverness' and that I have never lived at Twenty Three Torgorm Street, Inverness.

SIGNED by the said Angus McDuff at Glasgow on the   day of March 2006 before this witness

AND BEFORE

Notary Public of 999 Lally Street, Glasgow G2 6XX.

Note: This is an example of a situation that might arise, and which is fairly easily dealt with, but it is time consuming. It is also an example of why a form 10A report should be obtained as soon as possible, and not left till shortly before settlement. The form 10A report can be updated by a form 11A report shortly before settlement.

Generally, the transaction is going well, and settlement can now be contemplated. But, there are a few loose ends to be tied up.

Chapter 8

THE STUFF OF CONVEYANCING

'This registration of title is all very well, but it's not the stuff of conveyancing.'

(A Glasgow solicitor)

8.01 The great heyday of conveyancing is finally over. The relentless orderliness of the personal computer, the universality of land registration, and the great reforming statutes of 2004 (the year when they come into effect, rather than of their royal assent) have seen to that. Several good firms, which made a decent living from conveyancing, have either shrunk, merged, or simply disappeared. It is no longer necessary for conveyancers to cart about bags full of titles which have been examined several times before, and which might or might not constitute a health hazard. The conveyancer's skill is now one with that of the ship's riveter, much admired but not really necessary. The conveyancer's skill is, however, highly transferable.

A certain amount of the old skill is still required when we deal with non-registered titles, for instance when a security is renewed, or when property is transferred without consideration, perhaps to establish a gift as a potentially exempt transfer for inheritance tax purposes.

What exactly are we seeking in such transfers, and, indeed in all transfers although many of the questions we should be asking are automatically answered by land registration reports?

8.02 Missives having been concluded, it is now for the sellers' solicitors to show that the sellers have a valid marketable title, and for the purchasers' solicitors to be satisfied that this is so. This is truly the stuff of traditional conveyancing. In their book *Conveyancing* (2nd edn, 1999, Butterworths p 91) Professors Reid and Gretton define a marketable title as one:

(a)   which makes the buyer the owner of the property;

(b)   contains no heritable securities adverse to the new owner's interest;

(c)   contains no unusual conditions of title; and

(d)   contains no leases adverse to the new owner's interest.

To this might be added that, in land registration areas, a marketable title is one that can be sent to the Keeper immediately after purchase, and on the basis of which the Keeper will, without making further enquiries or requisitions, issue a land certificate without restriction of indemnity.

8.03 Modern conveyancing practice has placed much more emphasis on the preparation of missives than previously, and many of the matters formerly dealt with at the examination of title stage are now dealt with before missives are completed.

Thus, for instance, it is a usual stipulation of missives that the title shall contain 'no unduly onerous conditions or restrictions' (see para **8.05**). It is very hard to know exactly what is meant by this statement, and its meaning depends very much on the circumstances of each case. This is not satisfactory at all, as the word 'unusual' is subjective. If the sellers give this warranty in missives, purchasers can claim at a later date that there is, in their opinion, an onerous condition or restriction in the title, and the matter will have to be argued and compromised, although, at worst, the purchasers may withdraw.

The question of what is an 'unusual condition' is considered in *Whyte v Lee* ((1879) 6 R 699 at 701), where Lord Young commented on the phrase as follows:

> 'If a man simply buys a house he must be taken to buy it as the seller has it, on a good title of course, but subject to such restrictions as may exist if of an ordinary character, and such as the buyer may reasonably be supposed to have contemplated as at least not improbable.'

The leading case is *Armia Ltd v Daejan Developments Ltd* (1979 SC (HL) 56), where a property in Kirkcaldy High Street, which had been bought for redevelopment, was found to be subject to a servitude right of access, which included a ten-foot frontage with the street. It was held that this was a sufficiently unusual condition to allow the purchaser to resile.

In the case of *Morris v Ritchie* (1992 GWD 33–1950) a piece of ground being sold turned out to be burdened by a servitude right of access, which would have reduced the number of car parking spaces by 7 out of 18, and would therefore have a bad effect on turnover and thus market value of the property. This only became known to the pursuer after missives had been concluded, and a deposit had been paid. The pursuer was allowed to withdraw from the purchase because of the diminution in value of the ground. On a practical note, sellers who know of restrictions of this nature should disclose them to the purchasers before missives are concluded.

The chief ambition of the conveyancer must be never to let any matter near the court, as, at best, a reference to court entails expense and delay, and, at worst, an adverse decision, whether right or (even worse still) wrong. For that reason it has been suggested that the sellers' agents should obtain the titles, and as many other relevant certificates etc as possible, before exposing the property for sale. When an offer is received, containing the stipulation as to unusual or unduly onerous conditions, the sellers' agents should then send the title deeds, and other relevant papers, with the acceptance, and require the purchasers' agents to satisfy themselves prior to completion of the contract. This is good practice and will save arguments at a later date, probably arising shortly before the date for settlement.

8.04 For the purposes of this chapter, we shall assume that such matters have not been dealt with before missives are completed, and that the full examination of title takes place after completion of missives. It is not always possible to assemble title deeds and other papers, and as indicated previously the first intimation the solicitor may receive of a sale is when an offer drops through the letter box, requiring urgent attention. In that case, the missives must proceed on the basis of warranties given and proved to be correct when the title is available.

8.05 The obligations of the sellers for (a) a sasine transaction, (b) a first registration in the Land Register and (c) a subsequent dealing in registered land, are set out. In the disposition the sellers grant absolute warrandice, that is to say, they undertake to compensate the purchasers for any title defect. When a title is registered in the Land Register, the Keeper will issue a land certificate with a guarantee of indemnity. Check the real burdens, and make sure that these have not been breached in a manner which would allow interested parties to object. Fortunately we no longer have to deal with avaricious superiors, who were only interested in how much they may extract. Now it is only necessary to deal with proprietors with a genuine interest in the enforcement of the burden – which may be a mixed blessing. In the old days, you simply agreed a ransom with the superior to discharge the burden; now it has become a matter of principle.

Why then should the purchasers' agents have to examine the title in such detail? The reasons are: (a) professional pride dictates that the purchasers shall get a title that can be passed on without question when the purchasers eventually sell, be that next month or next century; (b) the person who prepared the sellers' title may not have had the same standards, or perhaps there has been an innocent mistake perpetuating itself over the years; (c) very often they have to certify the title to the purchaser's lender: (d) warrandice is not in practice a particularly effective remedy, as it depends on 'eviction' having taken place, and the victim has to go through the process of losing his case before he can claim warrandice (see *Welsh v Russell* (1894) 21 R 769). It should be noted that 'eviction' in this case means any interference with the property right, rather than being put out of the property. Even if there is a valid remedy under warrandice, you may not be able to trace the granters of warrandice, or if appropriate, their predecessors in title; (e) lawyers are not paid to get their clients into dispute, quite the opposite; and (f) the *caveat emptor* rule applies, in sasine transactions at least, although less so in Land Register transactions.

8.06 In a first registration, the procedure of examining title is very much the same as with a sasine title, but in a subsequent dealing, the title deeds are replaced by a land certificate. This contains all the essential parts of the title, and none of the non-essential, and should therefore be read very thoroughly. The fact that all inessential details are stripped out, and the remainder is clearly printed, should make this a very much easier business than reading through a lot of old titles written in spidery handwriting on disintegrating paper.

8.07 In a first registration, or in a sasine transaction, the first thing that you must do is to check the title deeds against the inventory and (assuming they are in order) return the inventory marked 'borrowed the above title deeds; to be returned on demand' and signed. Then put all the title deeds into order and check them against the search, making sure that all the deeds mentioned in the search or form 10A have been sent to you. Form in your mind a rough history of the property, and in particular spot any split-offs or acquisitions and the writs referred to for burdens.

8.08 Next, put to one side the writs that do not concern you, bearing in mind the following provisions of statute that are designed to make life easier for you (see paras **8.09–8.13**).

Prescription and Limitation (Scotland) Act 1973, s 1

8.09 Section 1 provides (in paraphrase) that where a person has possessed land openly, peacefully and without interruption for ten years, on the basis of a sufficient title, then after ten years the title shall not be challengeable on the ground that it was not valid *ex facie* (on its face), the

only exception being if it turns out to have been forged. This pr~
known as positive prescription.

It is not thought that many pieces of land are acquired in this way, yet
this is, for another reason, a vital provision for the conveyancer. What it
means, in effect, is that if you take the first transfer of the land that you
are buying, which is more than ten years old, and find that it is free from
an intrinsic objection (that is an objection showing on the face of the title,
and not requiring proof from outside sources) then that is a valid
foundation for a prescriptive title, and you need look back no further.
Therefore you may set aside all older transfers of the land, unless these
contain valid land obligations to which you must refer. You must,
however, check this foundation writ for any intrinsic objection, and check
everything after it to make sure that it correctly flows down to the
present seller. An intrinsic objection is one which can be observed from
the terms of the deed itself

An example of what might have been called an intrinsic objection is
given in *Cooper Scott v Gill Scott* (1925 SC 309), where a destination
detailed in the narrative clause did not correspond with a further
narration of the same destination in the dispositive clause. A majority of
the seven judges, however, held that this deed was not intrinsically null
and was therefore a good foundation for prescription (see also *Simpson v
Marshall* (1900) 2 F 447).

An extrinsic objection, that is to say an objection which can only be
proved from outside evidence, or an intrinsic objection that can be
proved only by extrinsic evidence, does not affect the use of the
disposition as a foundation of title.

8.10 As an example of the power of prescription, consider the disposition
a non domino (a disposition granted by someone who is not the owner). If
a piece of land lies vacant, and the owner cannot be traced, it is possible
for someone who does not own that land to obtain a disposition, granted
by anyone in favour of a grantee. Dispositions granted by the granter in
favour of himself are *ex facie* invalid and will not be a foundation writ for
prescription (*The Board of Management of Aberdeen College v Stewart Watt
Youngerson and Anor* [2005] CSOH 31). Only simple warrandice is given,
for the granter has no claim to the land at all. The disposition is then
recorded to make it public and the disponee occupies the land 'openly
and peaceably', as if it was owned, so that anyone who has a better title
may see the occupation and object. If no objection is made by anyone
having a better title, within ten years, the disponee then becomes the
owner of the land.

If prescription can cure a disposition that is so obviously bad, it will be seen that it can also cure any minor defect in a deed.

Prescription and Limitation (Scotland) Act 1973, s 8

8.11 Section 8 provides (again in paraphrase) that where a right has not been enforced or exercised for a continuous period of 20 years, then that right shall be extinguished. This is known as negative prescription.

Again, this does not clearly state the benefit to the conveyancer, who only need look back for securities over a 20-year period. Thus (writing in August 2006), if a bond was recorded before August 1986, and no interest has been paid on it in that time, and it has not been enforced, it can be said to have prescribed. The snag is to know whether or not interest has been paid. All kinds of out-of-date obligations can be cleared in this way.

Succession (Scotland) Act 1964, s 17

8.12 Section 12 provides that where a person for good faith and for value (ie the average house purchaser) acquires title to land from an executor, or from somebody who has derived title directly from an executor, the title shall not be challengeable on the ground that the confirmation of the executor was reducible, or had in fact been reduced, or even that the title should not have been transferred by the executor to the person who is offering the title.

Thus, for example, you may be offered a title by Xavier and Yasmin, who produce (a) a confirmation in the estate of their uncle (Victor), whereby Zak is appointed executor and (b) a docket in terms of the Succession (Scotland) Act 1964, s 15, transferring that property to Xavier and Yasmin, as, say, the persons entitled to take the property under Victor's will. Provided your client is buying in good faith and for value (ie the average house purchaser), it need not concern you (a) if someone produces a later dated will appointing Adam as executor and Brian the legatee, or (b) someone alleges that the will is a forgery. In summary, you need look no further than the confirmation itself.

An analogous provision is made in the Trusts (Scotland) Act 1961, s 2 which provides that titles acquired from trustees or executors are also protected from challenge on the ground that the transaction was at variance with the terms or purpose of the trust.

Conveyancing and Feudal Reform (Scotland) Act 1970, s 41

8.13 Section 41 provides that where a discharge of a security bears to be granted by a person entitled to do so (eg the creditor) subsequent acquirers of land *bona fide* and for value, shall not have their title to the land challenged after the expiration of a five-year period from the recording of the discharge, merely by reason of the discharge being reduced.

Thus, if a discharge is more than five years old, and appears to have been granted by the creditor of the security that is discharged, you need not examine the origins of that discharge any further.

8.14 The first step in examining title is to identify your foundation writ, and examine it for intrinsic defects. Then examine the writs that follow the foundation writ, ensuring that one follows on from another smoothly. If the grantee of one deed is not the grantee of the next deed, check whether there is a survivorship destination and, if not, examine the deduction of title, and ensure that the link in title is in order. (*Example*: if a writ is in favour of Brown, and the next deed is granted by Black, check exactly why Black is selling a house that appears to be owned by Brown. Generally there will be a good reason, and if Brown has died and Black is his executor, or if Brown is bankrupt and Black is the trustee, ensure that title is properly deduced in the second writ using confirmation to vouch this.)

Recall two reminders contained in the Halliday Report (Cmnd 3118, 1966) (ch 4):

(a) that only certain deeds in terms of C(S)A 1924, s 3 (dispositions of land, or assignations, discharges or restrictions of heritable security), may be granted by uninfeft proprietors. A surprising number of these deeds are granted by uninfeft proprietors, and are invalid until a recorded title is obtained, usually by means of a notice of title which is recorded, and which cures the defect by accretion. Formerly, heritable securities could not be granted by persons without a recorded title, but standard securities and their transmissions may now be granted by uninfeft proprietors in terms generally of CFR(S)A 1970, Pt II;

(b) that the style of deduction of title in C(S)A 1924, Sch A, form 1, requires a designation of the person last infeft, and is ineffective otherwise. Thus, the designation of the granter, which appeared in the narrative clause, must be repeated. While this may seem harsh and inconsistent with the liberal terms of C(S)A 1924, Sch D, note 1, that is nevertheless the law, and it must be followed.

8.15 Check carefully the first description of the land, either with your own observations or with a survey plan of the property and make sure that the first full description has been validly referred to throughout the progress in titles in conformity with the Conveyancing (Scotland) Acts 1874 and 1924. Note all additions to the land and disposals of any part of the land.

8.16 Check that all parties granting deeds had the capacity to do so, that the form of all deeds is correct, that they are properly executed and that the testing clause is correctly completed, that all deletions, interlineations, additions and erasures have been properly attested and that it has been correctly stamped and recorded in the General Register of Sasines.

8.17 Check for alterations having been mentioned in the survey report and that the building warrants for these are in place.

Once the works have been carried out to the council's satisfaction, they will issue a certificate of completion and you should ensure that this is present. Development and building control documentation will only be available after local government reorganisation in 1975.

8.18 Check that the house possesses suitable rights of access. This applies particularly to property in the country. Land is obviously useless unless it enjoys proper access, unless, of course, you own a helicopter. On 4 August 2002, it was reported in the press that a couple had bought a farmhouse (for £130,000) from a bank who had repossessed it. Unfortunately, however, the original owner still owned a small strip of land controlling access, and he wasn't selling it. This is the last thing you would want to happen. The common law may imply a servitude right through necessity, but you would not want to rely on this as a declarator may be required.

The problem is not so acute in the city and towns where, generally, but not universally, the streets have been taken over and are maintained by the local authority. In that case anyone can use the road, but the downside is that the local authority can paint yellow lines on 'your' road and, even worse, charge you for parking outside your own house.

The local authority maintains the road, and is responsible for any accident that occurs through lack of maintenance. Where the road remains private, and this can be found even in towns and cities, the frontagers own the road to the centre point, along the length of their frontage. They are responsible for maintenance, and usually don't trouble to do any, because of the near impossibility of getting agreement from all the frontagers to pay for the work. If there is an accident through lack of maintenance, the appropriate frontagers are responsible, but should be covered by the public liability of their household insurance.

If a road is built to a certain standard, the builders can, and will, ask the local authority to take over the maintenance of the road. Owners of existing private roads seldom do this, again usually for lack of agreement to spending money on turning their quiet road into a public highway.

In the country, purchasing solicitors must ensure that purchasers enjoy an unrestricted right to all necessary rights of access, and are not expected to pay a disproportionate amount of maintenance. A servitude right of access is a licence to use someone else's ground for certain purposes, and if the owners of the beneficial property exceed this use they can be interdicted. The division of large estates, and the sale of redundant estates and farm houses, has led to an increasing number of 'townspeople' now living in the country, often not happily with the country people. There have been an increasing number of cases that have illustrated the trend towards bad relations between the two (see an article on the subject by Douglas Patience (1993 SLG 127)).

In Caveat (a monthly article outlining the mistakes, hopefully, of others) (1993 JLSS 490), there is a cautionary tale of a couple who bought a house in the country, with an adjoining disused water mill as a holiday development. The access to the mill was over a farmer's land. There was nothing in the titles about this right, which had arisen from use, and positive prescription. The farmer objected to the proposed use of the road to the mill, which was intended for use as a holiday cottage. It was held by the court that the access had been created for use of the building as a mill, and not as a cottage. The solicitor who had acted for the pursuers was liable for the costs of forming an alternative access, and loss of income.

In addition, the owners of the benefited property cannot increase the burden on the burdened property, and cannot therefore increase the usage. Professor Halliday (*Conveyancing Law and Practice in Scotland* (2nd edn, W Green, 1996) vol II, 20.11), suggests that when a servitude of access is created, words such as the following should be used: 'The servitude has been granted with reference to the present state of the property and shall not be extended to apply to any substantially different condition thereof.'

Grants of servitudes should be drawn very carefully, and are construed *contra proferentem* (ie against the party who seeks to rely on it). For example, one frequently sees a servitude right of access for 'pedestrian and vehicular' use. Does that include the right to drive cattle over the road? You might argue that the word pedestrian is derived from the Latin word for feet, and that cattle have feet, however that is not the ordinary meaning of the word. Further, the law of servitudes is drawn from Roman law, and it had three classes of servitude: *via* (the right to use the road for carriages drawn by horses or other beasts of draught); *iter* (allowing a person a right of way to pass over the land of another on horse or on foot); and *actus* (the right of use for carriages drawn by men, and for driving cattle), indicating a more precise distinction between the uses.

Servitudes should be used *civiliter* (i e with civility). The owner of the burdened property is not under an obligation to maintain the ground, and should not obstruct the way. Where there is an agreement for the maintenance of a road, liability should be apportioned according to the extent of the respective uses.

8.19 The position with new houses is rather different. The builder will undertake, as part of the price of the house, to form the road to the appropriate council standard and to request the council to take it over, without it, of course, giving any guarantee that it will do so. (Provided the road is built to standard, a refusal to take over is virtually unknown.) Despite this partially incomplete work, the builder will nonetheless require the full price at the date of entry.

The builder should also provide a road bond. You may wonder why the purchasers should pay the full price before all work is complete. While payment is only made on completion of the house, the completion of roads is an exception, for it is useless to complete someone's road while there is work going on in the estate and the builder may have heavy plant using that road. A builder will normally complete all the houses in an estate, then finish the roads. The road bond covers the purchasers against the builder's insolvency in the intervening period between payment of the price and completion of the roads.

On the basis that good advice cannot be repeated too often, (1) the sellers' agents should obtain a letter as to roads from the appropriate council, normally incorporated in the PEC, the minute the sellers instruct the sale (see JLSS Council Notes, October 1982 as corrected in Council Notes, November 1982) and (2) the purchasers and their agents should deal with such matters before completing missives, by personal observation, inquiry and survey.

8.20 Approximately the same position applies with the supply of water, gas, electricity etc and with drainage. Most of us take these services for granted, but lawyers cannot do this, particularly when purchasing a property in a rural or even semi-rural area.

(a) Water. Scottish Water will not necessarily run water into every house, especially those that are isolated, and the water may be drawn from a stream or well situated in someone else's land (*aquaehaustus*) and be carried from the source to the house by a private pipe (*aqueduct*). Where this pipe crosses the land of another, make sure that there are clear servitude rights for running the pipe, and a right to gain access to the pipe if it requires maintenance.

In very rural areas the water system will be no concern of Scottish Water, and the conveyancer should ensure that the arrangement is adequate *tantum et tale* (both as to quantity and quality). Where the source is in someone else's land, make sure that the supply cannot be interfered with, and that the necessary servitude rights for pipes exist. Bear in mind the seasonal nature of water supply, even in Scotland.

(b) Gas, electricity and telephone. British Gas, Scottish Power, Scottish & Southern Electrictiy and British Telecom will take care of the servitude rights (or wayleaves) for cables and pipes, under statutory powers, and these will not therefore concern the average conveyancer in the active sense. In the passive sense, however, note should be taken of wayleaves for cable and pipes leading to other properties, which must not be disturbed by digging, or obstructed in any way, e g by building over the wayleave area. Thus, for example, if you have a mains water pipe in your property, or a gas pipe-line, you would be well advised to know about these and to leave them well alone. Modern pipe-lines are sunk to a great depth, but the same cannot be said of Victorian pipe-lines.

(c) Drainage. The position is as with water supply, but in reverse. In many rural areas drainage is not to a mains, but a private septic tank. It is a matter of survey to ensure that this tank is in order, and capable of treating the volume of waste generated by the household it serves. A properly constructed and maintained tank should do this without giving trouble. The local council should empty it from time to time. Check with the sellers as to whether there is a service contract. Again, if waste is piped through the land of another, the appropriate servitude rights must be seen to exist. There is, according to Professors Gretton and Reid (*Conveyancing* (2nd edn, Butterworths, 1999) para 13.02), a servitude of 'sinks' which covers this, although this is not one of the classic servitudes (perhaps it should be).

In the case of a new house, all services will be (or at least should be) 'laid on'. Each house in a new estate will be transferred subject to a variety of servitude or wayleave rights, which may be expressed as follows:

> 'There is reserved to us and our successors as proprietors of the remaining area or piece of ground of which the subjects form part of a servitude right of wayleave for all necessary water pipes, sewers, drains, electricity cables, communications underground and overhead cables, field drains and whole other necessary pipes and cables passing through the subjects and the grantees are prohibited from erecting any permanent construction on the lines of said water pipes, sewers, drains, electricity cables, underground and overhead communications cables and field drains if any within the subjects and shall not do or permit to be done any act which may cause damage to said water pipes, sewers, drains, electricity cables, underground and overhead communications cables and field drains; and the grantees shall further be bound to allow all parties interested in said water pipes, sewers, drains and whole other pipes and cables right of access to subjects on all necessary occasions for opening up, uncovering, inspecting, maintaining, cleaning, repairing and renewing the same on payment of compensation to the grantees for any surface damaged which may be thereby occasioned; further declaring that there is reserved to us and our foresaids in all time coming a right to lay on, in or over the subjects such water pipes, sewers, drains and whole other pipes and cables as we in our sole discretion shall consider necessary for the amenity of the subjects and of the remaining area or piece of ground of which the subjects form part but that always on payment of compensation for the grantees for any surface damage which may be thereby occasioned.'

8.21 Every new house, or every new extension or alteration to a house, must carry the following permissions:

(a) planning permission from the council under the Town and Country Planning (Scotland) Acts 1972 and 1977;

(b) building warrant from the council under the Building (Scotland) Acts 1959 and 1970 and completion certificate;

(c) the consent of any third parties who have an interest in enforcing burdens, eg neighbouring proprietors or conservation bodies listed in the Title Conditions (Scotland) Act 2003 (Conservation Bodies) Amendment Order 2003.

Planning permission and building warrants are often confused, perhaps because they cover roughly the same problems of decent building standards, and are obtained from the offices of the same council. They should not, however, be confused. They arise under different Acts and regulations, and are administered by different officials and committees.

The existence of one does not in any way guarantee the existence of the other. Separate applications must be made for each.

Planning permission covers, very broadly, the appearance of an area, and the zoning of that area. If an area is zoned as residential, you would be very unlikely to get permission to build a factory there; but you would probably get permission to build a house, assuming all the other requirements of the Council, as to density, the suitability of the roads etc are met. A building warrant is given (again broadly) where a planned building complies with the building regulations as to materials used, space available, hygiene arrangements, fire precautions, ventilation, lack of dampness etc. A completion certificate is granted when the building is complete to the building department's satisfaction, and only then may it be occupied. Failure to obtain these certificates can, in the worst cases, lead to an order being made to restore the land or building to its original condition.

Incidentally, even councils are not exempt from this provision of law: Dundee District Council was ordered by the Scottish Development Department to reinstate Camperdown House (built in 1824) to its original state after modernisation was carried out without planning consent. Retrospective consent had also been refused by the department (*Sunday Standard*, 14 November 1982).

Particular care should be taken with buildings of special historical or architectural significance, or which form part of a special townscape, and which are accordingly 'listed'. All alterations require listed building consent, and many owners may find the local councils and bodies such as Historic Scotland a bit pernickety. It is very pleasant to live in a listed building, until you come to alter it, when it can prove extremely expensive.

There is a dispensation contained in the Town and Country Planning (Scotland) Act 1972, s 84, to the effect that an enforcement action for breach of planning law is not enforceable after four years. It should be noted that this dispensation does not apply to a breach of building regulations. If obtaining permission or a completion certificate has been overlooked or forgotten, a retrospective warrant or certificate has to be obtained in cases of a serious breach. This can be extremely expensive, as the building work has to comply with current building regulations. Thus, even if a building was built in 1985, say, to comply with the regulations then, there is no guarantee that it would comply with the 1995 regulations. Alternatively, in less serious cases, the council may be prepared to issue a 'letter of comfort' covering the breach. An example of this, in a case where a completion certificate has not been obtained, might read:

> 'I would confirm that, following your application for confirmation of Completion, a survey of the above property has now been carried out. The purpose of this survey was to inspect the building operations referred to in the Building Warrant reference (*number*) and comment is therefore restricted to this. No responsibility for the condition of any concealed elements of the structure can be accepted.
>
> Following inspection of the property, it has been ascertained, as far as is practical, that the operations detailed in the documents relating to the aforementioned Building Warrant, and any relevant amendment(s), have been completed. I can therefore confirm that this Authority shall take no action with regard to the absence of a Certificate of Completion relative to these operations.'

This letter is pretty qualified in its terms, and does not bind the council at all, nor does the council accept any liability, which might arise in the future, for building defects, but it may provide some comfort which should be acceptable to a purchaser. In truth, a completion certificate does not offer a great deal more protection, as it can be changed anytime.

Similarly, all building work should have the consent of the former superiors and third parties, if this is written in the titles. Great care should be taken with these rights, especially where you have vigilant neighbours. Third parties can cause trouble, as groups of people are very difficult to deal with.

Care must be taken with replacement windows, to ensure that (1) in a listed building they are compatible with the building and have council approval; (2) they can be cleaned from the inside, unless they are at ground level; and (3) they permit escape in case of fire. Practice varies from district to district, and if you are in doubt the matter should be discussed with the local council.

8.22 Where a sale is made by a person or persons on behalf of someone else, or in default of someone else, care must be taken to ensure that the power of sale is competent, and that it was properly exercised.

(a) Trustees. Trustees have wide powers to sell, lease and grant securities over heritage under the Trusts (Scotland) Act 1921, s 4. The term 'trustee' includes (s 2) trustee *ex officiis* (namely trustees who are appointed by virtue of an office they hold, say a president and secretary of a bowling club, and who cease to be trustees when they demit office, giving way to the next incumbents automatically), executors-nominate, tutors, curators and judicial factors. This power of sale has now been extended to executors-dative by the Succession (Scotland) Act 1964, s 20.

(b) Creditors selling under a standard security. The power of sale may be exercised among other remedies when the debtor is in default.

The CFR(S)A 1970, s 25 imposes a duty on the selling creditor to advertise the sale in a medium that is seen in the locality of the property being sold. Reference may be made to the more defined rules of advertising of a sale under a bond, referred to in para (c) below; further, the seller shall take all reasonable steps to ensure that the price at which the sale is made is the best that can be reasonably obtained. The sale may either be made by private bargain (i e a sale normally concluded as outlined in previous chapters) or by public auction followed by articles of roup and a minute of preference stating the name of the successful purchaser and the offer made. The articles of roup and minute of preference have a similar effect to missives.

(c) Sellers under a bond and disposition in security. Prior to CFR(S)A 1970 the rules of sale under a bond and disposition in security were strict, in that the sale had to be by public auction, and certain rules of advertisement had to be implicitly followed (see Halliday Report, paragraphs 107–118 for a critique of these rules).

These rules were relaxed by CFR(S)A 1970, ss 33 ff, but only to some extent. Thus, in terms of s 35(1), the sale may now be alternatively made by private bargain, for 'the best price that can be reasonably obtained'. A calling-up notice may take place two months after the date of service of notice, or such shorter period as may be agreed with the debtor and postponed creditors.

The CFR(S)A 1970, s 35, provides that a creditor in a standard security may sell either by private bargain or by auction, provided that the sale is advertised and all reasonable steps taken to ensure that the property is sold at the best price. The CFR(S)A 1970, s 36, imposes certain rules of advertisement which may be briefly summarised (under the *caveat* that a perusal of the Act is essential if you are involved in a sale) as follows:

(i) Advertisements must be placed: (1) if the property is in Midlothian in a daily paper published in Edinburgh; (2) if the property is in Lanarkshire (as it then was) in a daily paper published in Glasgow; (3) if the property is elsewhere in Scotland in a daily newspaper circulating in the district where the property is situated and in one newspaper (ie a local paper that may be weekly or twice weekly) circulating in the district and published in the county where the property is situated.

(ii) When the sale is by public roup, one advertisement a week for three consecutive weeks must be made.

(iii)   When the sale is by private bargain, one advertisement a week for two consecutive weeks must be made.

These stipulations are the minimum requirements of law. The purchasers' agents must see copies of the advertisement certified as to date of publication by the newspaper publisher.

The final rule (CFR(S)A 1970, s 26), and one that can easily be forgotten, is that where a sale is by private bargain, the sale must be concluded within 28 days of the date of the second advertisement. This is taken to mean that missives must be concluded within the 28 days. If they are not concluded, the sale and every subsequent deed is invalid, so obviously this must be checked.

(d) Trustees in bankruptcy. Trustees in bankruptcy should, in terms of the Insolvency Act 1986, s 338, be qualified insolvency practitioners, as should liquidators, receivers and administrators of limited companies.

Sequestrations commenced after 1 April 1986 are governed by a completely new code introduced by the Bankruptcy (Scotland) Act 1985 (B(S)A 1995). This provides, in summary, that an interim trustee in bankruptcy shall be appointed by the sheriff to preserve the estate, and he will be replaced by a permanent trustee who is elected by the creditors. The property vests in the permanent trustee on behalf of the creditors. The Accountant in Bankruptcy issues Notes for Guidance (printed as an appendix to Professor William McBryde's commentary on the Act) which should be closely read by anyone practising in this field.

The interim trustee has no power to sell property. The decree in bankruptcy is registered in the Personal Register by the clerk of the relevant court (B(S)A 1985, s 14). The trustee cannot sell without the consent of the heritable creditors unless there are sufficient funds realised to pay off the heritable creditors, and the trustee cannot sell if a heritable creditor has intimated an intention to sell (B(S)A 1985, s 39). In the case of a sale of a family home (B(S)A 1985, s 40), the consent of the bankrupt's spouse (B(S)A 1985, s 40), or of the court if this is not forthcoming, is required. Inhibitions against the bankrupt need not be discharged (B(S)A 1985, s 31(2)). There is no requirement for any further sequestration orders to be lodged in the Personal Register.

Title to sell is deduced through the decree in bankruptcy from the last infeft proprietor to the purchaser, as with confirmation of a deceased person (see para **8.14**).

(e) A trustee under a trust deed. A trust deed is a document signed 'voluntarily' by the bankrupt, without the necessity of a court order. The trustee grants the disposition, deducing title through the trust deed, which will have been registered in the Books of Council and Session.

(f) Liquidators of limited companies. The deed to be granted here is in the name of the company and the liquidator, who signs on behalf of the company which now has no directors or secretary. As the conditions of the Companies Act 1985, s 36(3) (formerly CA 1948, s 32(4)), are not met, the signature must be witnessed. Title is deduced through the interlocutor ordering the winding up, if the liquidation is compulsory, and through the special resolution of the company, if it is voluntary. These documents should have been registered in the Companies Register as should the appointment of the liquidator.

Where the sale is by private bargain, as is usual, the consent of the creditors and of the Accountant of Court are not required (*Liquidator of Style & Mantle Ltd v Price's Tailors Ltd* 1934 SC 548) in the disposition. The powers of a liquidator are detailed in the Companies Act 1985, s 539 (formerly CA 1948, s 245), and include the power to sell, feu or otherwise dispose of property by public sale or private bargain.

In practice, the liquidation of a company is a matter of public knowledge, and is intimated widely in the *Edinburgh Gazette* and in newspapers which should be read by legal practitioners as part of their 'common knowledge', although in all cases of dealing with a limited company the searchers should be asked if there has been any liquidator, receiver or administrator appointed, or if the company has been struck off for failure to lodge documents. The question of the 'gap' between the appointment of a liquidator or receiver, and the printing of the advertisement is dealt with at para **8.32**.

(g) Receivers. In this case the floating charge should be carefully inspected to see that it has been properly executed and registered in the Companies Register within 21 days of its registration in the Land Register or Sasine Register (a requirement of CA 1985, s 410, and CA 1989, s 95). It should also be checked to see that it includes the property purported to being sold. The deed by the receiver runs in the name of the company and the receiver and is signed as with a deed by a liquidator.

(h) Administrators. This order proceeds upon a court interlocutor which is registered in the Companies and Personal Registers. Again, a disposition by an administrator runs in the name of the company and the administrator, and is signed by the latter.

Discharge of securities

8.23 Bearing in mind the valuable protection afforded by CFR(S)A 1970, s 41(1), it is important to check discharges which have been recorded within a five-year period. You should therefore check: (1) the details of the discharge—does it fully discharge the obligation that was created?; (2) the form of the discharge; (3) the execution of the discharge; and (4) the recording of the discharge.

As to the form of the discharge, the required forms are:

(a) *Bond and disposition in security.* (C(S)A 1924, s 29 and Sch K(3)). This is a very simple form of discharge, and contains no conveyancing description of the property or reference to burdens.

(b) *Standard security.* The form is provided in the CFR(S)A 1970, Sch 4 and form F. Again this is a simple form.

(c) *Ex facie absolute disposition in security.* This covert security may be discharged in one of two ways:

    (i) traditional method—a disposition back to the owner of the subjects, which takes the form of an ordinary disposition but which sets out in the narrative that the original disposition to the lenders was truly in security of a loan of £X which has now been repaid, and it is now 'right and proper' that the subjects be reconveyed. The lenders grant warrandice only from their own facts and deeds;

    (ii) shorter statutory method—CFR(S)A 1970, s 40 and Sch 9, provides for a short form of discharge, analogous to discharges (a) and (b). This has the effect (on being recorded) of disburdening the land and vesting the land in the person entitled to it.

Generally, it makes little difference which method is used. One school prefers to discharge securities in the manner in which they were created (*unumquodque eodem modo dissolvitur quo colligatur*); the other school prefers the shorter modern method.

In addition to being discharges, a security may also be partially discharged on part payment, or restricted to any part of the land, thereby freeing the remainder for sale. (For the appropriate forms see CFR(S)A 1970, Sch 4, forms C and D.)

Fences, walls and gables

8.24 As a general rule, fences, walls and gables that lie between the properties of two persons are owned to the centre line by each proprietor, with each proprietor having an interest in the other half. It is possible, however, that the wall is owned jointly, in which case the boundary of each property is the nearest outside face of the wall, and the wall is jointly owned and maintained. Obviously this must be closely checked from the deeds.

When there is no adjoining proprietor, the wall, fence or gable is usually owned and maintained solely by the houseowner. It may be provided, however, that at a future date when someone builds on the adjoining property and uses that fence, wall or gable then that person should refund one-half of the cost of building to the person who paid for it and become partly responsible for its maintenance.

When acting for purchasers of a house, particularly a new one, you should ensure: (1) the exact ownership of the fences or walls and (2) that there are no outstanding charges for formation or maintenance of mutual fences, walls or gables.

Rivers and lochs

8.25 Where a property is bounded by a non-tidal river, and there is no specification of the boundary, this is taken to be the middle line (*medium filum*) of the river. This includes the fishing rights, excepting salmon fishing which must be specifically transferred to the purchasers (see *McKendrick v Wilson* 1970 SLT (Sh Ct) 39). The same applies to non-tidal lochs. Care should be taken when purchasing a riparian property that the landowner has not retained a narrow strip of land between the property purchased and the loch or river. If this is the case, the purchaser is not a riparian proprietor and has no rights in the loch or river.

This should have been checked before missives were concluded, but better late than never.

Use

8.26 Many houses carry feuing conditions that prohibit certain uses: trade or business or profession. If your clients wanted the house for any particular business use you should really have cleared this up before completing missives. Even if your clients do not have a business use in mind, still note the restriction and inform your clients of it, in case at some time they want to pursue a business from the house. Another restriction that can occur is on keeping pets, and this must be cleared up, or much distress can be caused.

Clause of pre-emption

8.27 This clause gives a person who has sold land or buildings the choice to repurchase the first time they are resold. The duty to offer the land back now affects only the first sale after the commencement of the CFR(S)A 1970, and after the offer has been made and refused one time the right lapses (Conveyancing Amendment (Scotland) Act 1938, s 9, as amended by CFR(S)A 1970, s 46). Former feudal rights of pre-emption were capable of being preserved by the former superior recording a notice before the appointed day (28 November 2004). If the right of pre-emption exists against the granter, the former feudal may be able to enforce the right as a matter of contract.

The price at which the property is to be offered back is usually the amount of the highest offer received from other parties, although occasionally the contracting parties may fix another price (eg a price fixed at the date of agreement) in the contract containing the pre-emption clause.

From the sellers' point of view, a valid clause of pre-emption is particularly irksome, especially if they know that the right is to be exercised (say by a local authority who sold the land, but have now decided that they would like it back). The sellers must nonetheless go through the deception of a *bona fide* sale to establish the market value. The prospective purchasers are put to the trouble of obtaining a survey and submitting an offer. Yet if the sellers warn the purchasers of the true position, the sellers will not get a good offer for the superior to match.

The sole remedy of persons who have a right of pre-emption, which has not been observed, is to seek a court order to reduce the disposition granted without the right having been observed, and all other deeds flowing from it (see *Roebuck v Edmunds* 1992 SLT 1055).

The right of pre-emption is another point that should ideally be cleared up before missives are completed. If it is found that missives have been completed and that a pre-emption clause has been overlooked, the sellers cannot give a valid title without offering the property back to the person entitled to benefit from the clause. If that person then accepts the offer, the sellers will not be able to fulfil their part of the agreement to the purchasers and will be liable in damages.

It should be mentioned that, while the clause of pre-emption is a nuisance, it now only operates between the two contracting parties, and is not a perpetual nuisance as is the case with other land conditions and will not be affected by forthcoming legislation. If people do not like it, they should not have contracted for it.

Clause of redemption

8.28 This clause is similar in effect to the clause of pre-emption, but in this case the original owners may call for the land to be resold to them at any time they choose, and not just when a resale takes place.

In deeds executed after 1 September 1974 a clause of redemption is exercisable only within 20 years of its creation (LTR(S)A 1974, s 12). (The reason for this rather unexpected provision is to prevent owners circumventing the restriction on creation of residential leases for more than 20 years, by selling property subject to a redemption clause and then redeeming it some time after 20 years have expired.) You will not therefore see a redemption clause after 1974, but be carefully aware of such clauses granted before 1974.

Property bought subject to lease

8.29 Most houses are bought with vacant possession, but occasionally a house may be sold subject to a tenancy (colloquially 'with a sitting tenant'). Indeed a house may be sold to the sitting tenant (particularly local authority housing under the Housing (Scotland) Act 1987) (see ch 16). Where a house has a sitting tenant under the old Rent Acts the price will be accordingly abated where that tenant enjoys security of tenure. The value is (very roughly) around 50–60% of the value of the same house sold with vacant possession, but it depends on the circumstances (compare ch 16).

The intending purchasers of a house with a sitting tenant should realise what they are taking on: rent regulations, security of tenure etc. The purchasers do not of course get 'vacant possession' and the sellers' warrandice must exclude the lease from its scope ('and we grant warrandice subject to the Lease between us and (etc)'). If the house is a 'buy-to-let' property, a sitting tenant would prove attractive to the purchaser.

Moveable effects contained in missives

8.30 When the purchasers of a house buy furniture and furnishings with that house, the purchasers' solicitors should ask the sellers to confirm that they own these effects, and that there are no outstanding hire purchase, credit sale, leasing or other debts, which would mean that the sellers do not own the moveables they have sold.

National House-Building Council (NHBC)

8.31 Most builders are registered members of the National House Builders Council or other insurance schemes, and this implies that a certain standard of work may be expected from the registered builder. When a new house is built by a registered builder, the council will issue an agreement and certificate of registration. Ninety per cent of new houses in Scotland are covered by this scheme.

In the first two years of the certificate the builder (whom failing, through insolvency or any other reason, the council) is bound to make good any defect arising from a breach of NHBC requirements. This does not include, however, fair wear and tear and damage caused by shrinkage of plasterwork, cement and wood, as the house has a considerable water content which dries out when the house is occupied.

After two years and up to ten years, the builder (again whom failing, the council) is bound to make good any major defects in the structure. In inflationary times, the 'top-up cover' options should always be taken. This means that the cover will increase progressively over the years to meet the cost of any repair that may be required.

The registration certificate transmits automatically from owner to owner but the purchasers should ensure that this certificate is handed over to them at settlement.

Small builders, particularly in country areas, may not be registered with the NHBC. This implies no disrespect to most of them, as a good small builder may not find it worthwhile to join the NHBC scheme. In such a case, however, the purchasers should get a certificate from a qualified architect who is covered by indemnity insurance and who was involved in the building at all stages, that the house is complete (see para **8.21**).

Dealing with limited companies

8.32 Most limited liability companies are reputable, especially public limited companies which have to submit to very rigorous scrutiny, although they can quite suddenly get into serious financial difficulties. Unfortunately, however, not all limited companies are reputable, and it should never be forgotten that the forming of a limited company is a method of escaping unlimited personal liability in the event of liquidation. In terms of the Insolvency Act 1986, s 214, personal liability for a company's debts may be placed upon directors of a limited company where, before the commencement of the winding up of that company, they knew or ought to have concluded that there was no reasonable prospect that the company would avoid going into insolvent liquidation. Such personal liability was placed upon directors in *Re Produce Marketing Consortium Ltd (in liquidation)* ([1989] 3 All ER 1), but this may only be cold comfort for a disappointed creditor.

Some extra formalities are therefore required when dealing with companies, unless you are dealing with a company of outstanding quality. Such a company might rather resent being treated like a company, with two £1 shares issued, which was formed yesterday. This is a matter of personal judgment in all the circumstances, but you can never be wrong to ask.

There are a number of questions you should ask when purchasing, or taking security, from a limited company:

(i)   Has the company been properly incorporated and constituted? You do not want to buy property from a company that does not yet exist. This information may be received by instructing the searchers to search in the Companies Register. Further, is the company's name absolutely correct?

(ii)   Is the company incorporated in this country, and as such subject to the Companies Act 1985, and other company legislation and safeguards? This applies particularly to companies registered in the Isle of Man, Channel Islands, Cayman Islands and Gibraltar, which can have very British names, without having the protection of British law.

(iii)   Is the company properly registered, and has it been dissolved by the Register of Companies without formal liquidation in terms of CA 1985, ss 652, 653 (formerly CA 1948, s 353)? If you buy property from a dissolved company the disposition is invalid, and your only remedy is to petition the court for a restoration of the company to the Register. A search can be obtained from the Register of Companies certifying that the company has been continuously registered.

(iv)   Has the company power in its memorandum to do what it proposes to do? This has not been so crucial since the passing of the European Communitites Act 1972, s 9 (now CA 1985, ss 35 and 36), but it is as well to see the memorandum and articles of the company and to ensure that the action proposed is *intra vires* (within the power of the company as opposed to *ultra vires*).

This is of particular relevance in land registration (see chs 11 to 14).

(v) *Floating charges and receiverships.* Floating charges show up in a search in the Charges Register. A receivership is public knowledge which a solicitor should know. There exists the slight difficulty (see *Gibson v Hunter Home Designs Ltd* 1976 SC 23) that a deed has been recorded adversely, affecting the company's property, or that the company is no longer solvent, and that these events have occurred so recently that they have not been included in the search or advertised. In practical terms, and it is a practical problem, a personal warranty by the company's directors may be obtained (although there may be some resistance to this from the sellers' agents) in the terms following (adapted from JLSS Workshop 1):

'We, John Smith and Jane Smith both of 173 Cathedral Street, Glasgow, respectively a Director and the Secretary of Smiths Reciprocating Sprockets Limited (hereafter called "the Company"), HEREBY CERTIFY and WARRANT after due and diligent enquiry:

(i) that no deeds of any kind which are capable of being recorded in the Land Register in respect of or affecting the subjects of sale have been granted by the company other than as were disclosed in the Search (including Interim Reports in the Search) in the Companies Register exhibited to the said Messrs Campbell, Kinloch & Co, and

(ii) that the Company is solvent and no steps have been or are about to be taken by us or any third party to commence liquidation proceedings which would prejudice the validity of the Disposition of the subjects of sale now being granted to Steelhenge Property Co Ltd, or to appoint a Receiver or otherwise place the company in a position whereby it cannot execute and deliver to you a valid and unobjectionable title.

We further agree and acknowledge that in the event of Steelhenge Property Co Ltd incurring any loss, damage or expense as a result of any of the matters included in this certificate and warranty being untrue or proving to be unfounded we shall be liable personally and individually, and jointly and severally, to make good all such loss, damage and expense to Steelhenge Property Co Ltd.

Yours faithfully,'

In addition, a letter of non-crystallisation should be obtained from the floating charge holder.

CALEDONIAN BANK
Westport
Edinburgh EH1

The Directors
Smiths Reciprocating Sprockets Limited
173 Cathedral Street
Glasgow G4

Dear Sirs,

173 Cathedral Street, Glasgow

As holders of a Floating Charge over the whole assets of Smiths Reciprocating Sprockets Limited, dated 2nd July and registered 14th July 1986, we hereby confirm that:

(1)   As at that date we have taken no steps to crystallise the said Floating Charge, and we shall take no steps to crystallise the said Floating Charge within 21 days from this date, nor take any steps to impede the purchasers from obtaining a valid and marketable recorded title to the property specified in the heading of this letter.

(2)   We have no objection to the sale of the above building by Smiths Reciprocating Sprockets Limited.

(3)   We shall take no steps to deprive Smiths Reciprocating Sprockets Limited of right validly to convey the said subjects, provided that the Disposition thereof is recorded in the Land Register within 22 days of this date.

Yours faithfully,

Although there is still some uncertainty about this matter, this letter should meet the difficulties raised in the case of *Sharp v Thomson* (1995 SC 455), discussed in an article by Richard Leggett, 1994 SLG 99.

Adjudication titles

8.33 An adjudication may be granted against a person who either (a) does not pay a debt or (b) contracts to sell property under missives and then refuses or delays to transfer the property.

In case (a) the title given is a security title only, and the debtor may redeem within 'the legal', which is a ten-year period from the date of decree. Such a title should not be accepted by a purchaser until the legal has lapsed.

In case (b) the title is absolute and may be accepted by a purchaser or a lender in security.

A decree of adjudication is equivalent to a conveyance of lands, and the creditor (or 'adjudger' to give the proper name) completes title by recording the decree in the Personal Register, and then using the decree as a link in title to expede a notice of title which is recorded in the Register of Sasines.

Power of attorney

8.34 A power of attorney is granted by a person who, for any reason (be it illness or absence abroad or any other reason), is unable to deal with his or her affairs either temporarily or permanently. This person is known as 'the constituent' and the power is granted in favour of another person or persons known as 'the attorney'. The important point is that the power must contain an exact specification of the act or acts that are permitted to the attorney. Unlike a will, no powers are vested in the attorney by law. Thus, if a power does not give the attorney power to sign a disposition of heritable property, for example, then no such power exists, and the power is valueless for that purpose. Obviously, therefore, where a deed is granted by an attorney, the conveyancer must ensure that the terms of this deed were permitted by the power.

A power of attorney may be either in general terms, empowering the attorney to do literally anything, or it may be in particular terms, empowering the attorney to do only one thing, such as to sell a house. An example of such a power is as follows:

> 'I, (*name and designation*), CONSIDERING that I am about to be absent from the United Kingdom and temporarily absent abroad and to facilitate the management and sale of subjects at (*specify property to be sold*), owned by me it is convenient that I should grant a Power of Attorney and having full trust and confidence in the integrity and competence of (*name and design Attorney*)

THEREFORE I appoint the said (*name*) as my Attorney with full power to enter into any agreement for the sale of the said subjects and to sign all conveyances and other documents related thereto on my behalf and from the proceeds of sale to discharge any standard security or other form of security in connection therewith and to sign any documents related thereto; Thereafter from the net free proceeds of sale, to settle all expenses legally incurred in connection with the sale and generally to do whatever in his discretion my Attorney may think expedient for enforcing, carrying out and settling the said transaction; And I further grant to my said Attorney power to employ the firm of (*name and design*) to attend to the legal matters arising from the said sale; And I further authorise my Attorney to institute on my behalf, pursue to finality, defend, compromise, all and any suits or actions, disputes or differences arising from the execution of these presents or otherwise affecting me or my property; And I do hereby ratify and confirm and hereby promise to ratify, allow and confirm all and whatsoever my Attorney shall lawfully do or cause to be done in the premises in virtue hereof without prejudice always to my right demand just count and reckoning with me for the whole intromissions of my Attorney in terms hereof; And I declare that this Power of Attorney shall subsist until the same is recalled in writing; And I consent to registration hereof for preservation: IN WITNESS WHEREOF.'

A power of attorney may now be 'continuing', that is to say it continues after the constituent has become incapacitated. This has the tremendous advantage that a *curator bonis* does not have to be appointed, and the administration becomes much easier. On the other hand, it presents a temptation, for there is no real control over the attorney. For that reason the Law Society is very vigilant about solicitors who are appointed attorneys, and it is recommended that if an alternative person is available to act as attorney, then the solicitor should not be involved, except as agent for the attorney.

The Adults with Incapacity (Scotland) Act 2000 places all continuing powers of attorney under the supervision of the public guardian at Callander Park in Falkirk. Regulations have been made to ensure that these continuing powers are signed and used properly.

When a deed is signed under a power of attorney, it is signed by the attorney. The narrative of that deed may either (a) run in the name of the attorney narrating the power, and state in the testing clause that it is signed by the named attorney or (b) run in the name of the constituent without mentioning the power, and then state in the testing clause that it is signed by the attorney on behalf of the constituent, by virtue of the power, which is then specified. Either method may be used, but in both cases the power of attorney must be produced with the deed to authorise the signature of the attorney.

Uninfeft granters of deeds

8.35 You do not need to have a recorded title (or 'be infeft') to grant many deeds, in terms of C(S)A 1924, s 13, which allows an uninfeft granter to grant certain deeds using a mid-couple or link in title. Thus, if we take the example of William Brown who had a title to a house at 43 Goosedubs, Glasgow and who died on 4 February 2006. His Executor was his brother James Brown, who was confirmed as such on 10 March 2006. His brother then sold the house without taking title in his own name. The disposition is granted by James Brown as uninfeft proprietor, but must explain why James is selling William's house. The disposition therefore reads:

'I, JAMES BROWN, 14 The Elms, Glasgow, Executor nominate of the WILLIAM BROWN conform to Confirmation issued in my favour by the Commissariot of Glasgow and Strathkelvin at Glasgow on 10 March 2006 and as such Executor uninfeft proprietor of the property hereinafter mentioned HAVE SOLD at the price of ONE HUNDRED THOUSAND POUNDS and DO HEREBY DISPONE to MICHAEL MONK and his successors and assignees whomsoever heritably and irredeemably ALL and WHOLE the plot of land known as Forty Three Goosedubs, Glasgow registered under Title Number GLA 1234567; WITH ENTRY at 30 April 2006; which said subjects were last vested in the said William Brown residing at Forty Three Goosedubs, Glasgow and from whom I acquired right by the said Confirmation dated as aforesaid; and I as Executor aforesaid grant warrandice from my own facts and deeds only and bind the Executory in my charge in absolute warrandice: IN WITNESS WHEREOF.'

This form is easily altered for use by parties who grant deeds in a representational capacity, changing only the document that empowers them to sign on behalf of others.

8.36 These are some of the major points to be kept in view when examining and there are many more that could be mentioned. In a routine house purchase, however, there should not be too many other points which occur regularly. If you know of any that I have missed please do not hesitate to let me know.

Remedies for an unmarketable title

8.37 The purchasers are of course entitled to resile if presented with an unmarketable title, but we will presume that the purchasers and sellers are both keen to complete the purchase. There are many varied ways of reaching settlement, but the following should be considered:

(a) **Disposition** *per incuriam.* If a disposition has a bad mistake in it, for example you sell the flat '1/right' instead of '1/left', which is probably the commonest conveyancing mistake, you can grant this form of disposition. It simply narrates that *per incuriam* you have sold the wrong flat, and then goes on to dispone the correct one. The use of the Latin tag hides the fact that it was done (literally) 'by mistake'.

(b) **By skilful use of the Conveyancing (Scotland) Act 1874, ss 38, 39** (now the Requirements of Writing (Scotland) Act 1995, ss 4, 5). All manner of defects of execution and mistakes in the deed can be rectified by careful use of the provisions of these sections.

(c) **By use of the Law Reform (Miscellaneous Provisions) (Scotland) Act 1985, s 8(1)(a).** This useful provision of law allows a disposition to be rectified by the court if it does not reflect the agreement in missives.

(d) **Positive and negative prescription.** You should bear in mind that prescription cures all blemishes if it is appropriate.

(e) **The Keeper's discretion.** In land registration cases the Keeper has absolute discretion to record what he wants. Thus, for example, he keeps an 'elastic tape measure' for wrong measurements, which are not too wrong. Similarly he will turn a blind eye to other blemishes of title, which therefore disappear through not being shown on the land certificate. The only trouble is he will not tell you what he proposes to do, and turning a blind eye to something once does not mean that he will do it again. There is no doubt that judicious use of this power has made life much easier for conveyancers in operational areas for registration.

(f) **The insurance indemnity.** An indemnity policy can be taken out to cover a defect in title, which recompenses the purchaser if a claim arises from a third party. One insurance company advertises indemnity policies available against: absence of matrimonial affidavit, giving rise to a claim by a non-entitled spouse; *a non domino* disposition, where there is a claim by the true owner within the prescriptive period; failure to establish a link in title; lack of access rights; burdens imposed on the feu, and a possible claim by the former or third party superior when they have been contravened without having been discharged; discrepancies in the description of land and incorrect detailing of plans. A purchaser is not, however, obliged to accept an indemnity, as it does not render a title marketable. It is only an indemnity until prescription extends its healing balm.

(g) The *actio quanti minoris.* This remedy, which is now available automatically in terms of the Contract (Scotland) Act 1997, unless specifically excluded by contract, involves a reduction of the price where there is something wrong in the title of the subjects.

(h) *De minimis non curat lex.* ('The law does not care about little things'.) Try and persuade the purchaser that no court would accept the objection to your defective title.

8.38 *Environmental.* The purchaser's solicitors should ask the seller's solicitors for some evidence that the property is not potentially contaminated. Some local authorities provide this information in the property enquiry certificate, but if they do not, you should ask for an environmental search, provided by the Landmark Group. The outcome will either be passed or referred. If it is referred for a professional opinion, this will either be passed or recommend further action. Further action may necessitate an intrusive survey.

8.39 *Inhibitions and Adjudications.* A litigant may take out an inhibition either when the action is commenced ('on the dependence') and prior to a hearing of the case, or after decree is given. In either case, the effect is to prevent the debtor from granting a voluntary deed of all heritable property in ownership. It covers only voluntary deeds, and thus does not affect deeds that the debtor was under an obligation to grant. Thus, for example, it would not affect a standard security which the debtor was under an obligation to grant the security, given prior to the placing of the inhibition. An inhibition show up in the form 10A report, and the matter must be cleared up before any money is paid to the debtor, who cannot grant a deed of property.

An adjudication is a judicial transfer of the property, in satisfaction of an unmet obligation by the former owner. This is rarely encountered, because a rogue will divest himself of the property before the matter becomes serious. A recent example concerned a husband, who was divorced from his wife, and ordered to pay aliment. This was not paid. Then the wife found that the husband was living with another partner in a house in Aberdeen, which was in the husband's name, not the partner's name, or in the name of a nominee. Accordingly, the wife successfully took out an injunction, which transferred the property to her. Again such an order appears in the form 10A report, and must be dealt with prior to settlement because the debtor cannot transfer title.

8.40 *Letters of Obligation.* An example is given at para **7.06**(j), and is a little understood, but vital, part of any transaction. A final report, 10A or 11A, is received prior to settlement, but is not completely up to date. In the period between the report and 21 days after settlement, the purchaser is vulnerable, because the seller may be inhibited from selling, or grant a standard security over the property, without the purchaser's knowledge. In that event the seller's solicitor, who is covered by Professional Indemnity Insurance, is by the letter of obligation, obliged to make good any loss suffered by the purchaser. Thus the strength of the Indemnity Insurance covers the gap, and without this arrangement the situation could not be covered. It is thus a service given by the profession, 'unhonoured and unsung', basically because the profession doesn't explain its significance, and even if it did, the public would not understand! The Letter, which is signed by the seller's solicitors, and witnessed, is handed over at settlement.

Chapter 9

SETTLEMENT AND THE FINAL STEPS

'That I think is what we have done, that is what we continue to do and, as for the argument about the payment of council tax, let me tell him and he must know again in the comparison between our Government and his Government, that we gave in the response 39 per cent increase in real terms in council tax compared to the last five years of which he had some influence where there was an annual reduction of 7 per cent in real terms of contribution to councils for their council tax.'

(Rt Hon John Prescott in a parliamentary answer)

'I think there was so little English in that answer. President Chirac would have been happy with it.'

(Rt Hon William Hague in a supplementary)

9.01 The purchasers' agents consider whether or not they are satisfied with the title position and with the answers given to their queries. They write, if they have not already, to their clients setting out the salient features of the title and may warn the purchasers about any obtrusive conditions (particularly about any prohibition against trade, keeping animals, cutting down trees etc). They further apprise the purchasers of any financial commitment that may arise in the future. The clients should not, however, be swamped with inessential and confusing information. What is inessential or confusing obviously varies from case to case; broadly speaking a minimum of useful information will usually satisfy a residential purchaser, but a commercial purchaser may want a detailed report.

If anything is amiss in the title, and for present purposes we shall assume that it is not, the clients' instructions must be taken as to dealing with this, both at this stage and indeed at all stages of the transaction. If the purchasers' solicitors and their clients are not reasonably satisfied as to any important point, it must be cleared up before settlement takes place.

9.02 We must consider the financial arrangements to be made at settlement. The sellers prepare a state for settlement which is the sellers' account to the purchasers, and this is approved by the purchasers' agents. It should reflect the following items:

(a) The price of the house and the price of any moveables included.

(b) In non-domestic properties the apportionment of local rates. First of all, a short explanation of local government financing is required. The bulk of local government spending is funded by central government, but the remainder has to be raised locally. This was formerly done entirely from local rates, which were collected by regional councils, both on their own behalf, and of their constituent districts. Rates are now paid to the unitary councils.

Every five years (the quinquennium) a valuation is made of every item of heritable property, except agricultural land which is exempt. The official government valuer ('the Assessor') analyses rental evidence of all commercial property, which is only one element in the calculation of individual rates bills. For further information, see the Scottish Assessors Association website at www.saa.gov.uk. Much dissatisfaction was expressed at the fact that rates in the south of England are invariably much lower than those fixed for similar properties in Scotland. Scottish and English rates are now being equalised, but this is a lengthy and complex process. Rating tends to be a rather specialised subject confined to valuation lawyers and surveyors.

The rates of the property are apportioned on a daily basis as at settlement. The rating year runs from 1 April in each year until 31 March in the next year. Thus if the purchase date is, say, 15 November 1994, the sellers pay the rates for 229 days, and the purchasers pay for the balance of the year to March 1995, i e 136 days.

9.03 Meantime in domestic properties rates had been replaced by the community charge, otherwise known as the 'poll tax'. This was not a charge on properties but on persons who lived in properties, on the basis that if a person used a council service, then they should pay for it, and that the whole burden should not fall on property owners. While the reasoning behind this proposition was quite sound, you could not have called the charge controversial—at the end of the day, nearly everyone complained about it. It was also a beuraucratic nightmare as local authorities had to keep records on every citizen—hence the nickname 'poll tax', which stuck. It was, therefore, replaced on 1 April 1993 by the council tax, which remains in effect, and while it is unloved, as is any tax, it is seen as being reasonably fair.

Houses are valued as at their market value on 1 April 1991 or at their building date, or date of significant alteration, and are placed in bands, A to H, according to value: band A being the value up to £27,000, and band H being the value over £212,000. As was the case with the community charge before it, there are various exemptions: those living alone, students, student nurses, youth training trainees, apprentices, and persons under 18. In addition to rates there are water and sewage charges paid to Scottish Water. In the tax year 2005/06 these are respectively £166.50 and £188.10 at band D—the median band. Bands A to C are discounted and bands E to H pay more. There is little chance of these charges becoming less, as Scottish Water have to pay for years of under investment in infrastructure, eg pipes and reservoirs.

As at the date of settlement a notice of the change of ownership should be sent to the appropriate council, who will apportion the tax between the sellers and the purchasers.

Feu duty

9.04 This was formerly an area of the greatest complexity and danger, and the purchasers had to be satisfied that the feu duty was either redeemed or else paid to date of settlements and that no liability for arrears passed with the sale. Fortunately, feu duties were extinguished by Pt 2 of the Abolition of Feudal Tenure etc (Scotland) Act 2000, and the responsibility for compensating the superior rests with the seller, and does not transmit on sale of a property. In summary, the purchasers no longer have to concern themselves with the feu duty position.

Common charges

9.05 Where a flat in a tenement building is sold, the factor should be asked by the sellers' agents to apportion the common charges for maintenance of the building between the parties. This can be done when the factor is informed of the change of ownership by the sellers' solicitors. In modern practice it is usual for the factor to ask an incoming owner for a deposit to meet future charges. This deposit is set against these charges.

Factors, or property managers as factors prefer now to be called, are very wary about instructing repairs, let alone paying tradesmen without having received money from the owners well in advance. The reason for this is that they have incurred huge debts, paying tradesmen in the past, and which have not been repaid. The case of *David Watson Property Management v Woolwich Equitable Building Society* (1992 SLT 430), which held that a heritable creditor who has taken possession of a house on the default of the borrower is not responsible for common charges which the borrower had failed to pay, amply illustrates this point. Although *David Watson* possibly excuses purchasers from having to pay the sellers' common charges debts, it is the invariable practice for the purchasing solicitors to see a recent common charges receipt.

Interest

9.06 When settlement takes place properly on the agreed date of entry, the question of interest does not arise—that is to say when the full purchase price is paid by the purchaser and the property is made available with the disposition, the titles and the keys. Where, however, one party or the other cannot meet their obligation, the question of interest arises.

> **Example.** Mr and Mrs A contract to sell their house to Mr and Mrs B for £150,000 as at 16 December 2005. For some reason personal to them Mr and Mrs B cannot pay this sum at 16 December. Their building society loan may have been held up, or the proceeds of the sale of their own house may not yet have come through. What do Mr and Mrs B do?

The position at law is that the purchasers are obliged to pay the price at the date of entry, failing which they are in default, and the obligation can be enforced by the sellers. Thus at law (*ex lege*) the sellers may raise an action of implement, including a crave for interest at the legal rate, which is currently well below what the sellers would have to pay their bank if they take an overdraft to cover the lack of money received from the purchasers.

Additionally, interest runs only from the date of warranting the action, and not from the date of entry, unless the parties have entered, or enter into an agreement to the contrary. But the parties may agree (*ex pacto*) that a different provision shall apply (see para **4.23** and *Lloyd's Bank v Bamberger* 1994 SLT 424) and that interest at a stated rate shall apply if there is a delay or default by the purchasers. If no such agreement is made, there must be doubts as to whether overdraft interest can be demanded by the sellers without entry being given in return, on the basis of a statement in *Erskine* (III, 3, 79) to the effect that the sellers cannot gain interest as well as enjoy the 'fruits of the property'—whatever these may be (see *Thomson v Vernon* 1983 SLT (Sh Ct) 17 discussed by Professor D J Cusine, 1983 JLSS 273).

If the sellers are unable to settle on the date of entry, there is no obligation upon the purchasers either to take entry or pay interest (see *Bowie v Semple's Executors* 1978 SLT (Sh Ct) 9). If, however, the purchasers wish to take entry they may do so on consigning the price on deposit receipt with a bank. This is in terms of *Prestwick Cinema Co v Gardiner* (1951 SC 98). When the money is on deposit receipt neither party has control over it without the consent of the other. While this may seem to be a very convenient arrangement, it is spoiled as a practical remedy by the extremely poor rate of interest offered by banks on deposit receipt.

A clause in the missives requiring a defaulting purchaser to pay interest on the price at a realistic rate from the date when the purchaser defaulted until payment is made is standard in modern conditions. Alternatively, the seller may cancel the sale and resell the property at the defaulting purchaser's expense, with interest being payable from the date of the first sale until final settlement of the second sale. A heavy penalty upon the defaulting purchaser, maybe, but it is perfectly fair. The defaulting purchaser should have met the terms of the agreement struck with the seller.

The most practical solution to this reasonably common problem is for the purchasers to ask their bank for a 'bridging loan', that is to say, a short-term loan, usually given on the basis of the probability of the borrower receiving funds on a certain future date. Thus the purchasers can say to their bank: 'Our building society loan is coming through next week and we'll repay you then'. It should be emphasised that bridging loans are expensive and should only be taken on a short-term basis; further the bank may ask for an 'arrangement fee' for arranging the loan which may make these loans unattractive, save in an emergency.

Banks are not, however, so keen on lending against a payment on an uncertain future date; for example, if the purchasers are still selling their own house and have not found a buyer yet, their bank may not be willing to provide 'the bridge'. Banks like their loans to be short term and repayment to be certain, unless they make a specified arrangement as in a 'personal loan'. This provides for regular payments to account, and the banks charge more handsomely for a personal loan.

If the purchasers cannot therefore get a bridging loan, or if the parties decide it is unnecessary, a possible arrangement is for the purchasers to pay the sellers what money they have in return for possession, and for interest to run on the balance at an agreed rate until settlement. This rate of interest might be the rate that would have been payable by the purchasers to their building society. This, of course, is not necessarily recommended, as it is fraught with danger, but in many circumstances it would be unreasonable for the sellers not to co-operate with such a request, and to insist on implement of the contract strictly. When both parties agree to this, the sellers get a good rate of interest on their money and the purchasers get possession of the house although they have technically been in breach of contract. What has happened is that the contract has been partially reconstructed by agreement. This is a common feature of conveyancing practice—an unsatisfactory provision of law is altered by contract as in the law of tenement, passing of risk and mineral reservations, all of which are discussed in this book.

This agreement can, however, run deeper. (See Professor A J McDonald 'A Question of Interest' 1980 JLSS 103; Professor J M Halliday 'Delay in Settlement' 1981 SLG 68; and Professor Noble 'Delays in Settlement' 1984 JLSS 116, which contain a comprehensive review of the law.) The legal arguments on this matter are so complex that there is every reason for the conveyancer to seek to avoid such a dispute by:

(a) inserting a suitable '*ex pacto*' clause in missives to cover delays (see para **4.28**);

(b) ensuring that the buyers have made satisfactory financial arrangements;

(c) choosing a sensible and realistic date of entry; and

(d) keeping the transaction running on schedule until settlement.

9.07 The sellers who receive an interest payment without deduction of tax should account for this in their next tax return. They should, in turn, issue a tax receipt for the payment to the purchasers, who should use (if applicable) this to claim tax relief on the payment. Similarly when a bridging loan from a bank is taken, the bank should issue a certificate of interest paid for tax purposes. Interest payments made to persons resident overseas should be made after deduction of tax by the person paying interest, and that person should account to HM Revenue and Customs for the tax deducted, because the Revenue has no power of collection once the money has left the country.

9.08 When the state of settlement has been agreed and entry is near, both solicitors should ensure that they are ready to settle, and that there are no loose ends which could cause settlement to be postponed. In particular the purchasers' solicitors should ensure that they have received sufficient money from the purchasers to enable them to settle. They should at this stage also render their fee and get this settled while the clients still depend on the solicitors. This may sound cynical but the lawyers have by this time earned and deserve their fee, and any lawyers will tell you sad stories of highly grateful clients who have become quite the opposite when faced with a bill. We shall, however, deal with the question of fees in ch **9.18**.

The purchasers' cheque should therefore be given to the solicitors in plenty of time for it to be cleared through the purchasers' bank. This cannot be stressed sufficiently. A solicitors' cheque from clients' account is treated like cash, because of the strict rules (Solicitors' Account Rules) that solicitors shall ensure that at all times they have enough in their clients' bank account to meet the total amount that the firm is due to clients (irrespective of any money owed to the solicitors by clients). If, therefore, solicitors issue a cheque, and then are informed that the clients' cheque paid to the firm has not been met by the clients' bank, the solicitors may not order the firm's own bank to refuse payment of the firm's cheque. The loss in other words is the solicitors, and any attempt to shift that misfortune to the sellers may amount to professional misconduct. This point is brought home in a statement by the Law Society (1981 JLSS 357) which is worth repeating verbatim in view of the importance of the matter:

> 'A solicitor acting for a purchaser in a conveyancing transaction has a duty to ensure either that he has cleared funds in his clients' account for the settlement of such a conveyancing transaction or that any cheque which he has received for his client will be met by the paying bank. There is a principle that a cheque drawn by the solicitor acting for a purchaser on his client bank account and handed over in settlement in a conveyancing transaction to the solicitor acting for the seller should not be stopped except in exceptional circumstances.
>
> Such exceptional circumstances would arise in the event of circumstances amounting to breach of contract on the part of the seller, as for example when the purchasers are unable to receive vacant possession or if the subjects have been destroyed (and these circumstances are contrary to the terms of the missives) or in the event of a postal settlement where the disposition which is delivered contains a defect in execution.'

In this unfortunate event the purchasers' solicitors would be well advised to inform the Law Society before they stop their cheque.

Golden rule: always make sure you have cleared funds in your bank on settlement date, and before you write a cheque on the clients' account. It is normal that a cashier would refuse to make out a cheque unless and until it is confirmed that funds have cleared.

9.09 The sellers' and purchasers' solicitors should arrange a time and place for the settlement. Except in unusual circumstances the rule is 'the cheque goes to the disposition'—that is settlement takes place at the sellers' solicitors' office. Both parties should make a check list of what they require for the settlement.

If it is not convenient for the sellers to hand the keys in to the solicitors, as is often the case, they may be left with a third party, eg the selling estate agent. Then when the sellers' solicitors have the cheque, they telephone the third party and ask them to release the keys to the purchasers.

9.10 The cheque is exchanged for the disposition, letter of obligation, land certificate, keys, the receipted state for settlement and any other papers. Please note that this ceremony amounts to delivery of the disposition, in its technical sense.

Ideally settlements should be done face to face, so that the cheque and the disposition are exchanged at the same time. This was the traditional manner of settlement, but many settlements nowadays are carried out by post or courier, owing to constraints of time. To get round the difficulty of the cheque or the deed reaching the other solicitor before the other part is returned, and being misused, the sender of the cheque or disposition writes a short letter to the other solicitor saying: 'We enclose the cheque/ disposition and settlement papers, which please hold as undelivered until you dispatch the disposition and settlement papers/cheque to us.' This is a request that mirrors the obligation in missives and must be adhered to, as delivery is postponed until the event happens.

9.11 Alternatively the price may be 'telegraphed' from the buyer's solicitor's bank account to that of the seller's solictor. This, of course, entails in the buyer's solicitor having cleared funds in their clients' account, and a certain amount of careful planning. Incidentally do not assume that a telegraphic transfer will be an instant transfer—the process sometimes takes several hours. Banks do not like to explain why this should be so.

9.12 The sellers' solicitors then bank the cheque and pay any outlays (such as estate agents, advertising accounts and their own fees). They then send the balance to the sellers with a statement of their outlays.

9.13 Other loose ends may remain.

Stamp Duty Land Tax—Land Transaction Return. When introduced, in 2004, there was a hiatus from practitioners. Not only had HM Revenue and Customs failed to take account of the particular aspects of Scottish Conveyancing procedure but also a massive form had to be completed (by hand) and a certificate would eventually follow without which the deal would not be registered. The system has since been refined, much to the credit of the Law Society's Tax Law Committee, and an online form is available at www.hmrc.gov.uk. There is now a same day presentation in

Edinburgh and also the 16 day special urgency services for cases where the certificate has not been sent 16 days after the effective date (the date of entry). See SDLT under 'Conveyancing Essentials', on the Law Society website.

9.14 The sellers' agents make sure that the sellers' home insurances are cancelled, and that refund of premium is obtained for the remainder of the insurance year, and that all advertising is cancelled, if not already done.

9.15 After settlement the purchasers' solicitors complete the testing clause, and when the SDLT certificate arrives then send the deed to be registered in the Land Register, together with the deeds being sent in support of the registration, a cheque for registration dues unless your firm subscribes to Registers' direct debit scheme and form 1/2/3 as appropriate and form 4 *in duplicate*. Before the deeds are sent to the Keeper, these should be carefully checked to avoid a deed being returned by the Keeper. Make sure that the form 1/2/3 is signed at the bottom of the first page by a partner of the firm. You may also have the seller's discharge, relative forms 2 and 4 (the latter also *in duplicate*) and cheque for registration dues.

The deed then goes through the registration process at Registers of Scotland and is carefully checked. If there is anything wrong—for things that do go wrong, see the annual report by the Keeper—Register House will either send the deed straight back to you in serious cases (eg forgetting to sign a form or not recording within a time limit, or a defective form of deed) or telephone you in less serious cases to see what you want done (eg a small mistake in the testing clause or an unauthenticated erasure of a minor nature).

9.16 The land certificate is duly returned having been registered (sometimes up to two years later), together with the deeds sent with the application. The purchasers' solicitors should check that there is no restriction of indemnity contained in the land certificate, and that the land certificate contains no mistakes. In the latter case, the certificate is returned to the Keeper for correction. Having satisfied themselves, the purchasers' solicitors discharge the letter of obligation (usually by writing the word 'implemented' on it and dating and initialling it) and return it to the sellers' solicitors. The file is then checked for loose ends, for useful papers to be retained, and is put away.

9.17 The land certificate and the charge certificate, if appropriate, are now in the hands of the purchasers' solicitors. They should report this to the purchasers and ask for instructions as to safekeeping of the land certificate, which is the property of the clients subject to any right of lien the solicitor may have. If a lender is involved, the land and charge certificates are sent to the lender in terms of their instructions. If there is no lender involved, should the solicitors keep the land certificate or the purchasers' bank, or the purchasers themselves? The first two courses are preferable. 'In the tin box under the bed' is not to be encouraged, but it is the clients' choice.

In the case of the now redundant title deeds these should be sent to the purchasers telling them that the land certificate is now the title, and that the old deeds are redundant, and you are sure that the purchaser would like these for historical or sentimental reasons. The purchaser may decline with thanks, in which case the old titles may be discarded, but it is useful to ask the local archivist first, to see if the deeds are of any value to the archivist.

Finally, do not forget that if the fees have not been paid, the solicitors have a lien over the title deeds until payment. It is recommended (1984 JLSS 198) that conveyancing files be kept for ten years, or at least until the property is successfully resold.

Feeing-up

9.18 You have done the work and you are worthy of your fee, but the question is how much?

Fees were fixed by Law Society scales until 1985 when, under intense pressure from free traders, the Law Society was forced to abandon these fixed charges based on the value of the property. The weakness in scale fees was that they encouraged 'price fixing', placed low fees on small property transactions, which were often the most work-intensive, and high fees on large property transactions, which were often the least work-intensive. It should be noted, however, that estate agents, architects, surveyors, and indeed the government, can still charge fees based on the value of the property.

In place of scale fees the Law Society in 1985 issued a set of guidelines which should be followed:

(1)   The fee shall be fair and reasonable to both the solicitor and the client.

(2)   The fixing of every fee is a balanced judgment rather than an arithmetical calculation.

(3)   The solicitor should keep detailed records in respect of work carried out (i) to ascertain total time and (ii) to justify the fee fixed if need be.

(4)   The fee may consist of charges for detailed items charged at the current unit rate recommended in the General Table of Fees (now abolished).

(5)   Alternatively the solicitor may charge according to circumstances, taking into account the following seven factors:

    (a)   importance of the matter to the client;

    (b)   amount or value of any money or property involved;

    (c)   complexity or difficulty or novelty of the question raised;

    (d)   skill, labour, specialised knowledge and responsibility involved;

    (e)   time expended;

    (f)   length, number and importance of any documents prepared or perused; and

    (g)   place where and the circumstances in which the services are rendered, including the degree of expendition required.

(6)   It is important to establish an hourly charge rate for each fee earner in the firm.

(7)   Once hourly charge rates have been set, the first step is to determine the product of the rate charges and the time expended. The result should then be appraised to see if it is reasonable to the client.

(8)   The fee may contain an element which reflects all other relevant factors as set out in reg 4 of the General Table of Fees (now abolished).

(9)   There may be factors producing a negative weighting, eg property of small value or very routine work.

(10)   The practioner should then 'step back' and take an overall view to check if the fee thus fixed is fair and reasonable.

(11)   Where a solicitor does business which is fairly standard, the solicitor may prepare his or her own table of fees for such work, but it must be prepared in conformity with these guidelines.

(12)   Where a first registration of land is induced, some additional weighting is normally appropriate, but negative weighting is appropriate in dealings in a registered interest.

(13) Before embarking on business involving sale or purchase of property, the enquirer is entitled to know the approximate cost in fees and outlays.

Fees should, therefore, be charged at a rate to enable your firm to reflect the work done, to reflect the resources used (your time at university and training, office rental, stationery, equipment, cost of indemnity insurance, responsibility, continuing legal education, and so on) and to make a decent profit, to make the whole exercise worthwhile.

The Law Society formerly issued a General Table of Fees which did not include fees charged on the basis of the value of the property. These were judged to be anti-competitive, and dropped several years ago, although estate agents fees, SDLT, and recording dues are all related to value and not to the work actually involved. The table of fees included a permissible time charge—in 2005, the last year when this charge was fixed, a unit of six minutes cost £11.85. This was, however, judged anti-competitive, and the Law Society no longer fixes a unit value. The unit rate may seem very high, but reflect on the following—I go to the hairdresser who has me out of the door in about six minutes, because it is an increasingly small job. For this he charges me £6, which is not significantly below the unit rate, and the hairdresser doesn't have to keep detailed accounts, files, records of haircuts made, title deeds, computers, a huge staff, and a large office and is not subject to the attentions of various regulatory bodies.

As a rule of thumb, you can perhaps look at the old scale of fees, and see what would have been allowed, although these fees are probably on the high side for modern conditions, bearing in mind the remarks of the Reid Report, in 1963. Also bear in mind that to open a file and a cash card and to vet the client for money laundering and general financial reliability will probably cost a minimum of £100, before you do very much.

The effect of competition should always be borne in mind—many firms, who had what they considered 'dripping roasts', are now having to quote competitively for the provision of these legal services, which they formerly considered as a job for life. This is of course, in general, a good thing, although it may seem a fairly mixed blessing to those firms. Even large firms have to submit to 'beauty parades' at which they have to make a competitive presentation of services offered and fees charged to firms for whom they have worked for years. A sad story was related in *The Times* recently of a London firm who worked at minimum cost to set up the Tate Modern art gallery in London, involving the critical financing of the project. At a subsequent beauty parade, their services were not accepted, despite their earlier work.

Estimates should be pretty accurate, although one cannot prepare for the unexpected, and your firm's engagement letter should contain a provision allowing the quoted fee to be increased in the event that the work proves more complex. Value added tax is not, however, unexpected, and should be fully reflected in the quotation. If a normal figure cannot be arrived at, a list of the relevant fee earners' hourly rates should have been appended to the engagement letter. It would be usual to restrict the fee, the better to maintain an ongoing relationship with the client.

The best distilled wisdom in this feeing-up process is contained in guideline number 1: the fee shall be reasonable to both the client and the solicitor. A fair fee to the solicitor covers the overheads of the practice, and a reasonable profit margin. (For a further discussion on this topic, please see an excellent article by Brian Allingham 'Conveyancing: The profit motive' 1992 JLSS 439.) It should also be remembered that, as a business, the level of your fees essentially depends on what your competitors are charging.

9.19 Unless otherwise stated in the missives, each of the parties pay their own fees to their own solicitors. It used to be the case that builders insisted on buyers of new houses paying both the builders' and their own fees. This was not, however, popular, and the practice was scrapped. The builders' legal fees are now, therefore, presumably included in the price of the house.

9.20 Value added tax at 17.5% is currently payable on all legal fees. Value added tax is not, however, chargeable on recording dues in the Land Register (although if you order an extract deed from the Keeper, VAT is payable on that charge) or stamp duty land tax. Value added tax is also payable on Land Register reports. For the position of VAT on land prices (if applicable in a minority cases of tenanted land) see *Jaymarke Development Ltd v Elinacre Ltd* (1992 SLT 1193).

9.21 In addition a loan fee is payable, which is based on the principles enumerated in para **9.17**. Where the same lawyers act for the borrowers and the lenders, less work would be involved, and the fee would presumably be smaller than if completely different solicitors acted for the lenders, and had to go through the title new. Under the old table of fees the reduction in fees was from scale fee based on the amount of the loan to 40% of that fee. Value added tax is payable on these fees, but there is no stamp duty land tax on security documents.

Recording dues or Land Register dues are payable for the recording of the security. If, however, the security is presented at the same time as the conveyance to the purchaser, an abated charge of £22 is payable.

9.22 Registration due and rates of SDLT.

Table A

	Consideration or Value	Fee
Does not exceed:	£10,000	£22.00
	£15,000	£33.00
	£20,000	£44.00
	£25,000	£55.00
	£30,000	£66.00
	£35,000	£77.00
	£40,000	£88.00
Fees increase by £11.00 for every £5,000 until:		
	£200,000	£440.00
	£300,000	£500.00
	£400,000	£550.00
	£500,000	£600.00
	£600,000	£650.00
	£700,000	£700.00
	£800,000	£800.00
	£1,000,000	£900.00
	£1,500,000	£1,500.00
	£2,000,000	£2,000.00
	£3,000,000	£3,000.00
	£5,000,000	£5,000.00
	Exceeds £5,000,000	£7,500.00

Notes:
1. A separate charge may be made for completion of missives, arranging loan, redemption of feu duties etc. (See reg 21.)
2. A charge may also be made for posts and incidents which is normally about 10%. (See reg 14.)
3. The seller will also incur dues of property enquiry and other searches and Land Register reports.

9.23

Table B

	Amount	Fee
Does not exceed	£20,000	£22.00
	£30,000	£33.00
	£40,000	£44.00
	£50,000	£55.00
	£60,000	£66.00
	£70,000	£77.00
	£80,000	£88.00
Fees increase by £11.00 for every £10,000 until:		
Does not exceed	£200,000	£220.00
	£300,000	£250.00
	£400,000	£275.00
	£500,000	£300.00
	£600,000	£325.00
	£700,000	£350.00
	£800,000	£400.00
	£1,000,000	£450.00
	£1,500,000	£750.00
	£2,000,000	£1,000.00
	£3,000,000	£1,500.00
	£5,000,000	£2,500.00
Exceeds £5,000,000		£3,750.00

Notes:

1 Loan fees are quoted in table 'B' of Registration Fees. These are based on the amount of loan. There is no stamp duty land tax on loan documents.
2 In the case of endowment loans the fee may be increased as extra work is involved.
3 Where a security is recorded together with a disposition in favour of the borrower, the dues of recording the standard security are £22.
4 All data is believed to be correct at date of publication but as these figures are liable to frequent change they should be treated as illustrative only. Recording dues are not generally subject to annual upward revision. The apparently automatic rise in house prices has had the effect of increasing the level of dues.

Stamp duty land tax

Land transactions with an effective date on or after 23 March 2006.

Rate	Land in disadantaged areas— Residential	Land in disadvantaged areas— Non-residential	All other land in the UK— Residential	All other land in the UK— Non-residential
Zero	£0-£150,000	£0-£150,000	£0-£125,000	£0-£150,000
1%	Over £150,000-£250,000	Over £150,000-£250,000	Over £150,000 £250,000	Over £150,000-£250,000
3%	Over £250,000-£500,000	Over £250,000-£500,000	Over £250,000-£500,000	Over £250,000-£500,000
4%	Over £500,000	Over £500,000	Over £500,000	Over £500,000

Note: Disadvantaged Area Relief for non-residential land transactions **is not available for non-residential land transactions with an effective date on or after 17 March 2005**.

- the completion of contracts entered into and substantially performed on or before 16 March 2005.
- the completion or substantial performance of other contracts entered into on or before 16 March 2005, provides that there is no variation or assignment of the contract or sub-sale of the property after 16 March 2005 and that the transaction is not in consequence of the exercise after 16 March 2005 of an option or right of pre-emption.

9.24 Land Register report fees (as at April 2006)

Forms 10, 12, 14, P16, and P17	£ 27.00+VAT
Forms 11 & 13	£15.00+VAT
Form P16/10 and P17/12	£40.00+VAT

The Registers of Scotland Amendment Order 2005.

9.25 The purchase file for 3 Miller Drive, might continue as follows:

To: Wendy Robertson<wrobertson@bjw.co.uk>

Sent: 15 March 2006 11:03

From: Veronica Vanbrugh <vvanbrugh@bjw.co.uk

Subject: 3 Miller Drive, Newton Mearns

Dear Wendy

You may remember that Mr Pink asked me to keep an eye on the diary and to send out reminders of various time limits etc. This is just to remind you that the settlement of 3 Miller Drive, Newton Mearns takes place on 30 March and that you should now be thinking about settlement. Please let me know if I can help in any way.

Veronica

To: Veronica Vanbrugh <vvanbrugh@bjw.co.uk>

Sent: 15 March 2006 1:15

From: Wendy Robertson<wrobertson@bjw.co.uk>

Subject: RE: 3 Miller Drive, Newton Mearns

Dear Veronica

Thanks for your note. I am sending out some letters today, and have, I think, everything covered. Copies enclosed.

Wendy

9.26 Letter to O'Neill Middleton dated 15.03.06

Dear Sirs

As this transaction is due for settlement on 30 March we shall be pleased to receive the draft disposition for engrossment together with your draft form 11 for approval. We enclose draft forms 1 and 4 for your approval and return.

Yours Faithfully

Notes: The form 11 is a request to the Keeper to bring the search almost up to the date of settlement. It is roughly equivalent to the old interim report on search which was obtained in General Register of Sasines days, but it is much more up-to-date. This is an immense improvement, because it cuts down the 'blank' period between interim report and settlement, which had to be covered in the letter of obligation against the possibility of of any dirty tricks—perhaps the granting of an inhibition against the seller, or perhaps even a second, fraudulent, sale.

The form 1 requests the Keeper to effect registration and give his indemnity. It also asks certain questions about the property which must be answered to allow indemnity to be given.

The form 4 is an inventory of writs sent to back up the request for registration.

9.27 Letter from O'Neill Middleton dated 16.03.06

Dear Sirs

As requested, we return your draft Disposition and enclose our form 11 for approval and return. We also enclose our State for Settlement, for your approval and draft form 1 and 4 duly approved.

Yours faithfully

9.28 Draft form 11

 **eFORMS FORM 11**

(Form 11)

(Land Registration (Scotland) Rules 1980 Rule 24(2))

APPLICATION FOR CONTINUATION OF REPORT PRIOR TO THE REGISTRATION OF THE SUBJECTS DESCRIBED BELOW

Note: No covering letter is required and an existing Search should not be submitted.

VAT Reg No. GD 410 GB 888 84 10 64

Please complete in BLACK TYPE

From		FOR OFFICIAL USE	
Name	O'Neill Middleton	Report Number	
Address	LP53	Date or Receipt	
	Glasgow	Fee	

County	RENFREW	Previous Report No,	9615726REN
Search Sheet No¹	6140	FAS No,	1024
Applicant's Reference	BTB/RXR/FAC/@DUF43.2	FAX No.	0141 221 4567
Telephone No	0141 221 3456	FAX Response Required	✓

POSTAL ADDRESS OF SUBJECTS

Street No.	3	House Name		Street Name	Miller Drive
Town	Newton Mearns			Postcode	G77 10EU

OTHER:

Description of Subjects

I/we apply for the Report to | 24/02/2006 | (dd/mm/yy)[2] against the above subjects to be brought down to date

1. Number obtainable from previous Report
2. Date obtainable from previous Report

The following parties (in addition to those noted on the report) should be searched against in the Register of Inhibitions and Adjudication, viz

1. Surname(s) [   ]   Forename(s) [   ]

Address(es) [   ]

1. Surname(s) [   ]   Forename(s) [   ]

Address(es) [   ]

2. Surname(s) [   ]   Forename(s) [   ]

Address(es) [   ]

3. Surname(s) [   ]   Forename(s) [   ]

Address(es) [   ]

4. Surname(s) [   ]   Forename(s) [   ]

Address(es) [   ]

5. Surname(s) [   ]   Forename(s) [   ]

Address(es) [   ]

6. Surname(s) [   ]   Forename(s) [   ]

Address(es) [   ]

Note: Insert full names and address of the persons on whom a Report is required

Date: 20/09/07

Additional Info

[   ]

Please state the Date and Time you require report   Date | **30 Mar 06** | Time | **12:30**

Registers of Scotland

9.29 Draft state of settlement

STATE FOR SETTLEMENT

Property: 3 Miller Drive, Newton Mearns, East Renfrewshire

Sellers' Agents: O'Neill Middleton, Glasgow

Purchasers' Agents; Brown Jarvie & Walker, Glasgow

Date of Settlement: 30 March 2006

Price agreed by Missives	£249,000
Price agreed for moveable property	£1,000
Total Price due	£250,000

Note: East Renfrewshire Council have been requested to apportion the Council Tax and will issue separate accounts.

The council tax year ends on 30 March 2006 so there will be no apportionment at all—the sellers will pay all council tax for 2005/06; the purchasers will pay all council tax for 2006/07.

9.30 Letter to Mr and Mrs James dated 17.03.06

Dear Mr and Mrs James

This is to remind you that the settlement of your purchase is due on 30 March. It is therefore important that we have cleared funds in our account by that date. Please therefore send a cheque for the sum requested, or, better still, ask your Bank to send an electronic transfer of the funds to our Bank (details underneath), which entails them having cleared funds in their hands. Please therefore arrange this at the earliest opportunity.

The sum requested by us is as agreed in earlier letters.

We enclose drafts of Wills by you and Mrs James which are basically in favour of each other. There is however, in both cases, a transfer of your share in the house to your children. This will, as the law presently stands, transfer the half share and take advantage of the nil tax exemption—your half share of the house is valued at around £125,000 which is well below the current tax threshold of £285,000. Transfers between husbands and wives are tax exempt. This should therefore greatly reduce the ultimate tax liability of the survivor of you both.

Yours faithfully

Bank Details: City of Glasgow Bank, Glasgow Head Office. Clearing Number: 01.1506. Account Number: 00248833

Number: 00248833.

Sum requested;

Price of house	£249,000.00
Price of Moveable items	£1,000.00
Stamp Duty Land Tax @ 1%	£2,490.00
Our fee as agreed	£450.00
VAT thereon @ 17.5%	£78.75
Land Registration Fee	£500.00
	£253,518.75

Note: Remember the importance of having cleared funds in the bank. Cheques to you should be banked at least seven days before settlement, to ensure that they are met before you start signing cheques. Alternatively you may get an electronic transfer into your account, which guarantees that the funds are cleared. Please remember that an electronic transfer is not made instantly, and allow, say, a day for it to happen. Why electronic transfers cannot be made more quickly remains a mystery to all but the banks.

9.31 Draft will of Stuart James

I STUART JAMES residing at Three Miller Drive, Newton Mearns, East Renfrewshire in order to settle the my means and estate after my death DO HEREBY PROVIDE as follows:

One. I appoint my wife Mrs Henrietta James also of Three Miller Drive, Newton Mearns and Henry Pink, Solicitor of Messrs Brown, Jarvie & Walker, Glasgow and the survivor of them with such person or persons to be assumed by them or either of them as Executors, to be my Executors.

Two. I leave my whole interest in the house at Three Miller Drive or such other house as I may own to my children JOHN JAMES of Four The Beeches, Skelmorlie, Ayrshire and KATRINA JAMES of One Hundred Acacia Avenue, Bonkle, Lanarkshire equally between them.

Three. Subject to the foregoing provision, I leave the residue to my wife the said MRS. HENRIETTA JAMES, whom failing, should she not survive the time of my death, to my said children equally. And I declare that if they or either of them fail to survive the time of my death their share the share bequeathed to them shall pass to their issue. And I further declare that if either line should fail to inhereit the share shall accresce to the other line.

Four. I confer upon my Executors the fullest powers and immunities whether or not authorised by law or not including:

a. Power to pay or transfer any share of my estate or the income from any share to any pupil or minor beneficiary or, in their sole discretion, to his or her legal guardian or to any other person or persons acting or willing to act a such, whether legally entitled to that office or not, the receipt by such guardian or other person being a sufficient discharge to my Executors, or, in their sole discretion, to hold any share of residue and income therefrom on behalf of the beneficiary concerned until he or she shall attain the age of twenty one.

b. Power to hold any investments owned by me, and to purchase any other property of any kind wherever situated, and whether of Trustee status or not.

c. Power to take any action deemed by them to be in the interests of the beneficiaries, including power to make loans to tutors and curators of minor and pupil children to provide suitable accommodation for the enlarged family.

d. Power to purchase or sell and transfer heritable property by public roup or private bargain.

e. Power to carry on any business in which I may be engaged and that for such periods as my Executors may think fit.

f. Power to appoint any one of their own number as brokers, law agents, or accountants for the Executry, with the usual remuneration, and power to resign office at any time.

And I revoke all previous testamentary writings previously made by me and I declare that I am domiciled in Scotland:

IN WITNESS WHEREOF these presents are signed by me on the date and before the witness detailed below

Date: ....

Signature:.. .

Witness's signature: ....

Witness's Name: ....

Witness's Address: ....

Note: This is a clever move. The James have been given good tax advice, and now the firm is drawing up wills to effect this advice without extra charge. It is a small gesture which should pay off in years to come in client loyalty. Clients are mainly quite loyal to their professional advisers, but such loyalty must be earned and maintained by gestures like this.

1 The will of Mrs James is a 'mirror image' of the one above. His name is changed to hers, and her name is changed to his.

2 If the will extends to more than one page, please do not forget that EVERY page must be signed.

3 Domicile is largely a matter of circumstances, but the statement by Mr James may help in deciding which law shall apply. In fact there is little difference in Scottish and English practice on this point, and certainly there is no tax advantage in one or the other, inheritance tax being a UK tax.

9.32 Letter from Brown Jarvie & Walker to O'Neill Middleton dated 20.03.06

Dear Sirs

We enclose the draft Disposition together with the engrossment for signature. We also enclose the draft form 11 and State for Settlement, both duly approved.

Yours faithfully

9.33 Letter from Mr and Mrs James dated 20.03.06

Dear Sirs

Thank you for your letter telling us how much we owe you. We enclose cheque for £253,515.75 which we trust is in order. We approve the draft Wills and shall be pleased to have copies for signature. We would like to thank Messrs Brown Jarvie & Walker for their kind work on our behalf.

Yours faithfully

To: Veronica Vanbrugh <vvanbrugh@bjw.co.uk.; Wendy Robertson<wrobertson@bjw.co.uk>

Sent: 21 March 2006 13:04

From: Henry Pink <hpink@bjw.co.uk>

Subject: 3 Miller Drive, NM

Please see accompanying letter from Mr and Mrs James. Well done! I have incidentally passed the cheque to the cashroom and asked them to bank it today! They will let you know when it has cleared. HP.

To: Wendy Robertson<wrobertson@bjw.co.uk>

Sent: 27 March 2006 10:53

From: Nisha Banerji <nbanergi@bjw.co.uk>

Subject: Mr & Mrs James JAME323

Please note that cheque from Mr and Mrs James cleared today. You may now write cheques on the client account.

Note: The money is now safely in the client account, and accordingly cheques may be written for the price, the SDLT, the registration fees, and the firm's fee against a properly vouched fee note. Expenses incurred by the firm on their own behalf, salaries, rent, stationery etc. must be paid from the firm account which should be kept quite separate from clients' account. There should be no mixing of the two, for that way disaster lies.

To: Wendy Robertson<wrobertson@bjw.co.uk>

Sent: 29 March 2006 08:38

From: Veronica Vanbrugh <vvanbrugh@bjw.co.uk

Subject: 3 Miller Drive, Newton Mearns

You will need the cheque signed by a partner of the firm, in good time for settlement.

Please note that Mr Pink will be out of the office this afternoon, and thus not available for signing cheques.

Please get from O'Neill Middleton:

Keys
Signed Disposition
Details of signature
Title Deeds
Signed Letter of Obligation and draft for comparison
State for Settlement, receipted, and draft for comparison

Any other papers to be delivered, eg Property Enquiry Certificate, Coal Authority letter.

Please arrange house insurance.

Veronica

9.34 Note of telephone call by Wendy Robertson to Casualty Insurance dated 29.03.06

Phoning Casualty Insurance and asking them to hold the property at 3 Miller Drive, Newton Mearns insured with immediate effect. Sum insured £300,000. Account to be sent to clients at their address.

Note: This does not mean that the property has increased in value by £50,000 overnight. This is simply the replacement, as opposed to the market, value. This is generally greater than the market value because the house would have to be rebuilt using traditional building materials.

9.35 Note of telephone call by Wendy Robertson to Mr and Mrs James 30.03.06

Telling them transaction is now settled, and if they could collect the keys from us when convenient.

9.36 SDLT form

| Land Transaction Return |

For official use only

Your transaction return

How to fill in this return

The guidance notes that come with this return will help you answer the questions.

- Write inside the boxes. Use black ink and CAPITAL letters.
- If you make a mistake, please cross it out and write the correct information underneath.
- **Leave blank any boxes that don't apply to you** – please don't strike through anything irrelevant.
- Show amounts in whole pounds only, rounded down to the nearest pound. Ignore the pence.

- Fill out the payslip on page 7.
- Do not fold the return. Send it back to us unfolded in the envelope provided.
- **Photocopies are not acceptable.**

If you need help with any part of this return or with anything in the guidance notes, please phone the Stamp Taxes enquiry line on **0845 603 0135**, open 8:30am to 5:00pm Monday to Friday, except Bank Holidays. You can get further copies of this return and any supplementary returns from the Orderline on **0845 302 1472**.

Starting your return

Sample

ABOUT THE TRANSACTION

1 Type of property

Enter code from the guidance notes

2 Description of transaction

Enter code from the guidance notes

3 Interest transferred or created

Enter code from the guidance notes

4 Effective date of transaction

D D M M Y Y Y Y

5 Any restrictions, covenants or conditions affecting the value of the interest transferred or granted? Put 'X' in one box

Yes ☐   No ☐

If 'yes' please provide details

6 Date of contract or conclusion of missives

D D M M Y Y Y Y

7 Is any land exchanged or part-exchanged? Put 'X' in one box

Yes ☐   No ☐

If 'yes' please complete address of location

Postcode

House or building number

Rest of address, including house name, building name or flat number

8 Is the transaction pursuant to a previous option agreement? Put 'X' in one box

Yes ☐   No ☐

ABOUT THE TAX CALCULATION

9 Are you claiming relief? Put 'X' in one box

☐ Yes   ☐ No

If 'yes' please show the reason

☐ Enter code from the guidance notes

Enter the charity's registered number, if available, or the company's CIS number

☐☐☐☐☐☐☐☐☐☐☐☐☐

For relief claimed on part of the property only, please enter the amount remaining chargeable

£ ☐☐☐☐☐☐☐☐ . ☐☐

10 What is the total consideration in money or money's worth, including any VAT actually payable for the transaction notified?

£ ☐☐☐☐☐☐☐☐ . ☐☐

11 If the total consideration for the transaction includes VAT, please state the amount

£ ☐☐☐☐☐☐☐☐ . ☐☐

12 What form does the consideration take?
Enter the relevant codes from the guidance notes

☐☐ ☐☐ ☐☐ ☐☐

13 Is this transaction linked to any other(s)?
Put 'X' in one box

☐ Yes   ☐ No

Total consideration or value in money or money's worth, including VAT paid for all of the linked transactions

£ ☐☐☐☐☐☐☐☐ . ☐☐

14 Total amount of tax due for this transaction

£ ☐☐☐☐☐☐☐☐ . ☐☐

15 Total amount paid or enclosed with this notification

£ ☐☐☐☐☐☐☐☐ . ☐☐

Does the amount paid include payment of any penalties and any interest due? Put 'X' in one box

☐ Yes   ☐ No

ABOUT LEASES

If this doesn't apply, go straight to box 26 on page 3

16 Type of lease

☐ Enter code from the guidance notes

17 Start date as specified in lease

☐☐ ☐☐ ☐☐☐☐

18 End date as specified in lease

☐☐ ☐☐ ☐☐☐☐

19 Rent-free period
Number of months

☐☐

20 Annual starting rent inclusive of VAT (actually) payable

£ ☐☐☐☐☐☐ . ☐☐

End date for starting rent

☐☐ ☐☐ ☐☐☐☐

Later rent known? Put 'X' in one box

☐ Yes   ☐ No

21 What is the amount of VAT, if any?

£ ☐☐☐☐☐☐☐☐ . ☐☐

22 Total premium payable

£ ☐☐☐☐☐☐☐☐ . ☐☐

23 Net present value upon which tax is calculated

£ ☐☐☐☐☐☐☐☐ . ☐☐

24 Total amount of tax due – premium

£ ☐☐☐☐☐☐☐☐ . ☐☐

25 Total amount of tax due – NPV

£ ☐☐☐☐☐☐☐☐ . ☐☐

Check the guidance notes to see if you will need to complete supplementary return 'Additional details about the transaction, including leases', SDLT4.

Sample

ABOUT THE LAND including buildings

Where more than one piece of land is being sold or you cannot complete the address field in the space provided, please complete the supplementary return 'Additional details about the land', SDLT3.

26 Number of properties included

27 Where more than one property is involved, do you want a certificate for each property? Put 'X' in one box

Yes ☐   No ☐

28 Address or situation of land
Postcode

House or building number

Rest of address, including house name, building name or flat number

Is the rest of the address on the supplementary return 'Additional details about the land', SDLT3? Put 'X' in one box

Yes ☐   No ☐

29 Local authority number

30 Title number, if any

31 NLPG UPRN

32 If agricultural or development land, what is the area (if known)? Put 'X' in one box

Hectares ☐   Square metres ☐
Area

33 Is a plan attached? Please note that the form reference number should be written/displayed on map. Put 'X' in one box

Yes ☐   No ☐

Sample

ABOUT THE VENDOR including transferor, lessor

34 Number of vendors included (Note: if more than one vendor, complete boxes 45 to 48)

35 Title Enter MR, MRS, MISS, MS or other title
Note: only complete for an individual

36 Vendor (1) surname or company name

37 Vendor (1) first name(s) Note: only complete for an individual

38 Vendor (1) address
Postcode

House or building number

Rest of address, including house name, building name or flat number

ABOUT THE VENDOR CONTINUED

39 Agent's name

40 Agent's address
Postcode

Building number

Rest of address, including building name

41 Agent's DX number and exchange

42 Agent's e-mail address

43 Agent's reference

44 Agent's telephone number

ADDITIONAL VENDOR

Details of other people involved (including transferor, lessor), other than vendor (1). If more than one additional vendor please complete supplementary return 'Land Transaction Return – Additional vendor/purchaser details', SDLT2.

45 Title Enter MR, MRS, MISS, MS or other title
Note: only complete for an individual

46 Vendor (2) surname or company name

47 Vendor (2) first name(s)
Note: only complete for an individual

48 Vendor (2) address

Put 'X' in this box if the same as box 38.
If not, please give address below
Postcode

House or building number

Rest of address, including house name, building name or flat number

ABOUT THE PURCHASER including transferee, lessee

49 Number of purchasers included (Note: if more than one purchaser is involved, complete boxes 65 to 69)

50 National Insurance number (purchaser 1), if you have one. Note: only complete for an individual

51 Title Enter MR, MRS, MISS, MS or other title Note: only complete for an individual

52 Purchaser (1) surname or company name

53 Purchaser (1) first name(s)
Note: only complete for an individual

54 Purchaser (1) address

Put 'X' in this box if the same address as box 28.
If not, please give address below
Postcode

House or building number

Rest of address, including house name, building name or flat number

55 Is the purchaser acting as a trustee? Put 'X' in one box

Yes No

56 Please give a daytime telephone number - this will help us if we need to contact you about your return

57 Are the purchaser and vendor connected?
Put 'X' in one box

Yes No

58 To which address shall we send the certificate?
Put 'X' in one box

Property (box 28) Purchaser's (box 54)

Agent's (box 61)

59 I authorise my agent to handle correspondence on my behalf. Put 'X' in one box

Yes No

60 Agent's name

61 Agent's address
Postcode

Building number

Rest of address, including building name

62 Agent's DX number and exchange

63 Agent's reference

64 Agent's telephone number

ADDITIONAL PURCHASER

Details of other people involved (including transferee, lessee), other than purchaser (1). If more than one additional purchaser, please complete supplementary return 'Land Transaction Return – Additional vendor/purchaser details', SDLT2.

65 Title Enter MR, MRS, MISS, MS or other title
Note: only complete for an individual

66 Purchaser (2) surname or company name

67 Purchaser (2) first name(s)
Note: only complete for an individual

Sample

68 Purchaser (2) address

Put 'X' in this box if the same as purchaser (1) (box 54).

If not, please give address below
Postcode

House or building number

Rest of address, including house name, building name or flat number

69 Is purchaser (2) acting as a trustee? Put 'X' in one box

Yes   No

ADDITIONAL SUPPLEMENTARY RETURNS

70 How many supplementary returns have you enclosed with this return? Write the number in each box. If none, please put '0'.

Additional vendor/purchaser details, SDLT2

Additional details about the transaction, including leases, SDLT4

Additional details about the land, SDLT3

DECLARATION

71 The purchaser(s) **must** sign this return. Read the guidance notes in booklet SDLT6, in particular the section headed *'Who should complete and sign the Land Transaction Return?'*.

If you give false information, you may face financial penalties and prosecution.
The information I have given on this return is correct and complete to the best of my knowledge and belief.

Signature of purchaser 1   Signature of purchaser 2

Please keep a copy of this return and a note of the unique transaction reference number, which is in the 'Reference' box on the payslip.

Finally, please send your completed return to:
HM Revenue & Customs, Stamp Taxes/SDLT, Comben House, Farriers Way, NETHERTON, Merseyside, Great Britain, L30 4RN, or the DX address is: Rapid Data Capture Centre, DX725593, Bootle 9

Please don't fold it – keep it flat and use the envelope provided. Fill out the payslip on the next page and pay in accordance with the 'How to pay' instructions.

How to pay

 Please allow enough time for payment to reach us by the due date. We suggest you allow at least 3 working days for this.

MOST SECURE AND EFFICIENT

We recommend the following payment methods. These are the most secure and efficient.

1. Direct Payment
Use the Internet or telephone to make payment. Provide your bank or building society with the following information
- payment account
- sort code 10-50-41
- account number 23456000
- your reference as shown on the payslip.

2. BillPay
You can pay by Debit Card over the Internet. Visit **www.billpayment.co.uk/hmrc** and follow the guidance.

3. At your bank
Take this form with payment to **your bank** and where possible to **your own branch**. Other banks may refuse to accept payment. If paying by cheque, make your cheque payable to 'HM REVENUE & CUSTOMS ONLY'.

4. At a Post Office
Take this form with your payment to any Post Office. If paying by cheque, make your cheque payable to 'POST OFFICE LTD'. The Post Office also accept payment by Debit Card.

5. Alliance & Leicester Commercial Bank Account
Alliance & Leicester Commercial Bank customers can instruct their bank to arrange payment.

OTHER PAYMENT METHODS

By post
If you use this method
- Make your cheque payable to 'HM REVENUE & CUSTOMS ONLY'.
- Write your payslip reference after 'HM REVENUE & CUSTOMS ONLY'.
- Send the payslip and your cheque, **both unfolded**, in the envelope provided to
  HM Revenue & Customs SDLT
  Netherton
  Merseyside
  L30 4RN

By DX
As above, but send to
Rapid Data Capture Centre
DX725593
Bootle 9

FURTHER PAYMENT INFORMATION

You can find further payment information at **www.hmrc.gov.uk/howtopay**

9.37 In summary the purchasers have got a good deal here. They have bought a good house, at a good price; they have a registered title; they have been given good inheritance tax advice; they have got wills that put this into practice.

What of the solicitors? Their fee will not make their fortune—there are solicitors in London who charge this amount for an hour's work! The secret is that the lawyers will do well if they do enough transactions of this nature, and if they keep a handle on their costs.

They have probably secured the loyalty of the James, who will tell their friends and, if the solicitors remember the three horsemen of competitive business—costs, quality and service—they should have few fears of a competitive situation.

Chapter 10

BORROWING ON HERITABLE PROPERTY

'Unsurprisingly, 65% of first time buyers felt daunted by buying a mortgage, and more than three quarters did not know who they could trust and expressed a desire for more impartial information about mortgages.'

(Scotland on Sunday, 30 October 2005)

'Although I worked for a financial company, I knew nothing about mortgages, and everyone was throwing all these terms at me and I didn't have a clue what they meant. I was only in my early 20s and suddenly my ears were ringing with 'fixed rates', 'tracker mortgages', 'early redemption periods'. It is all extremely daunting, but it would have been worse without my mum to guide me throughout.'

(Paula Ritchie quoted in Scotland on Sunday, 30 October 2005)

'A rise of 66% in repossession orders against home buyers across the country was disclosed yesterday. Londoners were hit even harder, with an 81% increase. The Citizens Advice Bureau said that some providers of consolidation loans were increasingly aggressive and willing to go to court. Grant Thornton, the accountants, said 'Consumer debt is at a historical high of about £1.1 trillion and amounts to more than the whole external debt of Africa and South America combined. Contributing to this debt mountain is the fact that consumers have a heady total of more than 66 million credit cards at their fingertips—five times the European average'

(Daily Telegraph, 15 October 2005)

10.01 Although we have been dealing with a conveyancing transaction without the complications of a loan, the time now has come to talk of loans, which are generally known as 'mortgages', a word borrowed from French through English law. The Financial Services Agency maintain a very useful website on the subject of mortgages at: www.mortgageslaidbare.info

First of all let us explain some jargon words:

(a) Mortgage. A loan secured by a standard security granted by the borrower to the lender. The loan, plus interest, is repayable over a certain agreed mortgage term.

(b) APR. This stands for annual percentage rate, which should help the borrower to compare the cost of different mortgage offers. It does not stand, as one borrower thought, for the monthly payment being due in April. It states the true rate of interest payable on the loan taking into account when interest payments are deducted, eg yearly, monthly or daily, upfront fees and other costs, all bonuses, incentives and payment holidays, the length of the term of the mortgage and certain other charges by the lender, such as any arrangement fee for setting up the mortgage. This figure is very important when comparing two loan offers, say one at a fixed rate of 4.9% with a £500 arrangement fee, and one at 5.2% with an arrangement fee of £100. The apparently cheaper deal may in fact be more expensive.

(c) AER. Annual equivalent rate, applies to interest paid on savings. This will reflect rates boosted by introductory bonuses, which disappear after six months.

(d) EAR. This should not be confused with AER, although it often is. This indicates the true cost of overdrafts and other personal loans. It takes into account when interest is actually deducted from the outstanding loan, plus any additional costs, but not payment protection premiums, from which lenders make much money, and often aren't worth having, being only expensive accident cover.

(e) Bank of England Base Rate. The rate can go up or down from time to time and is announced by the Bank's Monetary Policy Committee, which make its decision in light of the state of the economy. The lenders normally charge several points over the base rate, which is known as the standard variable base rate. In 1990 the rate varied between 10.5% and 14% making borrowing a very dear option, but it has now settled down—at time of writing in November 2005—to a more reasonable 4.5%.

(f) Capped rate. Interest under this arrangement doesn't go above a certain level –'the cap' during the capped rate period. The borrower can thus enjoy rate reductions in the knowledge that the rate will not go above the cap.

(g) Cap and collar loans. These are loans with a fixed maximum and minimum interest rates. The borrower can be sure that the interest rate charged will not exceed the maximum, but will by the same token not fall below the minimum rate.

(h) Consolidation loans. Much advertised on daytime TV, this is a method of borrowing from a finance company enough to repay all credit card etc loans, and only have one lender, to whom a monthly payment is made. It sounds very attractive on TV, but the loan is secured on the borrower's house and the borrower grants a standard security to the lender. The house may be repossessed if the payments are not strictly adhered to, and finance companies are less lenient with non-payers than traditional lenders.

(i) Daily interest. The interest charged on the amount of mortgage outstanding, worked out on a day-to-day basis.

(j) Discounted rate. A discount on the loan standard variable base rate interest, available during the discounted rate period available for a set period.

(k) Early repayment charge. This charge is designed to deter borrowers from chopping and changing their loans to the cheapest currently available. If the borrower pays off the mortgage, in whole or in part, or transfers to a different mortgage rate before the end of the special rate period, the charge is then made.

(l) Exit fee. Even though the loan is repaid in due course, the lender may, however, charge a fee for closing the arrangement. This may be from £200 to £500.

(m) Equity. This is the difference between the amount owed by the borrower and the current value of the property. In other words it is the profit that a borrower has made, but not yet realised, on the investment. Alternatively, the borrower may have over -borrowed, or house prices may have fallen, in which case there is negative equity.

(n) Fixed rate. A rate of interest guaranteed not to change over a certain fixed period. This is fine when rates are going up, but not so good when they are going down. There is currently (2006) a trend fixed rate loans for a long period reflecting current monetary stability, which did not previously exist.

(o) Higher lending charge. A fee or premium sometimes charged by lenders, to reflect the greater risk, if a mortgage represents a high percentage of the property's value.

(p) Interest-only mortgage. While the borrower generally pays a sum to reflect repayment of capital and interest, the borrower doesn't repay any capital under this arrangement, only interest. The lender must be satisfied that, at the end of the mortgage period, the borrower will have sufficient funds (eg a pension plan, trust funds or share options) to repay at that time.

(q) Key facts illustration. A key facts illustration ('KFI') sets out details of the mortgage product that the borrower is interested in. All lenders are required to set out the details in a KFI on the same format, in order that different KFIs may be compared.

(r) LTV. This means loan to value and is the proportion of the value or price of the property (whichever is the lower) that the borrower borrows on the mortgage. For example, a £126,000 mortgage on a house valued at £140,000 would mean a LTV of 90%.

(s) Payment holiday. The borrower can arrange to stop making payments for a limited period agreed with the lender. Interest is generally charged during this period.

(t) Remortgage. Where the borrower switches the mortgage from one lender to another, without moving home.

(u) Buy to rent mortgage. A loan made to property investors who do not intend to occupy the property themselves, but to rent it to others. This mortgage is regarded as a slightly riskier arrangement.

(v) Repayment mortgage. This is where the monthly payment includes partial repayment of capital as well as interest.

(w) Self certifying mortgage. To save time and expense, the borrower does not have to provide proof of income but simply issues a certificate stating what the income is. This is a convenient method for both parties, but carries an obvious risk of fraud, and for that reason is usually slightly more expensive.

(x) Tracker mortgage. A loan on which the interest is fixed against the base rate, and rises or falls accordingly.

10.02 We have assumed to date that the sellers are not repaying a loan, and that the purchasers are not taking a loan on the new house. In fact, most transactions are aided by loans, but the main bulk of the work has already been done, and a discharge of an old security and a new security by the purchaser does not present any great difficulty, provided that you have followed the scheme of things so far.

Most loans are made by banks or building societies, or former building societies that have become banks, but have not yet achieved full banking status. Other bodies may be lenders, such as local authorities, particularly in the purchase of public sector housing. Broadly speaking, however, the procedure is the same whoever the lender may be. We shall refer to mortgage lenders as 'lenders' and the persons taking the loan as 'borrowers'. Lenders are now represented by a central body known as the Council of Mortgage Lenders ('CML'), the mortgage lenders' representative body, which produces a Handbook detailing the practices of various lenders, and issuing standard forms. The handbook can be downloaded from the CML website (www.cml.org.uk) and it should be studied carefully as CML represents most of the mortgage lenders.

Obtaining a mortgage no longer means that the borrower has to go on bended knee to the lender, and save with the lender or await a quota of mortgage funds, and it is now a normal commercial arrangement, with a variety of lenders competing strenuously with each other to lend funds. Borrowers may bid for funds on the internet (www.mortgagebundles.com).

Generally lenders will permit conveyancers acting for the borrower in the purchase of a house, to act on the lenders' behalf, provided the conveyancers are on their approved list. This practice, which is specifically exempted from the Solicitors (Scotland) Practice Rules 1986 preventing solicitors acting for two or more parties, with conflicting interests, means a substantial saving on duplication of work, and thus a saving of costs payable by the borrowers.

If the lenders insist on using conveyancers chosen by them, then two sets of conveyancers become involved in doing the same work and satisfying themselves as to title. The fee of the lenders' conveyancers is payable by the borrowers, as well as that of their own conveyancers, all in terms of the Standard Security, (CFR(S)A 1973, Sch 3, standard condition 12).

10.03 When the same conveyancers acts for both lenders and borrowers, that is perfectly in order despite the apparent conflict of interest (Solicitors (Scotland) Practice Rules 1986). If however, a genuine conflict of interest does emerge, the conveyancers must immediately stop acting for both parties, and choose which, if either, they are going to represent. The conveyancers must not reveal information to one client and not the other, eg information as to prices paid for the property. This was clearly established in *Mortgage Express v Bowerman & Partners* ([1996] 2 All ER 808). If conveyancers find themselves in possession of information that is clearly detrimental to one of the parties, they are under a duty to reveal it to the other party, for whom they also act. If they feel unable to do so, they should then withdraw from the agency of one party, or probably both parties.

10.04 Similarly, when conveyancers are asked to act for a married couple in a conveyancing transaction, they may do so as acting for related parties is exempted from the general rule of conflict of interest, laid down by the Solicitors (Scotland) Practice Rules 1986. There is a temptation to treat a married couple as one unit, but this temptation must be resisted, as a husband and wife have separate interests, especially if the marriage is in danger. The conveyancers must ensure that both partners signing the standard security understand the security, and the conveyancers must recommend that, where a wife is asked to sign a standard security over the marital home, in support of the husband's business, it is mandatory that both parties obtain separate advice to the extent of the obligation, from another solicitor, or at least another partner of the firm concerned.

This arrangement, known rather inelegantly as 'sexually transmitted debt' was the subject of a number of cases, such as, most notably in Scotland, *Smith v Bank of Scotland* (1997 SC (HL) 111), *Broadway v Clydesdale Bank plc* (2001 GWD 14–552) or *Forsyth v Royal Bank of Scotland plc* 2001 SLT 1295. The matter is, however, best summarised by an English case *Royal Bank of Scotland plc v Etridge (No 2)* [2001] 4 All ER 449. This case laid down very strict conditions on conveyancers acting for a married couple, which may be summarised thus:

- The conveyancer who is to advise the wife must explain why this meeting is being held, and the consequences of her signing the security. The husband should not be present at this meeting, and the conveyancer should explain matters to the wife in non-technical language.

- The conveyancer should be satisfied that the wife wishes the conveyancer to advise her.

- The conveyancer should be satisfied that there is no possible conflict of interest.

- The conveyancer should explain the documents and what legal effects they might have.

- The conveyancer should also explain the risks involved.

- The conveyancer should obtain from the lender detailed information as to the husband's accounts with the lender, and the application for the loan.

- The conveyancer should state what debts are being guaranteed, eg business debts, and the amount.

- The conveyancer should explain that the amount of the debt, and that the terms may change, without reference to the wife.

- The conveyancer should discuss with the wife her own financial means and her husband's means.

- The conveyancer should explain to the wife that she has a choice in the matter and establish that she wishes to proceed.

- The conveyancer should check that the wife wishes the firm to write to the lender confirming that she has been given legal advice.

The object of these rules is to ensure that the wife has given informed consent, and has not merely been hustled into giving consent, with some shallow explanation, as in the cases mentioned.

Of course, a wife may persuade a husband to sign a standard security which guarantees her business, in which case the same principles apply, changing that which has to be changed.

10.05 Assuming that the same conveyancers act for the purchasers and the lenders, the following steps should be taken by the conveyancers.

- The conveyancers receive and carefully peruse the lenders' instructions. After examining title, they draft a standard security and any other papers required by the lenders.
- They have the standard security and other papers signed by the borrowers. In the event of the title standing in the name of one spouse only, a form of consent by the non-entitled spouse has to be signed (see Matrimonial Homes (Family Protection) (Scotland) Act 1981 and App **I** hereof.) Naturally the advice given in para **10.04** applies when dealing with the non-entitled spouse.
- The conveyancers then send the report on title to the lenders, with the firm's opinion that the title is in order, and request the loan cheque. This should be done in good time for settlement, allowing several days for it to be drawn and posted.
- When the disposition has been stamped and being sent to the Land Register, the standard security is also sent, with a completed and signed form 2 and form 4 in duplicate. Any assignation of, say, an assurance policy is intimated to the assurance company in duplicate to validate the transfer, and on return one receipted copy is put with the title deeds and the assurance policy.
- The lenders will in all probability insure the property against fire and other damage as 'heritable creditors' and in the name of the borrowers as proprietors in reversion. If the property is destroyed the lenders will be entitled to the proceeds of the insurance claim, as long as there is part of the loan outstanding. This is only fair, as otherwise the borrowers might collect the money and disappear, leaving the lenders with the ruined property and no insurance money. The property is insured from

the time the lenders receive the report on title. This insurance provision is all in line with CFR(S)A 1970 Sch 3 and standard condition 5. The conveyancers need not worry about the insurance of the property, which the lenders will arrange for reinstatement value (which may not bear any relation to the market price, particularly in the case of a traditionally built building of stone and marble which might cost much more than its market value to reinstate) and for index linked compensation. The borrowers are entitled to obtain alternative quotations from other sources, and may make a considerable saving in this respect but the lenders must be satisfied with the arrangement.

- When the titles are all in the hands of the conveyancers, they should be then sent to the lenders, and a receipt obtained. Titles should not be sent piecemeal.

Golden rule: The lenders' instructions must be carefully read and rigorously followed.

10.06 When property is sold and there is an existing security created by the sellers, the sellers' conveyancers will in all probability (see para **10.02**) be asked to act for the lenders in its discharge. In that case, the conveyancers should do the following:

(a) The sellers' conveyancers inform the sellers' lenders that a sale has been agreed, and of the date of entry, ask for the sum required to repay the loan, and obtain the title deeds on loan.

(b) The sellers' conveyancers then draft a form of discharge and send the draft to the purchasers' conveyancers for revisal.

(c) On return of the draft discharge, they have the principal discharge typed and signed by the lenders, who will send the signed document to be held as 'undelivered' pending repayment of the loan.

(d) At settlement of the sale, the sellers' conveyancers hand over the discharge together with a signed form 2 and forms 4 in duplicate. These are sent to the Land Register by the purchasers' conveyancers, and once the Keeper is satisfied with the discharge, the old standard security will simply be removed from the title sheet, and the new disposition and standard security will be registered.

(e) In due course the Keeper will issue a corrected land certificate and charge certificate to the purchasers' conveyancers. These will duly be passed on to the lenders, who will have custody of them until their loan is repaid.

10.07 If the lenders use their own conveyancers, a rather cumbersome 'three-cornered' settlement has to be arranged. This involves, in addition to the settlement of the purchase transaction, the lenders' conveyancer handing over the loan cheque in return for the disposition, standard security, forms 2 and 4, the land and charge certificates, with a letter of obligation by the purchasers' firm of solicitors undertaking to deliver the certificates within a certain time. Alternatively this can be done by post, with the cheque being held as undelivered, and therefore not negotiable, until the various papers are sent by the borrowers' conveyancers.

10.08 The interest rate on money borrowed for house purchase generally fluctuates with the base rate (see para **10.01**) The base rate is fixed monthly by the Monetary Policy Committee of the Bank of England, largely for economic reasons which have little to do with supply and demand, and everything to do with inflation rates and the state of world markets, and are thus quite unpredictable.

The only borrowers who are not affected by base rate changes are those with fixed interest loans (see para **10.01**) or with 'cap and collar' loans (see para **10.01**) which are loans with a fixed maximum and minimum interest rate.

10.09 There is now no tax relief on loan interest payable. On the other hand, the sale of a main private residence (as agreed with the HM Revenue and Customs) does not attract capital gains tax ('CGT'), which has proved to be a huge benefit to homeowners in times of sharply rising prices. CGT is, however, payable on a gain in value of second homes or investment properties. A homeowner is required to nominate a main private residence, but may change the property so nominated (eg on retirement when the homeowner elects to live in what was once a holiday house). Otherwise, generally speaking, a homeowner is not entitled to change the nomination, and certainly not to chop and change it according to the circumstances.

Even when CGT is payable, it is reasonably light in comparison to income tax. The tax is payable on a 'chargeable gain' made on disposal of an asset, which is defined to include land and buildings. To compute the gain on which CGT is payable, a deduction is made from the price received of: (1) the original price paid on purchase; (2) the incidental expenses of that acquisition and of the subsequent sale; (3) any 'enhancement expenditure', that is the cost of capital improvements, eg building costs rather than the expense of decoration and maintenance; (4)

an exemption (currently £8,200) may be claimed provided that this is not applied to any other gain; and, finally, (5) a tapering allowance is applied to strip out that part of the gain which is due to inflation, as opposed to pure profit.

CGT is payable on the chargeable gain at income tax rates on the taxpayers' top slice of income, making the gain relatively small in comparison to the profit made.

The longer a property is kept, the less the tax payable on sale. The exempt allowance in 2005 is £8,200.

10.10 An average lending by a lender used to be two and a half or three times the joint incomes, but this depended very much on circumstances and to a large extent on what the borrowers could clearly afford. Now, with credit being readily available from lenders, there are no hard and fast rules. There is even talk of five times proven income being available in certain cases, but don't count on it.

There are basically a number of methods by which the borrowers may repay their loan.

Golden rule: It pays to shop around.

The methods of repayment are as follows:

(a) Repayment of capital and interest method. By this method a sum is paid monthly to the lenders throughout the life of the loan. This sum is constant, except to allow for changes in the mortgage rate, and contains an interest portion and a capital repayment portion. The ratios of capital repaid and interest repayable of this monthly payment change throughout the life of the loan. At the start, the interest portion is very high and the capital repayment is very low. Gradually the capital repayment portion increases, and the interest portion decreases. About two-thirds through the life of the loan the capital repayment portion and the interest portion are roughly equal and thereafter the capital repayment portion becomes progressively greater than the interest portion, until near the end of the loan, the capital repayment is almost all of the monthly payment.

This is the traditional method of repaying a loan, and it has stood the test of time. The borrower should, however, take out a mortgage protection policy, which guards against the death of the borrower. It is a simple 'whole of life' policy which only pays out on the death of the borrower, is geared to the capital repayable, and nothing is refunded if the borrower survives the term of the loan. For that reason it is comparatively cheap. Insurance against redundancy and critical illness should also be considered, and this covers the mortgage repayments during the borrower's incapacity. (This observation applies to all methods of repayment in this paragraph.) The premium on an £80,000 loan for a man aged 35, non smoker, over a 25-year period is about £25 a month, but again the golden rule is shop around.

(b) Endowment repayment method. This was a very popular method when tax relief was available on premiums, and when the stock market was rising dramatically. Insurance sales people could more or less guarantee that the borrower would get a generous subsidy on premiums from the HM Revenue and Customs, and that at the end of the loan the borrower would have the loan repaid and be given a generous share of the profits made on the investments bought with the premiums. Alas, the tax concession was withdrawn, and then the stock market fell heavily. The result was that borrowers were often left with not enough to repay their loans, and there are now a number of cases of mis-selling of endowment policies. The words 'endowment policies' have acquired an unfortunate meaning, and basically borrowers are warned to steer clear of these policies. A number of good assurance names have become sullied because of this, and the payment of huge bonuses to employees which were not really earned, Financial Services Authority ('FSA') solvency requirements that require assurance companies to keep large sums invested in 'safe'(ie unspectacular) investments, and unsuccessful court actions costing millions of pounds.

It is reported that (February 2006) a 25-year mortgage endowment with a £50 monthly premium, payable to a major company, will mature in 2006 at £40,459, compared with £49,511 in 2005, and with £99,747 in 2002. This is not good news for the life assured, who is expecting to pay off a mortgage from the proceeds of the endowment policy.

Particularly badly hit were the holders of 'low cost' endowment policies which only called for a low premium and which were badly hit by stock market falls. These are very dangerous policies, and are not on offer now, because of the danger of mis-selling claims.

For those with strong nerves, the full cost endowment policy is still an alternative. The borrower takes out the policy, assigns it to the lender along with the usual security documents, and pays the premiums. No capital is repaid throughout the loan, and at the end of the loan, or on the earlier death of the borrower, the full sum is paid by the assurance company to the lenders, who then return the title deeds to the borrower. The assurance policy is then cancelled, and the borrower gets the share of profits (if any).

The untimely death of the borrower is covered by this method. It is very much more expensive than the mortgage protection policy, on the same assumptions as in method (a), the monthly premium is about £294.00, but, of course, the borrower only makes interest payments to the lender, and doesn't have to pay for additional life assurance.

(c) The pension mortgage. This method is open to borrowers who have private pensions, that is other than State or occupational pensions. By this method, the borrower takes out a personal pension plan, and pays in sums of money intended for retirement. The loan is repaid on retrial from the sum thus built up, the balance being used to pay a lump sum to the pensioner and to buy an annuity to provide a pension.

The tax advantages of this method are enormous. The premiums can be deducted from the top slice of the pensioner's income (equal to a subsidy of 40% in most cases), gains on the investment of the fund, but not the income, are tax free, and the lump sum is paid tax free.

The only difficulty is that pension schemes are personal, and cannot be assigned in security, as could an endowment policy. A low cost life assurance policy is therefore taken out on the pensioner's life, and is assigned to the lenders.

From April 2006 SIPPs will be available. These are self invested pension plans, which can be used to purchase investments to be held by pension trustees, including business property. It was thought that this would include houses, home and abroad, works of art, vintage motorcars, and even fine wines to be held in the fund, with consequent tax advantages. The Chancellor of the Exchequer ruled, in his November 2005 pre-Budget report, that this scheme would not after all apply to houses, works of art, vintage motorcars and fine wines. This caused outrage among the sellers of these objects, but that was an end to the matter.

(d) ISA and PEP methods. The ISA (individual savings account) replaced the roughly similar PEP (personal equity plan), but there will still be some PEP mortgages in force. The ISA mortgage is similar to the endowment mortgage, and is repaid by the interest only method, the capital being repaid at the end of the mortgage from the proceeds of the ISA, which are invested in Stock Exchange securities, or cash or other investments. There are considerable tax advantages in this method.

The death of the borrower before the loan is repaid by assuring the life by a simple Mortgage Protection Policy which is assigned in security to the lenders (see para **10.10**(a) above.)

(e) Equity release plans and lifetime mortgages. These methods are suitable for elderly persons who would like to release some of their equity in the family home, without selling it. This gives them money to spend as they like, or get rid of, in order to avoid inheritance tax. This is vulgarly known as SKIing—spending the kids' inheritance—and may not be entirely popular with the younger generation, but it does make some sort of sense.

Which, the consumer affairs group, published a report on these plans, on 4 January 2006 which was critical of the marketing of these plans (one company suggested that the recipient used the money for a holiday in New York), and said:

'Equity Release schemes should come with a warning: they are very expensive and can leave you with little or no equity in your property if you keep one for 20 to 25 years'.

One method is to transfer a share of the house to the lender, which means that the lender becomes part owner with the borrowers or their executors, which may cause difficulties of control. *Which*, advise people to avoid this scheme completely.

The other method, and probably the better, is for the borrowers to get a loan, or a series of loans, from the lenders, on which either fixed interest is payable on the amount of the loan, or no interest is payable or capital repayable until the borrowers die or go into long-term care.

These loans are designed for older, and thus more vulnerable people. Unfortunately there are some characters in the financial jungle, who cannot see vulnerable people without sharpening their knives for the kill, and thus these arrangements should not be entered into without taking skilled financial advice, from Age Concern if there is no available financial adviser.

One scheme which caused considerable hardship in the 1990s, was a scheme in which people mortgaged their house and the proceeds were invested in some dubious bonds to provide, supposedly, a good income. In times of a property slump and recession, the value of the bonds fell, as did the value of houses, and thus the borrowers lost out twice.

(f) Foreign currency loans. When interest rates in this country were very high, sometimes as high as 15%, it was tempting to borrow money in another country, at a much lower rate. Some great bargains were available, but the snag was that the loan had to be repaid at a future date, and if the foreign currency continued to appreciate against sterling (eg the powerful Swiss franc) the borrower was repaying the loan at a much appreciated rate of exchange. This method is not one for widows and orphans, and should only be used with great care. The relatively low rate of interest in this country, in any event, makes this method attractive to only a few.

(g) Offset mortgages. Where a person holds a substantial amount in current account, but does not wish to use this sum to reduce the mortgage, as for instance an account to guard against future liabilities, the borrower may arrange for an offset mortgage. The mortgage is one where a sum of interest from the current account is offset against mortgage interest.

(h) 'Sharia mortgages'. Inverted commas are used because this is not a mortgage in conventional terms. Islamic law forbids the charging or paying of interest on loans. To get around this difficulty the lenders buy the property and resell it to the borrowers at a higher price. Since 2003, the second of the double dispositions involved, does not attract SDLT as would have normally been the case.

Such an arrangement is subject to religious approval.

Whichever method is favoured, the implication on the borrower's means, tax position, and commitments should be carefully considered. In addition, the borrower should search for the best bargain (for quotations, see mortgagebundles.com), and not be hustled into an arrangement which is only good for the person selling it. Despite the best efforts of successive governments and the FSA, there are still many snake oil salespeople in the financial jungle.

10.11 Since 29 November 1970, all loans over heritable property must be constituted by a standard security (CFR(S)A 1970). The law of standard securities is contained in Pt II, ss 9 to 32 of the 1970 Act, and to a lesser degree by the Mortgage Rights (Scotland) Act 2001 (MR(S)A 2001).

A standard security may either be in terms of CFR(S)A 1970, Sch 2, form A or form B, which are provided to give some uniformity to securities, and yet provide some flexibility to cover the myriad of arrangements that are made. Form A is used where the personal obligation of the debtor and the details of the mortgage are contained in the standard security, and this is the one that is most widely used by lenders in residential mortgages. Form B is used where the personal obligation and the details of the mortgage do not appear on the face of the security, but are contained in a separate unregistered document. This method is widely used in commercial loans where the parties wish to keep these details private, as for example in loans by brewers to publicans and loans over offices and factories.

10.12 Form A is made up as follows:

Name of the borrower

Personal obligation of the borrower ('hereby undertakes to pay')

Name of the lender

Amount of the loan

Rate of interest and repayment details

Grant of security over the specified property

Incorporation of the standard conditions and the incorporation of any variations (see CFR(S)A 1970, ss 11 and 16)

Grant of absolute warrandice

Consent to registration for execution in the Books of Council and Session or sheriff court books in event of any default by the granter.

10.13 Form B is made up as above, but omitting the personal obligation, the amount of the loan, the rate of interest and repayment details, and the consent to registration for execution, which are contained in a separate unregistered minute of agreement. In commercial loans this document may also carry heavy variations of the standard conditions and trading conditions (eg brewer's loan.)

If any collateral security is given (eg a life assurance policy) an assignation of that additional security must be drawn up, signed and intimated to the ultimate payer of the fund (eg assurance company.)

10.14 Forms of discharge, partial discharges, partial discharge and restrictions of the security when there has been a partial repayment or a sale of part of the property, and assignations by the lenders of the security, are given in Sch 4 to the CFR(S)A 1970. These are very straightforward, and are registered in the Land Register. While the borrower is entitled to a discharge on repayment of the loan, it may be considered that £1 of the loan be left outstanding. This means that the lenders continue to look after the insurance of the property, and that if a future loan is required, it is not necessary to create new security documents. Lenders will generally be happy with this arrangement, as they keep the insurance commission, and keep in touch with the debtor for the purpose of selling other products. It is always advisable for the debtor to check that the insurance premiums being charged are competitive, eg quotations for a combined buildings and contents cover on a house in Glasgow G14, valued at £120,000, with contents valued at £35,000, given by ten Insurance companies, varied between £121 and £429 per annum (*Daily Telegraph*, 12 November 2005).

10.15 The lenders will reserve the right to assign the loan to someone else, simply by granting an assignation of the security in terms of CFR(S)A 1970, Sch 4, form A. The borrower's consent is not required and the assignation is simply intimated to the borrower. The cost of this procedure is met by the lenders, and not the borrower who is otherwise usually liable for expenses involving the security. This is quite a common way for lenders to raise finance, and is known as 'selling the loan book'.

It was used by Glasgow District Council which sold a large number of loans in 1985 to the Trustee Savings Bank for a consideration of £4,774,727.

10.16 Where a loan is made of a high proportion of the purchase price, the lenders may insist on the borrower providing an insurance indemnity. Thus, if the price on resale does not cover the loan in full, the policy will provide the shortfall to the agreed limit There is generally a single premium payable at the time of making the loan, which is payable by the borrower. If this premium is to be large the borrower should be warned of the sum due in advance, and should make financial allowances for it. If the borrower is unable to sell the property for a sufficient sum to repay the loan the insurers will pay what they have to, and if there is still a shortfall the borrower remains liable. The borrower, despite paying the premium, will in general have no rights under the policy.

10.17 A small proportion of mortgages go bad each year, and in these cases the lenders have the right to enforce the loan conditions, which include repossession and forced sale. When the MR(S)A 2001 was passing through parliament it was pointed out that an average of 6,000 repossession actions were raised in Scotland every year, from which 5,400 decrees were granted, and 2,000 properties were repossessed. In England the courts have the right to suspend such orders, on cause shown, but, as was pointed out in the case of *Halifax Building Society v Gupta* (1994 SLT 339), no such power existed in Scotland. MR(S)A 2001 modified this position, as will be considered later in para **10.30**.

10.18 The contract between the lenders and the borrower is contained in the standard conditions of the loan. While the lenders may have made a large loan over the property, the borrowers remain the owners and occupiers of the property. The standard conditions are intended to make sure that the borrowers do not imperil the security of the lenders, otherwise the lenders are entitled to several remedies. The standard conditions are either variable (V), non-variable (NV), or partially non-variable (PNV). Variable conditions may be, and are, varied by the lenders in the security or by a longer, separate deed of variations which is registered in the Books of Council and Session. Most large lenders (eg banks or building societies) favour the latter method, and print the variations and give a print to the borrowers. The standard conditions are summarised as follows, and their appropriate status is marked:

(1)   (V) The borrower is to keep the property in good and sufficient repair throughout the loan period, in order that the lenders' security is not endangered.

(2)   (V) The borrower is to complete buildings and make alterations only with the lenders' authority, to prevent DIY disasters.

(3)   (V) The borrower is to observe ground burdens, and observe requirements of law (eg statutory notices).

(4)   (V) The borrower is to deal with planning and other notices.

(5)   (V) The borrower is to insure the property for 'market value', and the proceeds of any claim are to be dealt with as directed by the creditor. 'Market value' is almost universally replaced in standard conditions by 'replacement value', especially in older buildings built with traditional materials and craftsmanship. In such cases, replacement value may well be in excess of the market value.

(6)   (V) The borrower is not to let the property without the lenders' consent. In practice this means that the lenders must approve the tenant, and ensure that the requisite notices are served to prevent the tenant getting security of tenure, which would affect the lenders' security.

(7)   (V) If the borrower does not fulfil these duties, the lenders may do so themselves, at the borrower's expense.

(8)   (V) Calling up—if the lenders wish to terminate the loan, as for instance where the borrower is unsatisfactory, the lenders may serve a calling up notice on the borrower in terms of CFR(S)A 1970, Sch 6, form A, requiring the borrower to repay the loan within two months. If the borrower does not so repay, the borrower is in default, and the lender may exercise the remedies given at standard condition 10.

(9)   (V) If the borrower is in arrears or has not followed the conditions, the lenders may serve a notice of default in terms of CFR(S)A 1970, Sch 6, form B, requiring the borrower to remedy the defect(s) within one month. If the borrower does not do so, the lender may exercise the remedies given at standard condition 10.

(10)   (V) Specifies the remedies given to the lenders if the borrower goes into default, or is declared insolvent or bankrupt or goes into liquidation, or if the sheriff court grants a petition to exercise remedies.

    (a)   (V) Any remedies given by the standard security which are outwith the Act.

    (b)   (NV) Sale of property—the sale must be properly advertised, and the sale made at the best price available (see CFR(S)A 1970, s 25 and *Rimmer v Usher* 1967 SLT 7).

    (c)   (V) Entering into possession of the property—this can only be done with the permission of the court.

    (d)   (V) Letting the property.

    (e)   (V) Granting leases of the property.

    (f)   (V) Repair, reconstruction and Improvement of the property.

    (g)   (NV) Foreclosure. This is a remedy carried forward from the C(S)A 1924, which enables the lenders, after an unsuccessful attempt to sell the property. To petition the court to convert a security title into an absolute one. It is probably not appropriate, as the CFR(S)A 1970 gives the lenders ample powers anyway.

(11)   (PNV) Redemption—the borrower may redeem the loan on giving two month's notice of intention. The two-month period is variable, but the remainder of this condition is non-variable. This provision was intended to prevent borrowers from being locked into loans on unattractive terms. However the two-month period proved unsuitable to commercial lenders and was made variable by the Redemption of Standard Securities (Scotland) Act 1971. Otherwise, the provision remains non-variable.

(12)   (V) The borrower is liable for the expenses of the standard security, any discharge or partial discharge or restriction of the security. The borrower is, however, not liable for the expenses of the assignation of the standard security to a third party (see para **10.15**).

The Variable conditions can be, and are, varied by the lenders, but the non-variable conditions (ie sale and foreclosure) can not be varied.

10.19 Probably it was the intention of the drafters of the CFR(S)A 1970 the lenders would, on default of the borrower, take possession of the property, repair it, and then sell it. In fact few lenders will take possession, to avoid liabilities of upkeep, and will simply sell the property at the best price, either by auction or by private sale. So long as they advertise the sale properly and obtain the best price, there is no objection to this. It should be remembered that most repossessed houses are in poor condition, but so long as the conditions of sale are observed, there is no obligation on the lenders to perform any remedial work. If the property does not sell for a sum sufficient to clear the loan, the borrower remains liable for the shortfall.

10.20 As was pointed out in Parliament, these provisions are very creditor friendly. Once the borrower is on the slippery slope, there is no way off. Most reputable lenders will give the borrower a chance, but not all are so obliging. Accordingly the MR(S)A 2001 gives the borrower a lifeline.

If the borrower is heading towards default an action may be raised asking the court to suspend proceedings, to allow the borrower time to straighten things out.

Under s 2(2) of MR(S)A 2001, the court shall bear four things in mind:

(a)   The nature and reasons for the default.
(b)   The borrower's ability to fulfil the obligations within a reasonable time.
(c)   Any action taken by the lenders to assist the borrower.
(d)   The ability of the borrower, and any other person living in the house, to find other suitable accommodation.

An example of how the sheriff court deals with such petitions can be found in *Abbey National v Briggs* (an unreported case in 2002, which is digested in Cretton and Reid *Conveyancing 2002* (Butterworths, 2003).

10.21 Further details on standard securities and their enforcement ar available in Cusine and Rennie *Standard Securities* (2nd edn, Butterworths, 2002).

Chapter 11

INTRODUCTION TO LAND REGISTRATION

'Objectives: to extend, as required by statute, the operation of the Land Register throughout Scotland in order to bring the benefits of cheaper conveyancing to the Scottish public and to phase out the General Register of Sasines.'

(Keeper's Report, 1993–94)

Land registration scheme

11.01 The applicable law, and the prescribed forms, are contained in the Land Registration (Scotland) Act 1979 (LR(S)A 1979) and also in the Land Registration (Scotland) Rules 1980, SI 1980/1413, as amended by the Land Registration (Scotland) (Amendment) Rules, SI 1982/974, SI 1988/1143, SI 1995/248 and SI 1998/3100. Practitioners should also have available the *Registration of Title Practice Book* (2nd edn, 2000) which is now available free online at Registers of Scotland website: www.ros.gov.uk).

11.02 Registration in the Register of Sasines was a perfectly sound system, but it had some major defects:

(a)   It was time-consuming.

(b)   It was repetitive, and potentially involved several people doing exactly the same work in a short space of time. Thus for example, solicitors A may note title for their client X. When everything is complete X sells to Y, whose solicitors B then have to repeat the same process, and so on *ad infinitum.*

(c)   Once the sellers' solicitors handed over the title deeds at settlement in a sasine transaction, the sellers' responsibility for the title ceased, unless a successful claim for warrandice was established. This was not the case with Land Register transactions where the sellers' responsibility for the title does not cease until the letter of obligation, which contains the obligation to obtain a land certificate without any exclusion of indemnity, is discharged (see para **11.09**).

(d)   If there were two solicitors involved in the same transaction, both had to do the same work, and the unfortunate clients had to pay for the repetition. Thus if A buys a public house, A's solicitors have to note the title; if simultaneously a loan is obtained from brewery B, their solicitors will also had to note title. In terms of the standard loan documents (CFR(S)A 1970, Sch 3, standard condition 12), A has the doubtful pleasure of paying both of them.

(e)   Much of the work and the process involved in a sasine transaction was out of date and labour intensive and better suited to more spacious days, when such work could be done cheaply. Because there was a lot of work involved, sasine registration was obviously expensive.

(f)   The Sasine Register was a perfectly good register, but it was created in the 17th century. It has been substantially modernised by the introduction of microfilming of record volumes, and optical reading of presentment forms, leading to a computerised presentment book, thence to a computerised Sasine Register. The staff of Register House are highly efficient and can find any deed you want within minutes even though there are tens of thousands of deeds. It was, however, as a system, susceptible only to limited further modernisation.

(g)   Further the Sasine Register was a register of deeds and not of land. The only information it could disclose is that disclosed by the deeds registered. If you do not know exactly what you are looking for, you may have great difficulty in finding what you want.

(h)   Many plans presented to the Sasine Register was badly prepared and inaccurate. Further they followed no consistent pattern of scales, or even north points, and matching plans of adjoining lands is difficult.

In difficulties in drawing up a coherent picture of the ownership of vast acres of land in Scotland, which may only be described in the Sasine Register by a general description. An example of this is 'the Lands of Assynt in the County of Sutherland'. Nowhere is there, at present, an accurate delineation of the Lands of Assynt, which it is believed extend to some 50,000 acres, and considerable knowledge of the area provides the only answer.

Only now is a comprehensive system emerging, with the assistance of Registers of Scotland. See www.whoownsscotland.org.uk. If you are feeling charitable, you may wish to donate towards this project.

The principal difficulty was that under the sasine system huge areas of land, thousands of acres in the country areas, can be transferred by deeds containing only a vague general description, and with no map attached to illustrate the land transferred. Thus no coherent record of land ownership in Scotland existed.

11.03 The idea of registration of title, which seeks to correct these defects, is by no means new. A system of this kind was established in Prussia in 1700, and it was introduced in the whole of united Germany in 1872.

In the English-speaking world, a system of registration known as the 'Torrens System' was introduced into South Australia in 1858 and this system spread widely in the Dominions. It was principally a system for virgin land and was not thought to be a suitable system for introduction to Britain, where some land holdings go back to Domesday.

In Scotland, however, as far back as 1903, Professor Wood wrote in his lectures on conveyancing: 'I am unable to see any real difficulty in the way of introducing registration of title into Scotland'.

In 1959 the Secretary of State for Scotland set up a committee under Lord Reid to investigate the introduction of registration of title into Scotland. This committee reported favourably (Cmnd 2032) and recommended that another committee be set up to devise a scheme. This committee under Professor Henry reported in 1969 (Cmnd 4137) with a workable scheme, which after a trial in Register House, was introduced by LR(S)A 1979.

To set things in context, in 1959 there existed only a few huge main frame computers, and the electric typewriter was the latest luxury. There was no thought of personal computers, with the same, or greater, power than the main frame computer. The fact that the Reid Committee produced a scheme that fitted personal computers so perfectly was fortuitous, and it is hard to see how the concept of registration of title could work so well without the personal computer.

11.04 The scheme is based on the Ordnance Survey of Scotland using the scale 1:1250 for urban areas where modern house plots are small, 1:2,500 in villages and small towns where plots are rather larger, and 1:10,000 for farms and moorland areas. Ordnance Survey maps are extremely accurate, and are consistently updated. It should be noted, however, that they reflect boundaries as they actually exist on the ground, and not as they exist in title plans registered in the Sasine Register. This difficulty is met by asking the Keeper, in a form P16 (see para **12.03**) to compare the title plan with the Ordnance Survey map.

It should be noted that the Land Register is based, like the General Register of Sasines, on the old Scottish county system, which was phased out for local government purposes in 1974. Thus regions and district, introduced by the Local Government (Scotland) Act 1973 have no significance in land registration, and the unitary authorities, introduced by the Local Government etc (Scotland) Act 1994 and took over from them in 1996. The old county system was left untouched so far as the Land and Sasine Registers were concerned, as any change would have been too complicated and expensive.

The original intention was to make all Scotland operational in nine years, starting year one on 6 April 1981 with the County of Renfrew; then in year two—The City of Glasgow; year three—Lanark; year four—Midlothian; year five—Rest of Central Belt; year six—Angus, Kincardine, Aberdeen; year seven—Ayr, Dumfries and Galloway; year eight—Southern Rural Areas; year nine—Northern Rural Areas.

11.05 This scheme (para **11.04**), however, proved wildly over-optimistic, and by 1990 only four counties were operational: Renfrew, Dumbarton, Lanark and Glasgow. It appeared at that time that the scheme was irretrievably stalled, for the Register was under-staffed, and could not keep pace with the applications pouring in, let alone the arrears that were building up. Long delays were commonplace, and the Keeper acknowledged this problem in his 1988 report, and explained that the backlogs on his shelves would generate a fee income of £9m, if only he could process them.

The property boom of the late eighties coupled with the success of the 'right to buy' legislation led to a soaring demand for the services of the Registers of Scotland at a time when the department was subject to both staffing and accommodation constraints. The situation was steadily deteriorating and invidious comparisons were being drawn with the English system, which had only covered 50–52% of the country after 63 years. Fortunately the position in both countries has since been rectified.

The Department of the Registers of Scotland was created Scotland's first executive agency in 1990 and the consequent removal of constraints enabled the agency to tackle its problems and meet targets set for it at its creation. These targets included:

(a)   to reduce turnround times on registering dealings (i e sales of registered land) in the Land Register from 39 to 15 weeks;

(b)   to present a phased programme for the extension of the Land Register throughout Scotland, to provide cheaper conveyancing, and to phase out the General Register of Sasines;

(c)   to have in operation by April 1993 a branch office of the Land Register in Glasgow;

(d)   to eliminate progressively the older casework by the end of 1996–97.

11.06 It is very pleasing to note that these targets have been met. In particular the land registration process picked up momentum, as shown by the extension of land registration to the counties of Clackmannan (1 October 1992); Stirling (1 April 1993); West Lothian (1 October 1993); Fife (1 April 1995); Aberdeen and Kincardine (1 April 1996); Ayr and Dumfries, Kirkcudbright and Wigtown (1 April 1997); Angus, Perth and Kinross (1 April 1999); Berwick, East Lothian, Peebles, Roxburgh and Selkirk (1 October 1999); Argyll and Bute (1 April 2000); Inverness and Nairn (1 April 2002); Banff, Caithness, Moray, Orkney and Zetland, Ross and Cromarty, and Sutherland (1 April 2003). Thus, the whole of Scotland is now on the land registration system. The Sasine Register now exists only for deeds 'without financial consideration' which means land given as a gift or, more significantly, newly created securities over land. There are a surprisingly large number of, particularly, the latter as houseowners take the opportunity of changing their mortgages in a more relaxed and competitive financial environment. Some land may never be registered (eg parks, landed estates remaining in the family) unless the owners apply to register the title voluntarily. The Scottish Executive are understood to be carrying out a voluntary registration of all the trunk roads in Scotland, because of the significant benefits to the Executive.

11.07 When an area becomes operational for land registration, all transfers for value must be registered (ie new securities on existing holdings and gratuitous transfers, as opposed to transfers for value, do not need to be registered). Transfers of long leases must be registered, whether gratuitous or not (LR(S)A 1979, s 3(3)).

Thus, if Mr and Mrs A had bought a house in the county of Renfrew in 1975, and if they had lived there continuously, the deed in their favour, and the standard security to their building society, would have been registered in the Sasine Register. The reason for this is that in 1975 the Land Register was not yet established.

If Mr and Mrs A then sold their house to B in 1994, the necessary documentation would then be registered in the Land Register.

If, however, Mr and Mrs A decided to transfer their house to their children as a gift (there are possible inheritance tax benefits in this action), the documentation would be recorded in the Sasine Register, as the transfer was not for valuable consideration. Rather oddly, if Mr and Mrs A gave the house to a child as a gift in contemplation of marriage (this has slightly greater possible inheritance tax benefits), that would then be treated as a transfer for valuable consideration, and the documentation would be registered in the Land Register.

If, however, Mr and Mrs A decided that they were staying put, but would get another loan, for their own purposes, the documentation would again be recorded in the Sasine Register, as a loan is not treated as being a valuable consideration.

Once, however, the title is registered in the Land Register, all relevant documents are registered in that register, irrespective of whether the consideration is valuable or not.

The Register of Sasines still operates in parallel with the Land Register, and will continue to do so until it is finally phased out. Paradoxically, the Keeper of the Registers report for the financial year 2001–02 shows that the intake in the Sasine Register is 35% over that forecast. This is thought to be because of the upturn in remortgages caused by lower interest rates.

It may be provided that all land shall be registered, whether transferred or not, to give a complete picture of land ownership in Scotland, kept on standard Ordnance Survey maps, and all stored on computer. That date is, however, still a rather long way off.

11.08 In 2003–04 the Keeper reported that there had been an intake of 76,094 titles for first registration, 26,169 transfers of part of a new registered title (eg new houses built by builders on registered land), and 240,145 dealing with the whole (eg sales of registered land). There were, in the same period, 132,968 registrations in the Register of Sasines, showing this register is a very healthy corpse indeed.

11.09 It should, however, be made plain that there is nothing tricky about land registration. The first registration does, however, require extra work as the sellers' solicitors not only have to satisfy the purchasers' solicitors as to the sellers' title, but the purchasers' solicitors have immediately to satisfy the Keeper of the Land Register that a sufficient title is being registered, and that no restriction of indemnity is called for. Whereas formerly the purchaser's solicitors may have been content to take a view on, for example, a copy deed without the recording stamp, the Keeper invariably will not and will requisition quick copies of the deed from the purchaser's solicitors. The purchasers' solicitors who will in turn revert to the sellers' solicitors, demanding answers in terms of the obligation under missives.

Thus it may be said that while the sasine system is one of *caveat emptor* (buyer beware), the land registration system is one of *caveat vendor* (seller beware), as there is much more of an onus on the sellers' solicitors to prove a good title than there is on the purchasers' solicitors to be satisfied that the title is good.

When the Keeper is satisfied, a comprehensive land certificate is issued, which contains all necessary information on the title (but not the planning or building or other information) and it is conclusive evidence of ownership, the extent of the property, and the land obligations affecting the land.

11.10 In the case of *Short's Trustee v Keeper of the Registers of Scotland* (1996 SC (HL) 14) the House of Lords decided that the Keeper was not obliged to register a decree reducing a transfer of land, as the appropriate course for the holder of the decree is to apply for rectification of the register under LR(S)A 1979, s 9. This section allows the Keeper to rectify the title sheet where an error is brought to his notice, or if ordered to do so by the Lands Tribunal. This provision is, however, restricted by the terms of s 9(3), which does not allow rectification to the prejudice of the proprietor in possession, except in very limited circumstances:

(a)   to note an overriding interest, which does not prejudice the proprietor because an overriding interest is overriding, whether noted or not;

(b)   where all concerned consent;

(c)   where the error is caused by the fraud or carelessness of the proprietor in possession;

(d)   where rectification relates to something for which the Keeper has previously refused to indemnify the proprietor in possession. An example of this would be where the proprietor in possession has only an *a non domino* title, but this has now been perfected by positive prescription, and the proprietor wants the title to be rectified to the extent that the exclusion of indemnity is removed.

In the Inner House hearing of *Short's Trustee* (1993 SCLR 242) Lord President Hope said that if a decree of reduction was automatically registrable in the Land Register, that would subvert the whole system of land registration in that any person dealing with the registered proprietor would require to check the previous history of the title, which

241

was what land registration was designed to avoid. However, this decision has now been undermined by the subsequent case of *Short's Trustee v Chung (No 2)* 1998 SC 105.

It should be noted that the Keeper asks (Annual Report 1992–93) to be cited in any action for rectification that is raised, although the action is not directed primarily against the Keeper. This is in order that he can enter an appearance if the integrity of the Register appears to be under threat in any way.

The Scottish Executive are presently considering reform of the Land Registration (Scotland) Act 1979, suggested by the Scottish Law Commission.

11.11 Furthermore if the registered title is successfully challenged in any respect, on the grounds of a matter on which indemnity has not been excluded, the loss is state guaranteed and falls on the Keeper. For that reason the Keeper inspects the title very carefully, and seeks certain information from the presenter of the title (see the questions in LR(S)A 1979, forms 1, 2, and 3) before full indemnity is given.

Due to the care taken by the Keeper and his staff, claims for compensation against the Keeper are relatively very low, but, obviously, the occasional mistake is made resulting in a loss of property rights. Such claims are dealt with sympathetically and quickly. There were 50 such complaints in 2003–04.

11.12 The first registration involves a considerable amount of detailed work for it is effectively a sasine transaction, with the land registration work added. A positive weighting of fees may be justified. The case of any future transfer should be a comparatively simple matter, but there should be a negative weighting in fees for the reduction in work involved. Under the old scale of fees, the positive and negative weighting allowed was 25%, but the guidelines for fee charging in para **9.18** should be followed in all cases. The government call for cheaper fees is thus met, by greater productivity, and fewer time-wasting procedures.

11.13 Thus the land registration system is a very good and modern one, with digitalised maps, optical reading, computerised land certificates either in operation or planned. The Abolition of Feudal Tenure etc (Scotland) Act 2000, Tile Conditions (Scotland) Act 2003, Tenements (Scotland) Act 2004, Land Reform (Scotland) Act 2000 and various other developments imply additional work for the Keeper and staff in bringing title sheets up to date, and deleting various obsolete burdens.

In addition to that the Keeper is working on automated registration of title to land (ARTL) which will be introduced in 2007. ARTL will allow agents to register titles electronically, signatures being added electronically in terms of the Electronic Communications Act 2000 and the relevant Regulations of 2002. Solicitors will add their signatures by a card, and must have the authority to do so.

Chapter 12

FIRST REGISTRATION

'The Land Register for Scotland is a State guaranteed register of title to interests in land. Registration of a property for the first time in the Land Register results in the creation of a Title Sheet. The Title Sheet defines precisely the property on the Ordnance Map and also gives details of current registered owners as well as charges and burdens upon properties. The accuracy of the Title Sheet is guaranteed by the State and indemnity is payable for loss suffered as a result of an error or inaccuracy in the Register.'

(The Keeper's Report 1993–94)

First registration

12.01 The basic scheme of a transaction is similar to a transaction in sasine registration, with the addition of certain steps characteristic of land registration. This chapter should be read with reference to the timetable at the start of the book, and to the specimen transaction involving the purchase of 3 Miller Drive. It should also be read with reference to the following land registration forms:

Form 4	(White) and Notes—Inventory of writs
Form 6	Land certificate
Form 7	Charge certificate
Form 10	Application for report prior to registration
Form 10A	Keeper's reply to form 10 application (similar to a search)
Form 11	Application for update of form 10A
Form 11A	Continuation of the report contained in form 10A (similar to an interim report on search)
Form 14	Application for report to ascertain whether subjects are registered or not
Form P16	(White)—Application to compare a boundary description with the Ordnance map

244

12.02 Every offer, including the standard clauses offers, will normally include obligations for the settler to produce such documentation as would allow the title to be registered. In the case of a first registration, the typical requirements are as follows:

'If the provisions of the Land Registration (Scotland) Act 1979 ("the Act") relating to a first registration under the Act apply, a valid marketable title together with: (i) a form 10 report brought down to a date not more than three working days prior to the Date of Entry and showing no entries adverse to the Seller's interest in the Property (the cost of the said report being the Seller's liability); and (ii) such documents and evidence including a plan as the Keeper may require to enable the Keeper to issue a Land Certificate in the name of the Purchaser as the registered proprietor of the Property without exclusion of indemnity in terms of Section 12(2) of the Act. Such documents will include (unless the Property comprises only part of a tenement or flatted building and does not include an area of ground specifically included in the title to that part) a plan or bounding description sufficient to enable the whole Property to be identified on the ordnance survey map and evidence (such as a form P16 report) that the description of the whole Property as contained in the title deeds is habile to include the whole of the occupied extent.'

The obligation is similar to a sasine obligation in that a marketable title and a valid disposition are to be produced, and the main differences from a sasine obligation are: (1) the search drops out and is replaced by a form 10A report; and (2) there is an extra obligation upon the sellers to provide 'such documents and evidence including a plan' as may be required to satisfy the Keeper and enable him to issue a land certificate with the full state guarantee, without any qualification. This is a clause characteristic of land registration which keeps the sellers' solicitors 'on the hook', and ultimately responsible for the quality of the title presented for registration (see para **12.09**).

12.03 As soon as instructed the sellers' solicitors should (as well as obtaining property enquiry certificates, planning certificates, matrimonial homes affidavits, planning permissions, building warrants, completion certificates, benefited proprietors' permissions (if required), timber treatment guarantees, replacement window guarantees, and any necessary links in title as before), send a copy of any deed plan they have from the titles together with a form P16 asking the Keeper to compare the plan with the Ordnance map. The title deeds should also be scrutinised to ascertain whether there is any obstacle to a successful sale, such as an obtrusive land obligation or a personal pre-emption right. If the title is registered there will be a land certificate; if not the assumption is that the title is not registered, but there may be some reason for a land certificate not being with the titles. If in doubt the form 10A report will clarify this (see para **12.06**). Other remarks as to the quality of plans should be noted (see para **11.04**).

12.04 The Keeper will reply to form P16 in one of the following ways:

(1)   *'The subjects are not identifiable on the Ordnance map.'* In this case there is a serious problem, and if missives have not been concluded, the seller should be advised to withdraw the subjects from sale while this is cleared up. If this is not clarified before registration the Keeper may restrict his indemnity so as not to cover loss suffered through this defect in title. For this reason the form P16 report should be ordered before a sale is made, but this is not always possible with an impetuous seller. In practice this reply may not necessarily be difficult to overcome—the property may be a 'floating polygon', ie it is not related in any way to adjoining geographical features, and the land could be situated anywhere. This can be easily corrected by the insertion of necessary details, such as streets or geographical features.

(2)   *'The boundaries of the subjects coincide with those on the Ordnance map.'* This is the answer you hope for, and if you get it, you can proceed without worry.

(3)   *'The boundaries do not coincide with those on the Ordnance map. Please see print herewith.'* This indicates a minor, but material, discrepancy, which will have to be cleared up. It does not, however, go to the root of the sale as does answer 1.

However, failing this discrepancy in the boundaries being clarified, the Keeper would have to give a qualified indemnity, because of the uncertainty of the boundaries. This is contrary to the obligation in the missives (see para **12.02**). This matter is clarified in the article by the Deputy Keeper in 1995 JLSS 15, which states:

If the comparison confirms that the Ordnance map is correct and there is a discrepancy between the legal extent and the occupied extent, what will require to be done will depend on which extent is the greater. If the legal extent is greater than the occupied extent and the latter is contained wholly within the former then, if the purchaser is prepared to accept a title to the occupied extent, the Keeper should be informed of this when the application is made and he will process the application accordingly. The second additional question provides an opportunity to do so. Where, however, the occupied extent exceeds the boundaries of the legal extent, remedial conveyancing will be necessary and should be completed before application for registration is made.'

12.05 If the discrepancy is not major, the Keeper will provide this answer, but will not deal with the matter until the deed is presented for registration. In all likelihood the discrepancy will then be dealt with informally under the Keeper's discretion, or by using the mythical—but indispensable—'elastic tape measure'. However, where the discrepancy cannot be overlooked, the boundaries may have to be set out in a s 19 agreement, signed by the adjoining proprietors. This agreement reads, in skeletal form, and each such deed will depend on the individual circumstances of the case, as follows:

'WE, Proprietor 1 (*name and design and specify title*) and Proprietor 2 (*name and design and specify title*) CONSIDERING that the boundary (*state circumstances*) of the subjects belonging to me the said (*Proprietor 1*) shown on the said Plan first referred to does not coincide with the mutual boundary depicted on the current Ordnance Survey map (*specify map*) AND FURTHER CONSIDERING that the parties hereto are satisfied that the said mutual boundary is correctly shown on the Ordnance Survey of which a print has been annexed and subscribed as relative hereto; therefore it is agreed between the parties hereto as follows (*state agreement*); and the parties hereto bind and oblige themselves and take their respective successors and assignees bound and obliged to accept the said mutual boundary as defined in terms hereof: IN WITNESS WHEREOF (*Testing Clause*).'

Each proprietor signs a Sasine Application Form, unless one already has a registered title. As the deed is usually prepared on the occurrence of a first registration on one or other property, the agreement is recorded in the Sasine Register prior to the land registration, and the appropriate correction is carried onto the land certificate.

A form P16 report will not be provided by the Keeper for a flat in a tenement, and should not therefore be requested.

12.06 Further before missives are concluded, the sellers' solicitors should send a form 10 to the register or searcher, which is 'an application for report prior to registration'. The Keeper responds with a form 10A report showing the prescriptive progress of the title. The form 10A report also contains a definitive statement as to whether the title has been registered or not, if, for some reason, this cannot be deduced from scrutiny of the title deeds (see para **12.03**).

Alternatively a form 14 report can be obtained to ascertain whether a title is registered or not ('application for report to ascertain whether or not subjects have been registered'), but this contains nothing the form 10A report does not contain. The main purpose of a form 14 report is where the enquirer has no knowledge of the subjects or the state of the title. The sellers' solicitors should ideally not, of course, be in this position. This is to some extent, it is admitted, a counsel of perfection— but often the first time solicitors know a house is to be sold is when an offer lands at their reception with a 12-hour time limit for acceptance.

12.07 When missives are complete the sellers' solicitors send to the purchasers' solicitors the following:

(a) The title deeds being sent to the Keeper (detailed at para **12.15**). It is not necessary to send any other deeds, including the search, although this may be helpful.

(b) Draft letter of obligation for approval.

(c) Any other relevant documents such as roads certificates, property enquiry reports, building warrants and completion certificates, guarantees, links in title, and matrimonial homes consents.

(d) A form 10A report with a draft form 11.

(e) A form P16 report.

(f) A draft discharge of any security.

12.08 The draft letter of obligation is in terms similar to:

With reference to the settlement of the above transaction today, we hereby (1) undertake to clear the records of any deed, decree or diligence (other than such as may be created by or against your clients) which may be recorded in the Property or Personal Registers, or to which effect may be given in the Land Register in the period from* tot inclusive (or to the earlier registration of your clients' interest in the above subjects), which would cause the Keeper to make an entry on, or qualify his indemnity in the Land Certificate to be issued in respect of that interest; and (2) confirm that, to the best of our knowledge and belief, as at this date, the answers to the questions numbered 1 to 14 in draft form 1 adjusted with you (in so far as the answers relate to our client or to our clients' interest in the above subjects) are still correct. Where the discharge of a security is awaited a further paragraph is added; and (3) undertake to deliver to you within 21 days of this date, the duly executed discharge of the existing Standard Security granted by our client with our relative forms 2 and 4 and our cheque made payable to the Keeper for registration thereof.

* Insert date of certificate of form 10 (or form 11) report.

† Insert date 21 days (or such other period as may be agreed) after settlement.

This letter of obligation is signed and witnessed. This letter keeps the seller 'on the hook' and is the letter of obligation called for in the offer. It is also a 'classic' letter of obligation.

12.09 The form 10 asks the Keeper to provide the following details:

(a)   A search in the Register of Inhibitions and Adjudication against the party(ies) last infeft for five years to date of certificate, and any other parties interested (eg their building society or other parties who have disposed of the house within the past ten years).

(b)   A list of deeds recorded within the prescriptive period (see para 8.13).

(c)   A statement of securities within 40 years prior to the date of certificate and for which no final discharge has been recorded (see para 8.13).

(d)   A statement of discharge of securities within the five years prior to the date of certificate (see para 8.13).

(e)   Deeds other than transfer, or deeds creating or affecting securities recorded within the 40 years prior to the date of certificate (any miscellaneous recorded deeds).

12.10 If there is a significant time gap between obtaining the form 10A report and settlement this report should be brought down to a date nearer settlement by sending a form 11 to the Keeper or searcher for a more current report (form 11A). This simply continues the form 10A report. It may be tempting to delay the ordering of a form 10A report until a date near settlement, and to save a little money on a form 11A report, but this is playing with fire, as the form 10A may disclose something prejudicial that you should have known much earlier.

The Keeper or searcher will normally reply to reports within two days and, in some cases, for a small additional charge will fax the report. An almost instant reply can be obtained by faxing requests for reports, and requesting a faxed reply. The Keeper and many searchers offer electronic submission and email responses, which speed up response times.

12.11 The purchasers' solicitors look through the title and the contents of the form 10A report and will prepare their observations on title, revise the draft letter of obligation, draft discharge of the sellers' security, and return these to the sellers' agents. They also send back the draft disposition they will have drafted, which is drawn in exactly the same manner as one for unregistered land (a much simpler form is used for subsequent transfers) and drafts of forms 1 and 4. The sellers' solicitors approve these and then return them.

12.12 Form 1 (know as the pink form in the days of typewriters) is an 'application (to the Keeper) for first registration'. The Keeper requires the applicant for registration to answer (as at 2006) 14 questions, which are self-explanatory (except for two). These questions should be answered truthfully. You are asking the Keeper to guarantee a title, and the form 1 is therefore like an insurance proposal, and is therefore to be completed in the utmost good faith. By granting a letter of obligation, your firm is confirming that the answers in the draft form 1 provided by the purchasers are still correct at the time of application.

Forms 1, 2 and 3 are (i) a request for registration; (ii) a form of proposal for insurance; and (iii) a list of questions that every conveyancer should be asking anyway, and as such, a valuable aide-memoire.

As with other forms, notes and directions are given for completion. The form itself and the notes are quite self-explanatory, and more or less straightforward, but it might be mentioned that the purchaser has to supply the following information to the Keeper of the Land Register:

(a)   a short description only of the subjects to which the deed being registered relates; that is an identifiable postal address, rather than a full conveyancing description;

(b)   the full name of the person granting the deed (i e the seller) or the party last infeft if it is not the granter. Thus, if John Smith owned the property, but has died, and his executors were granting the deed without having made up a recorded title, the purchasers' solicitors would insert the late John Smith's name here, as the person last infeft;

(c)   the name and address of the grantee (i e purchaser) who is applying for registration;

(d)   the price;

(e)   the purchasers' solicitors sign the application on page one 'I/ We certify that the information supplied in this application is correct to the best of my/our knowledge and belief and apply for registration in respect of Deed No   in the Inventory of Writs

(Form 4)'. This certificate and signature are equivalent to the warrant of registration that used to be placed on sasine dispositions, but not necessary here;

(f) the presenting solicitors' name, address reference and FAS number (for financial accounting purposes).

12.13 Further in form 1, Pt B a number of questions must be answered, most of which are self-explanatory, but three only require further explanation:

No. 3. 'Is there any person in possession or occupation of the subject or any part of them adversely to the interest of the applicant?'

Here the applicants' solicitors should give details of any tenancy under a lease or any tenant who may have acquired security of tenure. Also, any encroachment should be explained.

No. 5(c). 'Are there any over-riding interests affecting the subjects or any part of them which you wish noted on the title sheet?'

An 'over-riding interest' is defined by LR(S)A 1979, s 28(1), as including (in summary) a right or interest over land of lessee under a lease which is not a long lease who has acquired a real right by virtue of possession; a crofter or cottar; the proprietor of the dominant tenement in a servitude; the Crown or other authority under an enactment which does not require the recording of a deed in the register to complete the right; the holder of a floating charge, whether crystallised or not; a member of the public in respect of a public right of way; *regalia majora*; or any person having a right which has been made real other than by registration. This definition does not include properly constituted land obligations which are covered in the schedule of burdens (p 4 of the form). Section 28 would seem to refer principally to minor public services, rights of access acquired by prescription, etc.

No. 7. Where any party to the deed inducing registration is a company registered under the Companies Acts can you confirm:

(a) *that it is not a charity as defined in* s 112 of the Companies Act 1989 *and*

(b) *that the transaction to which the deed gives effect is not one to which* s 322A of the Companies Act 1985 *applies.*

This question refers to the *ultra vires* doctrine (within the company's powers), which used to be applied strictly, but is not so important nowadays, except for (a) where the company selling property is a charity and (b) where the company is transferring property to its directors. In both cases the power to transfer property in these circumstances must be seen to exist.

The questions asked in form 1 are helpful to solicitors and Keeper alike. For solicitors, they present a check list of questions that should be asked of the sellers' solicitors (e g where the deed inducing registration is in implement of the exercise of a power of sale under a heritable security—have the statutory procedures necessary for the proper exercise of such power been complied with? Yes/No). From the Keeper's point of view, it helps him to identify any problem at an early stage.

12.14 On form 1, p 4, you are required to state what heritable securities (if any) affect the property. Please note this covers only existing securities transferred with the property, and not any new security created by the purchaser which are dealt with as a dealing in registered land and by use of a form 2 (blue) for the security. Similarly you are also required to state the writs concerning the property which state land obligations.

12.15 The other form to be completed by the purchasers at this stage is form 4 ('inventory of writs relevant to application for registration'). Again the notes relative to this form require careful study, and most particularly one should note the definition of 'relevant deeds and documents'.

The Keeper does not require all the writs of the property, no matter how old or obsolete, through the acting of prescription. He does require:

- (a) a sufficient progress of titles including the deed inducing registration and unrecorded links in title;
- (b) all prior writs containing rights or burdens affecting the land;
- (c) a feu duty redemption receipt (if applicable);
- (d) any existing heritable securities and related deeds;
- (e) a deed outside the prescriptive progress which contains a plan;
- (f) form P16 (see para **12.04**)—this report must now be returned to the Keeper;
- (g) matrimonial and family homes affidavits, consents or renunciations, as appropriate;
- (h) any other relevant document.

12.16 On receipt of these documents from the purchasers' solicitors, the sellers' solicitors should then:

- (a) if not already done, send the form 10 and form P16 to the Keeper or searcher, and send the resulting reports to the purchasers' solicitors;

(b)   revise and return the purchasers' solicitors' forms 1, 4 and draft disposition;

(c)   answer any title queries and obtain anything further required by the purchasers.

12.17 The purchasers' solicitors then have the disposition engrossed and return it to the sellers' solicitors for signature, with the draft for comparison, and blank form of particulars of signing and witnesses. Forms 1 and 4 are typed in principal form. Everything is prepared for settlement as before.

12.18 At settlement the sellers' solicitors hand over in exchange for the price:

(a)   the signed disposition, draft and particulars of signing;

(b)   Form P16 report;

(c)   letter of obligation (in terms of para **12.08**). They also exhibit the draft letter of obligation to the purchasers' solicitors to enable them to check the principal;

(d)   the title deeds and any other relevant papers;

(e)   the receipted state for settlement;

(f)   form 11A report, which brings down the report to a date as close as possible to settlement. This should be applied for by the seller at least three working days before settlement. Sellers' solicitors who have applied for, but not yet received, a form 11A report at settlement, may obtain a telephoned or faxed report from Register House, at a small fee. This allows the sellers' solicitors to grant a letter of obligation with an easy conscience (para **12.08**);

(g)   the keys, or authorise their release.

12.19 The purchasers' solicitors then send off to the Keeper:

(a)   forms 1 and 4, the latter in duplicate;

(b)   the disposition;

(c)   the land transaction return certificate;

(d)   the various documents specified in para **12.15**.

The Keeper checks off the deeds against the form 4, and acknowledges receipt by returning the duplicate form 4, which also bears the new title number and the date of the registration, both of which can be regarded as conclusive.

The purchasers' solicitors then settle up the odds and ends of the transaction as they would have under the old system and answer any questions the Keeper may have.

12.20 Assuming that everything is in order, the Keeper will send out in due course a land certificate, form 6, which discloses the following:

(a)   **Registered number of the title.**

(b)   **Statement of indemnity.** 'Subject to any specific qualification ... a person who suffers loss as a result of any of the events specified in s 12(1) of the above [1979] Act shall be entitled to be indemnified in respect of that loss by the Keeper of the Registers of Scotland in terms of that Act.'

(c)   **Section A—the property section.** A description of the property and a coloured plan based on the Ordnance Survey scale 1:1,250 for densely populated urban areas; 1:2,500 for less densely populated urban areas and farms; or 1:10,000 for hill farms, mountains and moorland.

(d)   Section B—the proprietorship section. The name and designation of the proprietor, the date of registration (i e when the real right was created), the price and the date of entry.

(e)   **Section C—the charges section.** Details of charges affecting the property whether previously existing or created by the proprietor. There is also a separate charge certificate (form 7).

(f)   **Section D—the burdens section.** A verbatim note of all land obligations affecting the property, in so far as still relevant and existing. The Keeper discards what he considers all irrelevant information: such as narrative and ancillary clauses; descriptions; old and useless burdens, such as details of roads that have long since been formed; and retains only the relevant ones. The Keeper is walking a tightrope in this respect, for what may be considered to be irrelevant, may turn out to be painfully relevant and the Keeper will be responsible for any loss in respect of lost rights (see ch 20).

12.21 When the purchasers' solicitors receive the land certificate, they should read it to confirm it is in order and then discharge the letter of obligation (assuming that all other items on it have been met) and return it to the sellers' solicitors.

12.22 This wonderful document completely takes the place of the title deeds, and can be brought up to date in future, as and when required. If it is lost an office copy can be obtained from the Keeper who prepares this from the title sheet. You can, in theory at least, tear up all the title deeds—but before you do so remember: (1) it is better to keep them until the first sale, just in case there has been a mistake that has been overlooked; (2) they belong to the owner of the house who may very well want to keep them; and (3) the deeds may have archival interest to the local archivist who should be allowed to see any old documents before they are shredded.

12.23 If the purchasers sell the property in the course of registration, a difficult situation arises. The Keeper can be requested to return the title deeds, but this only delays the registration. Alternatively, the Keeper prefers to supply photocopies of the title deeds, but this is an expensive and time-wasting procedure. The Keeper in a circular to the profession suggested that, if there is any likelihood of the property being sold before registration is complete, the applicants' solicitors should take photocopies of the deeds presented before sending them. This is not very satisfactory either. This problem has become less acute as registration delays have decreased.

In any event, when the sellers' solicitors do get the title, or photocopies of them, they are sent to the purchasers' solicitors, and in all other respects the transaction proceeds as a normal dealing of a registered interest (see ch **14**).

12.24 Armed with the land certificate and after a great deal of hard work, the conveyancer's job is now a great deal easier. In summary, it might be said that the main difference between this transaction and a sasine transaction is that there is a greater burden on the sellers' solicitors in a land registration transaction. If they do not ensure that the papers presented to the Keeper are in order, they will have to rectify these sooner or later, under the terms of the letter of obligation. The purchasers' solicitors are essentially the 'middlemen' between the sellers' solicitors and the Keeper.

Chapter 13

THE DEALING

'Once a property is registered, subsequent transfers are much simpler to effect, thus providing scope for lower conveyancing costs.'

(Keeper's Report 1993–94)

13.01 A dealing is a second registration and subsequent registrations of the same subjects, together with a transfer of a part of a registered holding (see ch **14**), securities, discharges or other deeds granted affecting the subjects, at any time after, or contemporaneously with, the first registration (as opposed to part of the subjects only).

13.02 The land registration forms referred to in this chapter are:

Form 2 (blue)	Application for registration of a dealing
Form 4	Inventory writs
Form 6	Land certificate
Form 12	Application for report over registered subjects (similar in purpose to form 10 in a first registration)
Form 13	Continuation of form 12 (similar to the form 11 in a first registration).

13.03 The missives are completed exactly as previously, in the compendious form, which includes the obligation for dealings in land:

'In exchange for the purchase price there will be delivered a duly executed disposition in favour of the purchasers and there will be exhibited or delivered to the purchasers

If the title to the Property is already registered in terms of the Act a valid marketable Land Certificate containing no exclusion of indemnity in terms of Section 12(2) of the Act with all necessary links in title evidencing the Seller's exclusive ownership of the Property together with (i) a form 12 report brought down to a date not more then three working days prior to the Date of Entry and showing no entries adverse to the Seller (the cost of the said report being the Seller's liability); and (ii) such documents and evidence as the

Keeper may require to enable the interests of the Purchaser to be registered in the Land Register as registered proprietor of the Property without exclusion of indemnity under Section 12(2).'

The sellers' obligation is thus to provide a valid disposition, a clear title in the form of a land certificate without restriction of indemnity, and clear searches in the shape of form 12 and 13 reports.

13.04 The land certificate is sent to the purchasers' solicitors together with:

(a)   a draft form 12 (not a form 10 which is applicable only prior to a first registration). Form 12 is a report over registered subjects;

(b)   the property enquiry certificate, affidavits, links in title etc that may be required;

(c)   draft letter of obligation;

(d)   the charge certificate and draft discharge (if applicable).

The title deeds, of course, need not be sent as they are replaced by the land certificate.

13.05 The purchasers' solicitors inspect the various sections of the land certificate. This is a matter of comparative simplicity, because the land certificate contains all relevant information that would have previously required to be extracted from the title deeds. Everything now is nicely printed in a central document, and you do not have to hunt through a mass of spidery handwriting, on crumbling paper, to discover the land obligations affecting the land. This makes it all the more imperative that you read the land certificate very carefully—there are no excuses available if you do not.

The purchasers' solicitors also draw up a draft disposition. This document is simplicity itself, because you need only state the postal address of the property and the number of the land certificate, which provide a sufficient description. You do not require a traditional conveyancing description, nor need you mention the deeds referred to for the land obligations they contain. The disposition thus becomes a very short document. It is perhaps paradoxical that as missives have got longer and longer, the disposition, which is still the primary deed of transfer, has shrunk to almost nothing.

The disposition need contain only the following:

(a)   narrative clause—granter, grantee, and consents, and the consideration;

(b)   dispositive clause—words of transference, destination of grantee, postal address of subjects, and land certificate number;

(c)   ancillary clauses—date of entry, and warrandice;

(d)   testing clause.

A sample disposition might therefore read:

> I, Allister McAllister (*design*) in consideration of the price of ONE HUNDRED AND FIFTY NINE THOUSAND NINE HUNDRED POUNDS (£159,900) paid to me by JAMES MEIKLE (*design*) HEREBY DISPONE to the said James Meikle and his executors and assignees ALL and WHOLE the subjects 3 Miller Drive, Newton Mearns, Renfrewshire, registered under Title Number   ; with entry on Thirty first October Two thousand and five; and I grant warrandice: IN WITNESS WHEREOF (*Testing Clause*)

Note: There is no reference to burdens, no parts and pertinents and no warrant of registration.

13.06 Form 2 (blue) and form 4 are filled up in accordance with the printed form of instructions. This form 2 is substantially the same as form 1 (pink) (see para **13.08**), and nothing further need be added in this respect. The draft form 2 is returned to the sellers' solicitors for approval together with:

(a)   draft letter of obligation, duly revised or approved;

(b)   draft discharge, duly revised or approved;

(c)   draft form 12 (application for report over registered subjects) duly approved;

(d)   the draft disposition;

(e)   the land certificate and other papers sent by the sellers' solicitors;

(f)   draft form 4 (inventory of writs).

13.07 The sellers' solicitors revise the disposition and return it to the purchasers' solicitors, who in turn have this document engrossed and send the typed deed and draft back to the sellers' solicitors for signature by their clients. The draft disposition is also returned for comparison purposes.

13.08 The sellers' solicitors send form 12 to Meadowbank House or George Square, as appropriate, for a form 12A report which they exhibit to the purchasers' solicitors. The latter should satisfy themselves as to the sufficiency of the report, as with an interim report in preregistration procedures. If there is a significant time gap between obtaining the form 12 report and settlement this report should be brought down to a date nearer settlement by sending a form 13 to the Keeper for a more current report, observing a three-working-day period.

13.09 Settlement duly takes place and the disposition, form 2 (duly signed), form 4, land certificate and such other papers as are required (see para **12.13**) are sent to the Keeper. In due course the land certificate is returned, with the purchasers' name inserted in the proprietorship section. The letter of obligation, which is in the terms following, is returned to the sellers' solicitors.

> With reference to the settlement of the above transaction today, we hereby (1) undertake to clear the records of any deed, decree or diligence—other than such as may be created by or against your clients—which may be recorded in the Personal Register in the period from*   to†   inclusive (or to the earlier registration of your clients' interest in the above subjects) and which would cause the Keeper to make an entry on, or qualify his indemnity in, the Land Certificate to be issued in respect of their interest; and (2) confirm that, to the best of my knowledge and belief, as at this date the answers to the questions numbered 1 to 8 in the draft form 2 adjusted with you (in so far as these answers relate to my client or to my client's interest in the above subjects) are still correct.
>
> * Insert date of certification of form 12 report, or if a form 13 report has been instructed, the date of certification of that report. If there is a significant time gap between obtaining the form 12 report and settlement, the report should be brought down to a date nearer settlement by sending a form 13 to the Keeper, who will return a more up-to-date report.
>
> †Insert a date 21 days (or such other period as may be agreed) after settlement.

If there is a discharge, then the third clause narrated at para **12.08** should be inserted.

13.10 The land certificate and other relevant papers are kept carefully either by the client, or as instructed by the client. If the land certificate is misplaced, an office copy can be obtained from the Land Register (see para **14.07**). If a land certificate is irretrievably lost, a substitute one can be requested from the Keeper. The Keeper is, however, reluctant to issue one unless satisfied by due inquiry and certification that every reasonable effort has been made to locate the land certificate, which accordingly can be viewed as irretrievably lost, as distinct from misplaced.

Chapter 14

SOME OTHER REGISTRATION PROCEDURES

'Transfer of Part. A sale, lease, assignation or gift of a part of a registered interest. A new build or the division of existing property would fall into this category. A typical Transfer of Part might contain two deeds—a transfer deed and a mortgage deed.'

(From Glossary to the Keeper's Report 2004–05)

Application for registration of a transfer of part of registered holding

14.01 This procedure is similar to that under ch **13** ('blue form' procedure) which refers to the transfer of an entire landholding. Thus if A bought a house in 1993, registered the title, and then resold the house in 1999, the proper procedure is the 'blue form' procedure. If, however, a builder bought a two-acre field in 1993, registered the title and then sold off the field in 20 plots with houses, then the appropriate procedure for each house purchase is 'yellow form'.

Again the yellow form is largely similar to the pink and blue forms (forms 1 and 2) and there are similar official notes for its completion. The transaction will follow the same course as a 'blue form' transaction (see ch **13**). The disposition, however, is slightly different, as the proper conveyancing description must be prepared for the plot of land being split off the larger, registered, subjects.

If you refer to the sample disposition of 3 Miller Drive, Newton Mearns, in paragraph **13.05**, and then assume that part of the (presumably large) garden is being sold for the building of a small house, then the disposition would read along these lines:

'I, JAMES MEIKLE (*design*) in consideration of the price of £X paid to me by JEREMIAH JONES (*design*) HEREBY DISPONE to the said JEREMIAH JONES and his executors and assignees ALL and WHOLE that plot of ground in the County of Renfrew containing one-tenth of an acre Imperial Measure* delineated and shown within the boundaries coloured red on the plan annexed to this Disposition;

being part of the subjects registered under Title number REN .
(*Thereafter insert any new land obligations relating to the new
holding: the date of entry; warrandice; stamp duty clause; and
testing clause.*)'

Note:

1   This should be metric. Say 962m²?

Considerable difficulties in registration are caused by builders lodging
estate plans with the Keeper, of proposed building estates, and then not
adhering to them. This is not done maliciously, it's just that it's easy to
draw a site plan in the office, but hard to mark out the site accurately on
the ground, and the boundary markers are often misplaced, or run over
by a bulldozer. The fence is then placed in a position different from the
site plan, and this is the boundary that is picked up by the Ordnance
Survey when it maps the site. For this reason the Keeper will take some
time to produce a land certificate, as it will be necessary to obtain an
Ordnance map of the estate, and to see that all the land certificates in the
estate are consistent with each other.

Securities over land under registration procedures

14.02 The first thing to point out is that if you frame a new security over
unregistered land without a transfer of ownership for valuable
consideration in an operational area, this security is registered in the
General Register of Sasines, which continues to run in parallel with the
Land Register. Thus, for example, if A has a loan from Y building society,
but discharges this and creates a new security in favour of Z building
society, then both of these deeds are recorded in the Register of Sasines.
Similarly if A dispones a half interest in his house to his spouse for 'love,
favour and affection', that is not a valuable consideration and the
disposition is recorded in the Register of Sasines. If, however, you buy a
house for valuable consideration in an operational area, you must
register the title (pink form) and register any simultaneous or subsequent
security, using the form 2.

   You will see that the notes for the blue form say that this form is to be
used among other things for:

(a)   standard security over the whole of the interest;

(b)   standard security over part of the interest in one registered title;

(c)   discharge of a registered standard security (a discharge of an unregistered security will be registered in the Register of Sasines).

The standard security is sent to the Land Register, with a form 2 and the land certificate, and any existing charge certificate (which is prepared by the Keeper to conform with form 7), and any other writs which may be necessary (such as links in title, but see explanatory notes for fuller details).

The charge thus created is entered into section C of the land certificate (the charges section). A charge certificate (form 7) is also prepared, which is made to agree with the title sheet. The certificate certifies that the lender is a registered creditor in the heritable security on the date of registration. The standard security is also annexed to the charge certificate. Where a limited company is creating the security, a copy of the certificate of registration of charge in the Register of Charges (which is mandatory under the Companies Act 1985, ss 410ff) should be sent to the Keeper within 21 days of the registration of the standard security in the Land or Sasine Registers. Where separate solicitors act for the lender, as is usually the case, a letter of obligation is given to them by the borrowers' solicitors in the following terms:

(a) First registration or purchase of registered interest with immediate grant of a standard security

'With reference to the settlement of the above transaction today, we hereby undertake to deliver to you within twelve (or as appropriate) months of this date a Land Certificate issued by the Keeper of the Registers of Scotland in favour of our clients, showing the interest of our clients as registered proprietors of the above subjects, which Land Certificate shall be unaffected by any deed, decree, or diligence—other than such as may be created by or against your clients—given effect to in the Land Register in the period from*   to†   inclusive, or to the earlier date of registration of 'your clients' Standard Security over the above subjects, and further will disclose the Standard Security granted in favour of your clients; provided that it is presented for registration in the Land Register within fourteen days of this date.'

* Date of certificate 10/11/12/13.

† Twenty-one days after settlement.

'Further we (1) undertake to exhibit to you along with the said Land Certificate all deeds, documents and other evidence which were submitted to the Keeper in support of our clients' application for registration of their interest as heritable proprietors of the above subjects; and (2) confirm that, to the best of our knowledge and belief, as at this date the answers to the Questions numbered 1 to 8 in the draft form 2 adjusted with you—in so far as these relate to our clients or to our clients' interest in the above subjects—are still correct.

We further undertake to exhibit to you within fourteen days of this date the duplicate form 4 lodged with our clients' application for registration with the Keeper's acknowledgment thereon.[1]

Yours faithfully,'

Note: Where purchasers' solicitors lodge the purchasers' application with the Keeper; or where there are two lenders, one of whom will present that application.

(b) Where borrower is already registered proprietor of the interest to be secured

'With reference to the settlement of the above loan transaction today, I hereby (1) undertake to clear the records of any deed, decree, or diligence—other than such as may be created by or against your clients—which may be recorded in the Personal Register or to which effect may be given in the Land Register in the period from* to† inclusive (or to the earlier date of registration of your clients' interest in the above subjects) which would cause the Keeper to make an entry on, or qualify his indemnity in, the Title Sheet relating to my clients' interest in the above subjects; and (2) confirm that, to the best of my knowledge and belief, as at this date the answers in Questions numbered 1 to 8 in the draft form 2 adjusted with you—in so far as these answers relate to your clients or to my clients' interest in the above subjects—are still current.

I further undertake on behalf of my clients, to deliver to you within two months a clear Search in the Companies and Charges Register in terms of the Memorandum adjusted between us down to the date occurring twenty-one days after today's date.

Yours faithfully,'

* Insert date of form 12/13 report.

† Insert date twenty-one days from settlement.

Form 5 – Application for noting an over-riding interest or for entry of discharge of an over-riding interest or of additional information

14.03 An over-riding interest is defined in s 28(1), which is the definition section (see para **12.13**). Reference should be made to this subsection, but the interest is generally an interest in the land concerned, enjoyed, by a third party, and not constituted by a deed recorded in the Register of Sasines. Some examples given are:

(a)   the interest of a lessee under a long lease, provided that the leasehold interest has not been registered in the Land Register. On registration the interest ceases to come within the definition of an over-riding interest;

(b)   the right of a crofter under the crofting legislation;

(c)   the dominant tenement in a servitude;

(d)   a public right of way.

Such over-riding interests are generally to be notified to the Keeper on the pink, blue or yellow forms as appropriate, and they are noted on the title sheet. Any interest or discharge of an interest not thus notified, should be notified on form 5, in terms of the Land Registration (Scotland) Rules 1980, r 13.

Form 8 – Application for land or charge certificate to be made to correspond with the title sheet (Land Registration (Scotland) Rules 1980, r 16)

14.04 Where a certificate has been in existence for some time, without any dealings taking place, the Keeper may be requested in a form 8 to bring it up to date with his title sheet.

Form 9 – Application for rectification of the Register (Land Registration (Scotland) Rules 1980, r 20)

14.05 Where it appears to any party that there is a mistake in the land certificate, however trivial or however fundamental, the Keeper may be requested to rectify this mistake. Reference is made to LR(S)A 1979, s 9.

Form 14 – Application to ascertain whether or not the subjects have been registered

14.06 This form may be used in the course of a normal transaction but it is more usual to obtain this information from the relevant part of the form 10 (see para **12.06**).

Form 15 – Application for an office copy of a land certificate or charge certificate or any part of one of these

14.07 An office copy of the title sheet kept by the Keeper may be requested if a land certificate is in constant use or is misplaced. The office copy may be of the whole title sheet or any part of it, or of any document referred to in it. If a land certificate is irretrievably lost, see the comments in para **13.10**.

Rectification of boundaries

14.08 When the boundary disclosed on the deed plan and the boundary shown on the Ordnance Survey plan do not agree, as will happen from time to time, an agreement in terms of LR(S)A 1979, s 19, may be signed by the parties concerned and registered. This agreement should also contain a plan showing the agreed boundary. The agreement is registered in the Land Register, in the case of registered interests, or in the Register of Sasines, in the case of unregistered interests (for style, see para **12.05**).

Legal and occupational extents of boundaries

14.09 Forms 1, 2 and 3 pose the question: 'Is there any person in possession or occupation of the subjects or any part of them adversely to the interest of the applicant?' The main purpose of this question is to elicit whether legal and occupational extents correspond, and whether there may be a competition in title with, eg a neighbour.

Long leases

14.10 The transfer of an interest which is held under a long lease is also a registerable event. A long lease is defined in LTR(S)A 1974, as being a lease over 20 years' duration. In practice, many commercial leases will be for a long period, because only by registering a lease may a security over that lease be created. The LTR(S)A 1974, s 12, also prohibited the creation of leases of residential property for a period exceeding 20 years. This is therefore a matter principally for commercial leases, although a pre-1974 residential long-lease may still be registered, if it hasn't been already. Similarly an assignation of a registered long-lease, or a sublease, or a subunderlease, or a standard security over any part of the property contained in the registered lease, may be registered.

If an unregistered long-lease has less than 20 years to run, but its length was originally over 20 years, it may still be registered. Thus (writing in 2006) a lease for a 25-year period, granted say in 1987, may still be registered although it has only a life of a further six years. The registration of a long leasehold interest proceeds in exactly the same way as the registration of a right of ownership, although one must apply for the registration of an assignation etc, and not of a disposition.

Obtaining guidance from the Keeper

14.11 The Keeper and his staff are very helpful, and are willing to discuss any problems that you may have. If it is a general question, ask for the customer service centres at 68 Queen Street,Edinburgh or George Square, Glasgow, but if it is a specific question, ask for the appropriate county register, and specify the title number, or the property involved. The telephone numbers are: Meadowbank House, tel: 0131 659 6111; 68 Queen Street, tel: 0845 607 0161 and George Square, tel: 0141 306 4424. See also the Registers of Scotland website, which contains a lot of useful information: www.ros.gov.uk.

In return the legal profession owe consideration to the Keeper's staff. In particular, you should:

(a) Not bombard the Keeper with stupid or hypothetical questions. The story goes that the stupidest question ever asked was 'does a title in Paisley have to be registered?'

(b) Fill in the correct forms carefully and accurately. Do not forget to sign applications for reports and registration. Check all writs carefully before sending them—that they are properly signed and completed, and that the testing clauses are in order.

(c) Send duplicates of forms where these are specified.

(d) Check that you have up-to-date forms or use the eforms online service.

(e) Obtain quick copies of deeds that you do not have. Do not expect the Land Register to obtain these itself, just because it is in the same building as the Register of Sasines. It will not, as this would impose an intolerable extra workload. Keep copies on file of all important deeds sent to the register, in case a resale is necessary before the land certificate is sent.

(f) Make sure that if you have a note that the Keeper has already seen a common title in connection with another earlier application, quote that title number to the Keeper.

(g)   Pay fee notes promptly. Since the passing of the Land Registers (Scotland) Act 1995 it is important to remember to send a cheque for registration dues with the application.

Part Three
Transfers of Special Subjects

Chapter 15

TRANSFERS OF SUPERIORITIES—A HISTORICAL NOTE

'The feudal system, that is to say the entire system whereby land is held by a vassal on perpetual tenure from a superior is, on the appointed day, abolished.'

(Abolition of Feudal Tenure (Scotland) Act 2000; appointed day 28 November 2004)

15.01 The remarkable AFT(S)A 2000 completely abolished the feudal system with effect from 28 November 2004 and as a result we no longer have to concern ourselves with such mediaeval horrors as:

- *Dominium plenum, dominium directum* and *dominium utile*.
- Feu charters, feu dispositions, feu contracts, and charters of novodamus.
- Feu duties, whether *cumulo*, allocated or unallocated, ground annuals, teinds, skat, and standard charge. These charges have to be extinguished if the recipient took the necessary steps to request repayment, but arrears no longer attach themselves to the property.
- The demeaning nomenclatures of superior, feuar and, especially, vassal.
- Thirlage, which is the duty of the vassal to have corn ground at the local mill. This had long fallen into disuse, but had never been formally abolished.
- The rights of a superior to enforce real burdens, or, as it had become in modern times, to extract a payment from feuar for waiving the terms of the real burden. A former superior may enforce certain real burdens which have been kept alive by recording a notice or by the terms of the AFT(S)A 2000 provided that such burdens relate to common parts of a tenement or common recreation areas, facility burdens, amenity burdens, rights of pre-emption and redemption, service burdens conservation and maritime burdens.

- The superior's grossly disproportionate remedy of irritancy was abolished by the AFT(S)A 2000 with effect from 9 June 2000.

15.02 It follows that any comments on the creation, transfer and discharge of superiorities are superfluous. The only thing to note is that you may come across a disposition of the superiority in pre-registration titles. You may ignore it. The problem is distinguishing between it and a normal disposition. The only guaranteed way is by looking at the warrandice clause—if it grants warrandice but excludes from the warrandice all feu rights in the land that have been granted, then it is a superiority disposition.

Chapter 16

SALES AND PURCHASES OF TENEMENT PROPERTY

> 'Billy was born on 24 November 1942, right next to that alcove on the kitchen floor, all 11lb of him plopping out on to freezing linoleum. His family's living arrangements were similar to those of thousands of other inhabitants of Glasgow, a city that had come to be defined by row upon row of late 19th-century apartment buildings known as "the tenements". The Dover Street flat had only two rooms: a kitchen-living room, with a niche where the children slept, and another room for their parents. The family bathed in the kitchen sink and there was no hot water.'
>
> *(Pamela Stephenson on Billy Connelly's early years in 'Billy')*

16.01 As has been discussed above, there have been numerous legislative changes since the last edition, particularly on account of the Scottish Executive's desire radically to reform Scottish property law. The final part of the Executive's land reform package was root and branch reform of the law of the tenement, which was largely based on common law and considered to be arcane and anomalous.

The Tenements (Scotland) Act 2004 (in this chapter, the 'Act') implements the majority of the recommendations of the Scottish Law Commission Report on the Law of the Tenement (Scot Law Comm, no 162), published on 29 March 1998 (available online at www.scotlawcom.gov.uk) and thus, unlike some of its cousins, had a fairly unremarkable journey through the legislative process. The Act, with the exception of s 18 (obligation of the owner to insure), came into force on the 'Big Bang' for Scottish Property Law, 28 November 2004— which the Executive rather unimaginatively hailed as 'the Appointed Day'.

16.02 Previous editions of this book note that, in relation to the sale of a 'traditional' tenement flat, the disposition in favour of the purchasers would include:

(a) the ownership of the flat itself; and
(b) a fractional right to the common parts of the larger tenement building, typically including: the solum, foundations, outside

walls, gables, roof, attic, chimneyheads (but not the pots), the entrance, close, staircase, hatchway to the roof, rhones, gutters, all pipes, wires and sewers, the back garden ground and the walls surrounding it, the coal cellars and the street back lane and pavement in so far as not maintained by the council. In more modern buildings, these common parts may be extended to such common property as landscaped gardens, car-parking areas, door-entry systems, lifts and television aerials and satellite dishes.

The ownership and management of the common parts of more modern developments would typically be set out in a deed of conditions by the developer recorded in the Register of Sasines or registered in the Land Register. However, in the traditional style tenement building, the fractional ownership of common parts and the real burdens should have been detailed at length in every single disposition of every single flat to ensure that the real burdens are mutually enforceable by each of the proprietors. The purchasing solicitor would have to examine carefully the title to every flat in the development to ensure that the titles conform. This creates an enormous amount of repetitive work and does not always result in uniformity.

16.03 In cases where the title was silent or unclear on the respective ownerships or burdens, the common law developed minimum default provisions. It is worth noting that the provisions of the Act are in effect a codification of the previous common law to clarify the law on this subject. However, it is important to realise the limitations of the Act— where the titles specify either the extent of the pertinents, the common parts or the rules for the management of the tenement, then provisions in the titles should prevail in each case.

16.04 The scope of the Act encapsulates more buildings than would be imagined by the traditional understanding of what constitutes a tenement building. The Act defines a tenement as a building or a part of a building which comprises two or more related flats, at least two of which are, or are designed to be, in separate ownership and are divided from each other horizontally. In determining whether flats are related, regard shall be had to the title of the tenement and any tenement burdens. The Executive's explanatory note to the Act states that most tenements are residential blocks, but also that office blocks or subdivided houses will also fall within the definition.

The Act overrides the traditional understanding of a flat as a particular type of Victorian flatted dwellinghouse as described by

Pamela Stephenson above—and indeed the dictionary definition of a 'set of rooms, usually on one floor, used as a residence' (*Oxford English Reference Dictionary*). The statutory definition contained in s 29 of the Act provides that a flat includes any premises whether or not used or intended to be used for residential purposes or on the one floor.

16.05 The Act restates the common law in relation to the boundaries of the flats, which make default provisions in the event that the titles do not provide otherwise. In particular:

- each flat will own up to mid-point of the walls;
- a structure serving one flat only will belong to that flat (eg a bin store);
- the bottom flat will own the solum and the top flat will own the roof. A close (passage, stairs and landings) includes the solum and roof;
- the airspace above the tenement is owned by the owner(s) of the solum. In the titles this is likely to be common property, whereas in the statutory scheme it will belong to the owner of the ground floor flat; and
- where there is a pitched roof, the triangle of airspace between the extent of the actual slope of the roof and the imaginary horizontal and vertical lines from the highest and widest points of the building will belong to the owner of the top floor flat.

16.06 In the same way, the Act makes default provisions for common property or pertinents of the tenement. A close or a lift will be owned only by the owners who make use of them for access. Any land (other than the solum, a path, outside stair or other access) shall belong to the ground floor flat nearest to it. Any other pertinents (such as, for example, a path, outside stair, fire escape, rhone, pipe, flue, conduit, cable, tank or chimney stack) will be owned by the flat they serve or, if serving more than one, equally among them. The only exception to the latter rule is a chimney stack, which shall be determined in direct accordance with the ratio which the number of flues serving it in the stack bears to the total number of flues in the stack.

It should be remembered that, just as with the common law, if there is a gap in provision in the titles, then the statutory scheme will apply. Thus, if the titles make provision for the common parts of a tenement, but is silent on, for example, the chimney stack, then the statutory provisions will apply.

16.07 Many tenement titles make detailed provisions for the management and factoring of the common parts. Where this is not the case, the Act contains a default tenement management scheme (TMS). It is not proposed to consider the TMS in any detail—it forms Sch 1 to the Act, which can be downloaded from the Office of Public Sector Information (the publisher formerly known as HMSO).[1] Briefly the TMS allows owners of a tenement to make decisions by a majority vote, where the title deeds are silent on matters of decision-making. This is a huge improvement on the previous law, where it could have been impossible to make decisions on the maintenance and management of the tenement because the titles were silent on such matters and every owner had to agree. The TMS also introduces the new concept of scheme property, which comprises the main parts of a tenement that are so fundamental to the building as a whole that they should be managed and maintained in accordance with the management scheme of the tenement. The concept of scheme property will not, however, affect the ownership of the different parts of the building which remains unchanged. The TMS also contains default provisions on emergency repairs and the apportionment of costs.

Note: (1) http://www.opsi.gov.uk/legislation/scotland/acts2004/40011—a.htm#2.

16.08 The previous law of common interest in the solum and the roof is abolished, but is then promptly restated in statutory form as the right of support and shelter. The positive obligation is confined to the tenement building itself and does not include the solum or any land pertaining to the building. The obligation would not extend to a building that is beyond economic repair. Any owner (including a *pro indiviso* owner) can enforce the duty if he or she is, or would be, directly affected by the breach of the duty and a *pro indiviso* owner has a complimentary power to maintain the part of the building affected by the obligation without the need for the consent of co-owners. The negative obligation is framed more broadly: owners *and occupiers* are to refrain from interfering with the right to support or shelter, which also covers the former common interest right to light and covers the whole tenement, *including* the surrounding ground. Only owners may enforce the prohibition—an occupier, although bound, has no complimentary right to enforce the prohibition.

The right to support and shelter is so important that a minority (even one *pro indiviso* owner) is able to carry out works for support or shelter where a majority cannot be assembled, and to treat it as a TMS cost in the same way as if authorised by a scheme decision. This provision removes the frustrations of the previous law. That owner is then able to recover the cost of the repairs from remaining owners in equal shares as if the works had been carried out in pursuance of a scheme decision.

16.09 Section 17 of the Act creates a statutory right of access over other flats in the tenement on giving reasonable notice for the purposes of maintenance, inspection and also to determine whether the owner of the flat is complying with the right of support and shelter. An owner or occupier may refuse only if it is reasonable to do so. Reasonable notice may be dispensed with in cases of urgency.

There is also a statutory obligation to have buildings insurance for risks to be prescribed by the Scottish Ministers by order, whether by individual policies, or, more likely, by a common insurance policy covering the whole building.

An owner may lead pipes or other necessary service media through the tenement so long as it is not through, or attached to, another owner's flat.

16.10 If you are involved in the preparation of a deed of conditions, bear in mind that it is now competent to create servitudes when the benefited and burdened properties are in the same ownership. A good example of a style post-feudal deed of conditions can be found on the Property Standardisation Group website (www.psglegal.co.uk). The PSG are a bunch of experienced conveyancers, generally with the large blue chip firms, who have got together with the laudable idea of trying to streamline transactions and improve the quality of documentation by providing styles free to the profession. You should also liaise closely with the first factors to ensure that the provisions of your deed of conditions will suit them.

Chapter 17

PURCHASING OF PUBLIC SECTOR HOUSING

'Heseltine has said he regards offering council tenants the right to buy their homes as one of his greatest political achievements. "That's quite true." But hasn't that policy caused great problems for the inner cities? "I wholly reject that as a concept. Most of those council tenants were paying rent the same as mortgages, but they had nothing to show for it. I saw them as economically disenfranchised. I wanted the proceeds from the sales to go into capital projects. That's what went wrong: the money went into current expenditure, which is not what I had in mind at all."'

(Lord Heseltine in an interview with The Guardian, 11 March 2006)

17.01 A right for tenants to purchase the house they are occupying was given by the Tenants' Rights etc (Scotland) Act 1980 as amended by the Tenants' Rights etc (Scotland) Amendment Act 1984. This legislation has been consolidated in the Housing (Scotland) Act 1987, Pt III (ss 44–84). Prior to 1980, however, some local authorities were prepared to sell their housing stock to tenants voluntarily, and such sales proceeded in the manner already outlined, for private sales, in prior chapters. Not all local authorities by any means were prepared to do this, and the main 1980 Act introduced a right for the tenant to buy, whether the local authority consented or not. The amending Acts merely circumvented certain difficulties that had arisen from the objection of recalcitrant councils.

The 1987 Act also introduced a statutory procedure for sales under the Act, and this was substantially reworked by the Scottish Executive in the Housing (Scotland) Act 2001.

17.02 The procedure is fully detailed in the Housing (Scotland) Act 1987, which should be carefully studied before undertaking a transaction in this area. The 1987 Act has been so heavily amended by the 2001 Act that the practitioner should ensure that the version referred to has been fully updated. The application to purchase must be made on an official form which is available from the local authority concerned, with *'Notes for Guidance to Tenants on the Completion of the Application'*. A helpful booklet

'Your Right to Buy Your Home' is also available from Scottish Executive website at www.scotland.gov.uk/Publications/2002/08/15280/10372.

17.03 Tenants who have occupied a publicly provided house on a [unmodernised] secure tenancy for at least two years have a right to purchase such housing provided by:

  (a)   a local authority council, under the Local Government etc (Scotland) Act 1994, or as a successor to the New Town development corporations;

  (b)   Communities Scotland, formerly Scottish Homes;

  (c)   housing corporation;

  (d)   a registered social landlord, which in many cases began taking over the responsibilities from local councils from 2002.

Also included are a variety of other authorities, the most important being, a housing co-operative, a police authority, a fire authority, the prison service, the armed forces, a health board, the Forestry Commission, a State hospital, the Commissioners of Northern Lighthouses, HM Coastguard, the United Kingdom Atomic Energy Authority, the Ministry of Defence, and any other authority prescribed by the Secretary of State by order.

If the tenancy is a Scottish secure tenancy (commenced after 30 September 2002) tenants who have occupied the house for at least five years have a right to purchase housing provided by a local authority (including housing management co-operatives, a registered social landlord (RSL), a water authority or any other authority prescribed by the Scottish Ministers by Order).

17.04 Tenants can exercise the right to buy together with one or more members of their family, provided that the family members are at least 18 and have occupied the house as their only or principal home for a continuous period of at least six months before the application. The definition of a family member has been extended by the 2001 Act to include same sex couples.

17.05 Houses which are subject, not to a tenancy agreement, but a service agreement requiring the occupier to occupy the house for the better performance of the occupier's duties, and which must be surrendered on termination of the employment (eg houses in parks) are not included, as there is no secure tenancy (see *Naylor v Glasgow District Council* 1982 LTS/TB/129). Further a house which is provided with certain services (eg sheltered housing for the elderly or infirm) is not susceptible to purchase in terms of the 1987 Act.

17.06 The tenant who is qualified to purchase should first complete the official application and send it to the authority concerned by recorded delivery, keeping a copy. Where a joint tenancy exists and not all tenants wish to exercise their right, they must sign the application form as consentors. The consent of any spouse is also required, whether a tenant or not. Non-purchasing tenants should give careful consideration to their consent as the tenancy will lapse on the purchase being completed, and they may end up homeless. When the form is received the authority will arrange for the house to be valued by the district valuer, who is the official government valuer for a number of such purposes including assessment of gross annual values and valuation for capital gains tax. Alternatively the valuation can be made by another valuer, nominated by the landlord and accepted by the tenant, so the valuer should be informed of any such improvements at the time of inspection.

17.07 The authority concerned should issue an offer to sell within two months of the application, or a notice of refusal if it considers the applicant not to be qualified to purchase for any reason (eg if it is not a secure tenancy, or is sheltered housing, is specially designed for use by the elderly, or if it is required by an islands council for educational purposes). The 2001 Act gives authorities the right to reject an application based on the following: a ten year limitation for RSLs; the right to buy for SST tenants has been suspended by Ministerial designation of an area as a 'pressured area'; arrears of rent or council tax; or the authority is recovering possession on any of the conduct grounds set out in paras 1–7 of Sch 2of the 2001 Act. A notice of refusal may be referred to the Lands Tribunal by a disgruntled applicant, and the tribunal may order the authority to make the offer if it is satisfied that this should be done.

17.08 The offer to sell should then be checked to see that it contains the subjects intended. The authority should sell all rights possessed by (see *Annott v Midlothian District Council* 1982 LTS/TR/191). The offer should also stipulate the valuation made, the discount applied to the valuation, and the price thus reached. Further the offer may contain conditions stipulated by the authority. Any of these matters can be referred to the Lands Tribunal. For examples of decisions on unreasonable conditions, see *Clark v Shetland Islands Council* (1981 LTS/TR/599, 598, 597, 594, all summarised in 1984 JLSS 469), and *McLeod v Ross and Cromarty District Council* (1981 LTS/TB/150).

17.09 The time limits here are quite crucial. If the tenant is satisfied with the offer, an acceptance should be sent within two months. If the tenant needs a loan from the selling authority, the time limit in that case is only one month. If the authority will not alter conditions to which the applicant objects, the applicant may refer the matter to the Lands Tribunal, the time allowed being one month, starting from a date *one month* after the tenant wrote to the authority asking it to amend the offer to sell.

17.10 If the authority does not issue an offer to sell within two months of the application to buy, the matter may be referred to the Lands Tribunal which will investigate the matter, and which may, in the last resort, issue an offer on behalf of the defaulting authority.

17.11 When the valuation of the house has been agreed, a discount is then deducted in respect of the application being made to purchase by a secure tenant. It is, incidentally, a general principle that a tenanted house should be sold at a discount, because vacant possession can be given to no one but the tenant. The basic discount after two years' occupation is 32% and the discount rises by 1% for every year's tenancy to a maximum of 60%. In the authority's discretion a period of occupation prior to a break of between 12 and 24 months may be taken into account. The reason for the break should be stated on the application.

In the case of a flat, the basic discount is 44% of the value, rising by 2% each year to a maximum of 70%. A flat is defined as 'a separate and self-contained set of premises whether or not on the same floor, forming part of a building from some other part of which it is divided horizontally'. This definition includes the traditional tenement and 'four-in-a-block' type of houses, as well as high-rise flats. If the tenant only gained the right to buy on or after 30 September 2002, then they can, subject to qualifying, buy after five years' occupation. The discount starts at 20% and rises by 1% each year for all house types to a maximum of 35% of the market value or £15,000 whichever is the lower.

17.12 When agreement has been reached, and missives concluded, the transaction then proceeds, as previously outlined, to settlement. The applicant has a recorded title and may sell at any time thereafter. However, there is a financial penalty if a sale is made within three years of purchase. If a sale is made within one year of purchase, all discount is refundable, and this figure then decreases by 33 1/3% a year until it reaches nil at the end of the third year. The purchaser grants a standard security over the property in favour of the authority for the amount of the discount plus interest, which security ranks second to any security granted by the purchaser in respect of a loan to purchase the property. If the purchaser then defaults on repayment of the discount, or part of it, the authority may then enforce its security. On the expiry of the three-year period, it is not necessary to record a discharge of the security, as the security is discharged by operation of statute. If the owners insist on receiving a discharge, they will be expected to pay the legal discharge fee of the council.

17.13 If the tenant requires a loan to purchase, application to lending institutions should be made as in the normal case, but if two refusals are received, the authority is under an obligation to provide a loan based on the applicant's income and other circumstances. Please remember that in these circumstances there is only one month for acceptance of the offer to sell (see para **17.09**). Applications for loans therefore should be made as soon as the application to purchase is submitted, for time is very tight. As mentioned in paragraph **17.12**, the standard security in favour of the lender has the first ranking. Finally, if the authority does not offer a loan sufficient for the purchase to be made, the tenant may on payment of £100 reserve an option to purchase the house at the price currently fixed at any time within two years of the date of the original application to purchase.

17.14 In the past, there have been many complaints about long delays in processing applications, which were caused by a variety of reasons: title difficulties, in many cases councils had never completed the conveyancing formalities after compulsory purchase of land for building, staff shortages, and huge numbers of applications. This, fortunately, has settled down now.

17.15 When a house which was bought from a public authority in this manner is resold, the procedure is exactly the same as with any other house. If the house is disposed of within three years of its acquisition date, however, it is necessary to repay the discount (or part of it) and obtain a discharge of the standard security signed to protect the discount (see para **17.12**). Acquisition and disposal are defined respectively as the date on which the purchaser and the council complete missives.

17.16 While this scheme has proved to be very attractive to many, there are certain matters to be made clear to a potential purchaser. The new owner, in particular, will become responsible for repairs and insurance of the property, and should be advised of this new liability. In the case of high-rise flats particularly, repairs may be higher than expected, as recladding of the building or expensive lift repairs may be needed. While the former tenant pays only a small proportion of the account, it may nonetheless be a lot of money in real terms.

Further, many local authority houses were built of suspect materials and by unsatisfactory methods, which might give rise to a high level of repairs. The valuer's report will issue a warning where this is the case, and the purchaser must then decide whether to proceed or not.

17.17 In the case of *Clydebank District Council v Keeper of the Land Register* (1992 LTS/LR/1) the Lands Tribunal found that in terms of H(S)A 1987, ss 72 and 73, the sale of the subjects by an executor terminated the liability to repay to the council a proportion of the statutory discount on the purchase price of a house, and that the Keeper had acted correctly in cancelling the entry in the Land Register relating to the standard security for the amount of the discount. The missives had been concluded on 13 August 1990, the owner died in February 1991, and the disposition was registered on 5 November 1991.

17.18 Where elderly people are the tenants, they will be helped sometimes by younger relatives. This is, of course, in order, but the position of the younger relatives must be protected. Some authorities will allow the young relatives to appear on the deeds, in the destination clause, and you should enquire if this is possible. If not, the older persons should make wills in favour of the younger relatives, to protect their position against other relatives, with preferential or equal claims on the estates, who have not been involved in the purchase. The only trouble with that plan is that wills are revocable, and it may be preferable to set up a trust with the older persons as liferenters and the younger relatives as fiars. In addition the older persons can grant a standard security over the property to the younger relatives, to protect their interest. This standard security would rank third, behind: (1) a security to a commercial lender; (2) the discount security, for three years. The solicitor should be expected to give the best advice as to which course should be followed. Certainly there is a probable cause of action if the interests of the younger relatives are not protected in some way.

17.19 It was felt that tenants were getting an over-fair bargain under the Right to Buy scheme, and accordingly the Housing (Scotland) Act 2001 was enacted to make purchase rather harder. It provided that for leases entered into before 30 September 2002, the conditions of sale and the discounts available would remain as stated above. In leases entered into after that date the following conditions would apply:

1. The qualifying period of occupancy would be five years, as opposed to the former two years.
2. The discounts available were reduced to: 5–9 years occupancy, houses 22%, flats 24%; 10–14 years occupancy 25% and 29%; 15–19 years occupancy—30% and 34%; 20 years and over—35%. The maximum discount in all cases is £15,000.
3. There must be no arrears of rent or Council Tax.

A new power is given to local authorities to declare that public housing in pressured areas, to withhold housing from sale. An example of a pressured area in St Andrews where the public housing stock has virtually all been sold, and the demand for housing remains high.

Chapter 18

SALE AND PURCHASE OF BUSINESS

'How the price (360p a share) was finally arrived at reflects precious little credit on the Low board and its advisers . . . it is not the job of any board to recommend to its shareholders one opening offer (225p a share) which, within weeks, proves to be £100m less than that bidder is actually willing to pay for the business.'

(Alf Young, The Herald (discussing the sale of Wm Low to Tesco in 1994))

18.01 We think that we should first of all explain what this chapter sets out to do, and what it does not set out to do. We have reproduced at the end of the chapter a simple offer for a small retail business. Our main effort will be to show that such a business is simply a collection of assets, bound together by the goodwill of the business, and that the sale of the business is really only a transfer of the various assets, with certain safeguards built in for the purchasers.

We shall ignore businesses run as limited companies, for such organisations are outwith the scope of this subject. We shall merely leave the topic with the suggestion that the differences between a small retail business and, say, British Petroleum, is one of scale. We know that he shall be accused of over-simplification, but both businesses are collections of assets, and whereas the small business's transport is represented by one bicycle, BP's transport is represented by, say, a hundred super tankers, five hundred petrol tankers, ten thousand cars, and so on. When either business is sold, these assets are valued and the total forms part of the price to be paid by the intending purchasers.

18.02 The assets of a business are: heritable property (whether owned or leased), stock-in-trade, trade fittings and fixtures, work-in-progress (but not particularly with retail businesses), money owing, vehicles, trade name, trade marks, copyrights, patents etc, and any licences of franchises owned by the business. All of these assets are wrapped up in the goodwill of the business. The liabilities of the business, which are deducted from the valuation of the assets, are basically money owing to suppliers, employees, pension fund, the taxman, and so on. And lastly, we have the people of the business, who are probably an asset in a good business and a liability in a bad business, but not always so.

Heritable property

18.03 The property of the business is valued by a surveyor, and the offer should make the usual stipulations for the purchase of heritage; that is date of entry, clauses dealing with heritable and moveable property, clauses dealing with property enquiry certificates and outstanding notices, and so on. It should be remembered that there are certain statutory requirements for commercial property, particularly the Health and Safety at Work Acts, and the offer should stipulate that all requirements under these Acts have been met, particularly fire requirements, otherwise the purchasers may be faced with making extremely expensive alterations. Where the property is leasehold, the lease will be valued bearing in mind, among others, these considerations: (a) remaining life of the lease; (b) rent being charged; (c) frequency of rent reviews and the terms of the rent review clause; (d) use permitted by the lease; (e) planning position of the property; (f) restrictions of assigning and subletting; (g) general fairness of the lease to the tenant; and (h) location and trading prospects of the site.

Precaution should be taken that there are no outstanding liabilities to the landlord for, eg rent and dilapidations of the property (the cost of restoring the property to the condition it was in when it was first let). As well as receiving permission from the landlord for the assignation of the lease or sublet, a certificate should also be received from the landlord confirming that there are no outstanding liabilities, and that the proposed use of the property is approved.

Check that the property is not opted for tax with HM Revenue and Customs. If it is, and your offer does not provide that the price is VAT inclusive, your clients will get a nasty shock and will invariably blame you. There are different rules if the sale is a transfer of a going concern (T40) and you advise your client to speak to his accountant about this. You must make it clear in your letter of engagement that you are not providing tax advice or a claim may result.

Stock-in-trade

18.04 This is valued, at cost except in the case of old or slow-moving stock, by agreement of the parties. If so wished, a valuation can be made by a person specialising in stocktaking, with the account being divided equally between the parties. The stocktaking should obviously be done as near to the date of sale as possible, at a quiet time, perhaps in the evening or on a Sunday afternoon.

Trade fittings and fixtures

18.05 These include counters, scales, cash registers etc. Some of these items are expensive to buy and may be on hire purchase or other credit arrangement. This should be clarified in the offer to buy, and if the item is owned by a finance company, arrangements for the transfer of the item should be made subject to the amounts still payable under the contract. It should be carefully noted that VAT is payable on secondhand trade fittings and fixtures. Thus, if a price is quoted for these, without mention of VAT, it will be taken to mean that the price is VAT inclusive. With VAT at 17½% the VAT content is 7/47ths of the total. The purchasers should therefore get a receipt from the sellers showing the VAT content, in order that they may claim this as an input on their own return.

The purchasers of a business relying largely on internet or telephone orders, will also want to acquire the website and telephone number(s), and to make sure that the telephone company has not withdrawn the number, as happened with Atlantic Telecom, which went into liquidation, and withdrew all its numbers.

It is as well that the offer shall contain a fairly tight condition about the working order of any central-heating, refrigeration, air-conditioning or other mechanical plant, and the liability of the sellers to pay for any repairs. To avoid bad feeling, the purchasers should inspect the mechanical equipment concerned, and arrange for the sellers to pay for any necessary repairs, before parting with any money. The contractual position should, however, also be preserved.

Work-in-progress

18.06 This refers particularly to business people like solicitors or builders who do work and get paid at the end of that work. If the business is transferred while the work is continuing, a valuation should be made of the work done but not yet paid for, and that forms an asset of the business.

Money owing to the business

18.07 The debts owing to the business are generally retained in the ownership of the sellers, who collect them as and when they can. If the sellers are emigrating or retiring, however, this may not be appropriate, and the purchasers may take these over. The purchasers should then pay the sellers for this asset, and it should be remembered that the debts should be assigned to the purchasers, and the assignation intimated to each debtor, both to satisfy the technical rule that 'the right of a creditor in a debt is fully transferred by an assignation followed by an intimation' (Gloag *Law of Contract* (2nd edn, Caledonian Books, 1929) p 74) and to let the debtor know who the creditors are. The intimation can simply be printed on the account when it is rendered. A simple statement requesting the debtor to pay the account to the assignee should suffice.

Similarly the purchasers of a business, who take over the collection of the debts, can have the benefit (or liability) of any court actions in which their predecessors were engaged, or the benefit of any court decrees that they hold. There is a businessman in Edinburgh who specialises in buying causes of action from people, and then fighting the cases himself. This is a simple way around the monopoly of lawyers to appear in court cases.

The valuation of the debts of the business should reflect the likely outcome of the cases they have started.

Vehicles

18.08 Vehicles being taken over are valued at date of sale, by reference to *Glass's Guide*, a trade publication containing current values. These figures will probably have to be obtained through someone in the motor trade. Again care must be taken to ensure that there is no outstanding debt on these vehicles, or alternatively that the debt is allowed for in the price.

Trade name

18.09 Some trade names are beyond value and form a very valuable part of the business; others are of very doubtful value, and may be changed on takeover. Where an individual or partnership or limited company trades under a name that is not its own, details of the ownership of the trade names must be disclosed on letterheads and by a notice displayed in the place of business. This provision of the Business Names Act 1985 (formerly Companies Act 1981, ss 28–30) replaces the provisions of the Registration of Business Names Act 1916, which provided for such names to be registered in the Register of Business Names. That useful register is now discontinued, although an unofficial register is kept privately.

It should be noted that neither the old nor the new register conferred any right of ownership in a name, as was mistakenly thought. The old register was in fact designed to reveal the name of enemy aliens who might be trading under assumed names when anti-German feeling was at its height during the First World War. Unchallenged ownership of a trade name can only be acquired by use, and both registers provide the useful information as to when a name was first used.

A trend emerged in the 1980s for companies to take over other companies whose principal assets are their strong brand names (eg Rowntree Mackintosh, which was in turn taken over by Nestlé—the company had some very strong brand names, eg Smarties, KitKat and Polo). This led to some companies placing a valuation on their brand names in their balance sheet (eg Guinness). There is always the possibility that supermarket chains will introduce 'own brand' versions of popular goods, at a lower price than the original, which they will then market carefully to the detriment of the original. Often such own brand goods bear a startling resemblance to the original. In that case all the brand owner can do is to rely on the courts enforcing the law of 'passing off'—which is where the copy goods are similar enough to the original— see Penguin and Puffin biscuits and the various 'cola wars' between Sainsbury's and Coca Cola.

Intellectual property

18.10 A small retail business is unlikely to own any patents, designs, trade marks or copyrights, but a small electronics business, for example, might own all four, and be completely dependent on their existence. For example, Dyson own the patent of the method for their cyclonic cleaner, the design of the machine, the copyright of the packaging and instruction manual, and the trade mark of the name. They protect their intellectual property rigorously, as a number of cases against competitors have shown.

It is important, therefore, to check (a) that the sellers own the right to the particular intellectual property, (b) that the rights are validly registered, (c) their remaining years of life and the date of renewal in the case of a trade or service mark, (d) that they are properly assigned and intimated, in the case of trade marks and patents, to the appropriate registrar. The specialist advice of a chartered patent agent should probably be sought, as a mistake in this direction could be catastrophic. In addition intellectual property in overseas countries should be protected as well.

Licences and franchises

18.11 Many businesses depend almost entirely on a licence or franchise for their existence. There is little point in buying the business unless you can be sure the licence or franchise can be transferred to the purchasers. The purchasers may, therefore, wish to insert a suspensive condition making the purchase dependent on getting a transfer of the licence or franchise. The commonest example of the former is a hotel or shop licensed to sell alcohol, and of the latter, a business which owns a franchise outlet of one of the franchise companies (eg McDonalds, Dyno-Rod, Pronuptia, Holiday Inns etc).

An application for transfer of licence must be made to the licensing board set up by each council under the Licensing (Scotland) Act 1976. These boards meet quarterly, and an application for transfer must be submitted before the last date for submission, which date is intimated in the local press (usually a month before the board meets). The offer should therefore, unless circumstances dictate otherwise, be suspended in action until a day or two after the next licensing board meeting, or any adjournment of it (*Tarditi v Drummond* 1989 SLT 554).

If there are to be objections, which are fairly rare to transfers unless the transferee is of doubtful character, the purchasers will be told well in advance, and are given a chance to meet the objections. If no such indications are received, the parties can get on with arranging the formalities of the licence being transferred.

The purchase of a business which depends on a franchise will depend on the consent of the franchisers, who will probably prove extremely fussy about the ability of the purchasers to run the business, and pay for the supplies. Please remember that the franchisers, and other franchisees, will lose heavily if one of the franchises is badly run, especially in the case of a food shop.

Various other activities require a licence, eg road haulage, post offices, bookmakers and so on. The rules for the transfer of these licences are quite complicated, and specialist advice should probably be sought. In addition the Civic Government (Scotland) Act 1982 provides that metal dealers must have a licence. The same Act also provides that each council may adopt a licensing system for any of the following activities: the operation of taxis and private hire-cars, secondhand dealing, boat hire, street trading, private markets, operation of places of entertainment, late-hours catering, window cleaning, and sex shops. Requirements vary widely from area to area and enquiries should be made of the appropriate council when dealing in any of these areas.

Incidentally, if you think that our spelling is a bit variable we would refer you to Bill Bryson *Troublesome Words*: 'Licence, License. In British usage the first is the noun, the second the verb—"a licence to sell wines" but "licensed premises". In America "license" is preferred for both noun and verb.'

Franchises are licences privately granted authorising the licensee to use the business style of the licensor. See articles by the author on the topic in the Scottish Law Gazette, March 1985, p 7 and June 1986. Note the case under Art 85 of the Treaty of Rome where international franchises were considered and broadly ratified (under conditions) by the European Court (see *Pronuptia de Paris GmbH v Pronuptia de Paris Irmgard Schillgallis* (1986) CMLR 414).

Goodwill

18.12 Goodwill has been defined as 'the probability that the old customers will revert to the old place' (*Crutwell v Lye* (1810) 17 Ves 335 at 346 per Lord Eldon). But perhaps it is something more prosaic as suggested by Dr Samuel Johnson remarking on the sale of Thrale's Brewery in 1781: 'We are not here to sell a parcel of boilers and vats, but the potentiality of growing rich beyond the dreams of avarice.'

Goodwill is the only asset so far that cannot be precisely valued, and its valuation will vary widely from case to case. To some extent it will also vary with the purchasers' opinion as to whether it is a good business that can be extended, or it is a poor business that will require an investment of time and money to bring it round. You must always be careful, especially in small businesses, of highly personal goodwill that will simply disappear when the sellers leave. Customers or clients of a business are often resentful of having their custom being taken for granted, and sold like a pound of butter, as Saatchi and Saatchi discovered when they bought, in the 1980s, an advertising agency in the United States for $450m. Almost immediately they lost the three main clients of the business and consequently $300m of annual billings. You will probably wish to discuss this valuation with an accountant who will base a valuation largely on past figures, which is as good a basis as any, but a shrewd businessperson will have a sixth sense for the value of the goodwill.

Generally speaking, people do return to the old place despite a change of ownership, unless they are antagonised, or the takeover is too radical for their tastes. Goodwill was treated as heritable property for stamp duty purposes (until the Finance Act 2002), and had to be included in the disposition of the property, and the duty paid.

With no particular apologies we would mention that Saatchi and Saatchi had more troubles in 1994–95, when the founder of the business (Maurice Saatchi) was effectively sacked. He set up a new business, and took many clients with him. This underlines the dangers of a business where the only real assets are the goodwill and the staff. Please remember that both can simply walk out of the door. We will deal with this further under 'people'.

Value

18.13   The valuation of a business is part art and part science. An accountant will work it out almost exactly, but a good businessman will pay less, and a fool will pay more. All in all it is a matter of negotiation (see quotation at head of chapter). You can pay an asset valuation, but what value is there in a pile of assets which produce a loss every year or which need replaced regularly? A multiplier of income is probably a fair starting point for negotiations. Another starting point, and probably a more accurate one, is what it would cost your clients to set up a similar business, taking into account the initial losses your clients would probably suffer.

People

18.14   As I indicated earlier, a business is largely at the mercy of its employees. A good business which is being sold will probably have high calibre employees whom the purchasers will wish to retain. A bad business may have been brought to its knees by its employees, and the purchasers are unlikely to feel a great compulsion to inherit these liabilities.

Good employees may be hard to retain. They may feel upset at the business being sold over their heads, and the owner disappearing with a large sum, representing their unrewarded hard work. They may even decide that they could do the same thing, and will leave to start up their own businesses. Apart from advising on and drawing up service contracts, there is not much the solicitor can do here. It is more of a personnel management exercise, or 'golden handcuffs' to give them their vulgar name—that is a good reward to stay faithful to the employer.

If an employee is under contract for a number of years, and the employers are afraid that the employee is going to be disruptive and unco-operative, yet they are unwilling to cancel the contract, and let the employee immediately move to another firm, taking their secrets and customers with them, they can give the employee 'gardening leave', ie pay the employee to do nothing for a period, at the end of which the customers will have forgotten them. Unhelpful staff are rather easier to lose, but the rights conferred on them on redundancy or dismissal under the various Employment Acts may make this an expensive exercise for the purchasers.

It is no longer competent to provide in the sale agreement that the sellers shall dismiss employees before takeover, and pay their compensation, in order that the purchasers may re-engage only such of those as they wish to keep (see Transfer of Undertakings (Protection of Employment) Regulations 2006 and various cases under these Regulations). Formerly a clause would normally be put into a contract to the effect that the purchasers of a business would require the sellers to terminate all contracts before the sale and the sellers would deal with the employees' redundancy and unfair dismissal claims. The purchase would then re-employ such employees as might be required, as new employees without accumulated rights.

The TU(PE)R 2006 replaces the similar Regulations of 1981, which were badly drafted and raised many questions. At one point the Scottish courts adopted a different interpretation of the rules from the English courts. The matter was finally settled by the House of Lords in *Litster v Forth Dry Dock and Engineering Co Ltd* (1989 SLT 540) where it was ruled that employees, dismissed by the receivers of the company one hour before the receivership took effect, had continuity of employment, and, therefore, a claim for redundancy. A clause which purports to require the sellers of a business to dismiss all employees before transfer, and to be responsible for the employees' claims, is not competent.

Employees dismissed will also generally be entitled to a redundancy payment (see *Anderson and McAlonie v Dalkeith Engineering Ltd* [1984] IRLR 429). Consultations with workers' representatives must take place before any transfer, with a view to reaching agreement about changing conditions, and the Directive for Informing and Consulting Employees, which is adopted in the United Kingdom, requires employers to inform and consult employees representatives when they propose to make twenty or more workers in one workplace redundant. This must be taken seriously. Vendors of a failed scottish business were fined £750,000 when they failed to consult workforce representatives, and this is not an isolated instance.

It has to be said that most businesses and mergers result, sooner or later, in job losses—whatever pious intentions are expressed at the time of the happy event. The effect can hopefully be achieved by natural wastage, but the purchasers of a business who intend to trim the workforce should bear these provisions in mind, should consult and inform, and should adjust the price to be paid in accordance with the potential liability for redundancy and unfair dismissal payments that are acquired with the business.

What of the departing sellers? Hopefully they will have made enough to enjoy a well-earned retirement, but whether they have or not, they should be subjected to a restrictive covenant to prevent them from returning to business to compete with the purchasers. The covenant should be neither too loose to stop the sellers from competing unfairly, nor too tight to be declared unenforceable by the courts (see *Scottish Farmers Dairy Co (Glasgow) Ltd v McGhee* 1933 SC 148, and many subsequent cases on the topic).

Lastly, some other terms in use in this area of practice include:

'**Golden hello**'—where an employee is induced to change jobs by a 'headhunter' (recruitment agent) the employee is usually rewarded by an additional incentive. This is to cover the danger of the employee moving from a job for life, only to find that things are not working out, and thus having to leave. This happens frequently.

'**Golden parachute**'—an executive has a contract which provides extra rewards in the event of a hostile takeover of a firm, leading to dismissal.

'**Poison pill**'—a company makes provisions for certain things to happen in the event of a hostile takeover, which will make the company less attractive to a purchaser.

18.15 The question of creating a monopoly situation under the Fair Trading Act 1973, or of falling foul of Arts 85 and 86 of the Treaty of Rome, relating to the creation of monopolies or the abuse of a dominant position, should always be borne in mind. Where these conditions are not fulfilled, the national authorities, such as the Competition Commission, have jurisdiction. This has the effect of clearing up the confusion where a merger might face vetting both in Brussels and by a national body. While these provisions are relevant mainly to large companies, they could also apply where two quite small companies merge, and thereby control a quarter of the home market. If there is any doubt about this, the Office of Fair Trading and the appropriate office in Brussels should be consulted.

18.16 The sale agreement should, where necessary, call upon the sellers to grant warranties that the situation is as they have stated. The purchasers will also do 'due diligence', ie a thorough inspection of company records, which may cut down the need for elaborate warranties. Warranties may not be very effective unless there are also indemnities to cover them. For this reason agreements for the sale of large companies are very lengthy and complex, there being alone about 30 different kinds of tax liability that may arise after the sellers have received their money. This is, however, outwith the scope of this work, and is dealt with in other specialist publications.

18.17 Offer of a business—contract to be completed by acceptance

Messrs Talle, Darke & Hansom,
Solicitors,
33 Watson Street,
INVERNESS

6 November 2005

Dear Sirs,

On behalf of our client Mr Art Sidewright ('the purchaser') we hereby offer to purchase from your client Mr Humphrey MacKerrell ('the seller'):

(1)   the shop property at 44 Angus Avenue, Inverness together with all the heritable fittings and fixtures therein;

(2)   the goodwill of the business of Fishmonger and Poulterer carried on therein by the seller under the name 'Seafresh';

(3)   the fittings and equipments hereinafter specified; and

(4)   the non-perishable stock-in-trade;

and that at the price and on the terms and conditions following:

1.   The price for the heritable property shall be ONE HUNDRED THOUSAND POUNDS (£100,000) STERLING payable as at the date of entry aftermentioned. The price for the goodwill shall be FIFTEEN THOUSAND POUNDS (£15,000) STERLING payable as at the date of transfer aftermentioned.

2.   The seller will sell as at the date of transfer and at the price of THREE THOUSAND POUNDS (£3,000) STERLING to the purchaser the whole trade fixtures and fittings, trade utensils and equipment which shall include counters, refrigerators, cash registers and scales. By acceptance of this Offer the seller warrants that there are no hire-purchase or credit sale

agreements, diligences, liens or charges of any kind affecting any of these moveable items, and that the title of the seller thereto cannot be reduced or affected at the instance of third parties. It is further understood that this price is inclusive of Value Added Tax and that the seller will account for this and will hand over a valid receipt to the purchaser within two weeks of payment of the price.

3. The purchaser will take over the non-perishable stock-in-trade of the business as at the date of entry and transfer, at a price to be agreed between the parties. Failing agreement the Valuation shall be referred to a neutral Valuer to be agreed between the parties.

4. The date of entry to the heritable property and the date of transfer of the goodwill and other subjects of sale shall be at the commencement of business on Thursday, 27 October 2005.

5. The following conditions shall apply with reference to the heritable property:

   (a) It is understood that the Rateable Value is £2,800. It is understood that the property is liable for one-eighth of the common charges of the whole tenement in which it is situated. The current rates, ground burdens and common charges and other outgoings will be apportioned as at the date of entry.

   (b) In exchange for the price the seller will deliver a valid Disposition of the shop premises in favour of the purchaser or his nominees, and will deliver a clear Land Certificate.

   (c) It is understood that the minerals are included in the sale only in so far as the seller has right thereto.

   (d) It is understood that there are no burdensome or unusual conditions, servitudes or wayleaves affecting the subjects and that there are no Orders affecting the subjects under the Town and Country Planning (Scotland) Act or the Public Health Acts or other Acts or any Notices or Orders by the the Local Authority or other authority affecting the subjects. Full Planning Permission for the present use has been granted and not revoked.

(e) It is understood that there are no conditions of Title which would prejudice the free use by the purchaser of the premises for trading purposes.

(f) It is understood that the premises meet the requirements of the Offices, Shops and Railway Premises Act; Health and Safety at Work Act and all other statutory provisions applicable thereto and that a Fire Certificate has been issued and not withdrawn or revoked.

(g) It is understood that the roadway *ex adverso* the subjects of sale and the sewer service the same have been taken over and are maintained by the Local Authority.

(h) The subjects of purchase shall include the refrigerated cold store, and the refrigeration system, all thermostats, pipes, plant, valves, pumps, time clocks, laggings, and vents. It is understood that the purchaser or his engineer shall be entitled to inspect the said equipment in the week before the date of transfer, and satisfy himself that it is in full working order. In the event of any repair being necessary, the purchaser shall be entitled to withhold a reasonable part of the price pending execution of the required repairs.

Note: The purchaser may also wish to insert other clauses for heritable property, such as a clause dealing with local authority notices etc.

6. The following conditions shall apply with reference to the sale of the goodwill.

(a) The seller will be entitled to the whole sum due in respect of sales of stock prior to the date of transfer and be liable to meet the cost of all stock ordered and delivered to the shop prior to that date.

(b) The seller will maintain the business as at present between the date of acceptance of this Offer and the date of the transfer but shall not order stock for delivery after the date of transfer without the consent of the purchaser.

(c) All outgoings of the business shall be apportioned as at the date of transfer, and the seller will be entitled to all book debts owing to the business prior to the date of transfer, and will be responsible for their collection. The purchaser will assist the seller to collect such book debts, but without recourse to legal proceedings.

(d) The seller shall indemnify the purchaser against all liabilities whatever of the business incurred or arising in connection with the business transactions carried out prior to the date of transfer.

(e) The Books of Account relating to the business shall become the property of the purchaser on the date of transfer, but they shall for a period of six months thereafter be open to the inspection by the seller or his agents at all reasonable times for entries relating to the period prior to the date of transfer and twenty-one days thereafter.

(f) The seller will not in any way carry on directly or indirectly (unless with the written consent of the purchaser) within one year after the date of transfer and within one mile of 44 Angus Avenue either on his own account or as a partner with, or in the name of, or as a servant or agent to any person or persons, firm or company, the business of Fishmonger or Poulterer within the said area.

7. The whole subject of Offer will be maintained by the seller in good condition and repair to the date of entry and transfer and adequately insured against fire, theft and other usual risks to the said date.

8. The purchaser shall be entitled to take over all telephonic and telegraphic equipment, and any telephone numbers and email and website addresses presently used by the seller. The seller warrants that all accounts for telephonic services have been paid up to date, and that there are no proposals to withdraw any of the telephone numbers purchased with the business.

9. This Offer is for immediate acceptance only.

Yours faithfully,

SHORT, FATTE & UGGLY (*signed by a partner of the firm, and witnessed*)

Notes:

1   From this point completion of the contract will be reached by exchange of letters until all points are resolved and *consensus in idem* has been reached.

2   The total consideration for the business does not exceed £125,000 and therefore there is no stamp duty payable. As it is a marginal case, however, HM Revenue and Customs may demand evidence that the valuations of the property are correct.

3   Stamp duty is no longer payable on sales of goodwill (Finance Act 2002).

Chapter 19

ASSIGNATIONS OF LEASES

'During the course of the year the Agency made a total of 18 payments, totalling £62,779.96 in respect of indemnity claims. Of this amount over £55,000 was paid out in respect of 3 claims, 2 of which were a result of omissions from, or misleading information in Agency reports, and the third was in respect of leasehold casualties omitted from the title sheet.'

(Keeper's Report 1992–93)

19.01 In certain areas it was traditionally the practice to grant long leases (or tacks to use the old Scottish term) of property, rather than feudal rights. The lease would usually be for a period of 99 or even 999 years, or in one case noted by the Scottish Law Commission, 9,999 years. If you buy a leasehold property with some 800 years of the lease to run, it may seem little different from a feu, but it is quite a different concept, and there are certain differences of emphasis. The most obvious difference is that you never own the property, and the lease will come to an end one day, no matter how remote that day may be.

Thus certain unfortunate tenants on Seafield Estates, in the north east, were faced with losing their houses simply because their leases were about to expire, and they were being asked to pay substantial sums to buy houses that they had considered as their own. It is perhaps difficult to understand why this miscomprehension had arisen, but that is the way things stand, and no statutory relief was offered. Presumably these unfortunate people will now have had to pay for what they considered, however wrongly, to be 'their' houses. They should have been told, or perhaps were told, but chose not to hear, that if a lease is granted, the tenant is only entitled to occupy the property for the term of the lease, and that anything that is built on the land belongs to the owner of the land. Perhaps they got confused with the security of tenure provisions under the Rent Acts, but these apply to relatively recent leases. The length of such leases is now restricted to 175 years, to prevent the creation of an alternative feudal system (AFT(S)A 2000, s 67).

19.02 It is perhaps also unfortunate that advantage was not taken of the provisions of the Long Leases (Scotland) Act 1954, Pt I, which allowed such tenants to convert their leases into feus on a small payment to the landlord in compensation. Sadly the benefits of that Act ceased to be available after 1 September 1959, and have never been renewed.

The model village of Eaglesham in Renfrewshire was largely let on long leases by the Earl of Eglinton, who had, however, to sell the village some years later to make up for his disastrous losses when he staged a jousting tournament at his castle on one of the wettest days apparently ever remembered. The rentals charged were one or two old shillings per house, with the only notable condition being a requirement on the villagers to pay for a piper for the Earl when required. The successors to Eglinton Estates were happy enough to convert their leases into feus, and will, I believe, still do so, if asked by anyone who has not yet done so. Not so Seafield Estates, who rest on the contracts signed by their predecessors.

19.03 When a leasehold property is sold, the land is not sold, merely the right to occupy it for a certain number of years. A disposition is not therefore the competent deed, it is an assignation of the lease in the form provided by the Registration of Leases (Scotland) Act 1857, Sch A.

An assignation of lease takes this form:

'I, (*name and address of seller*) IN CONSIDERATION of the price of (*price*) paid to me by (*name and address of purchaser*) of which price I hereby acknowledge the receipt HAVE SOLD and DO HEREBY ASSIGN to the said (*purchaser*) the tenant's right and interest to and in a Tack (*specify details of the Tack*); and further I assign in so far as necessary my title thereto which is recorded (*specify Register and date of registration*); Together with (first) the parts privileges and pertinents of the Leasehold rights hereby assigned; and (second) my whole right, title and interest present and future therein; WITH ENTRY as at (*date*); And I grant warrandice: IN WITNESS WHEREOF.'

Similarly if money is borrowed on the security of the long lease, the competent security was a bond and assignation in security, in terms of Sch B to the 1857 Act. Nowadays, of course, in terms of CFR(S)A 1970, s 9, it is competent to grant a standard security over any interest in land, including a leasehold interest.

It should, however, be made perfectly clear that, as a practical matter, no institution will lend money over a leasehold property of which the lease has only a few years to run as this does not constitute a reasonable security, nor over an unregistered lease.

19.04 Purchasers acquiring a lease should be satisfied that the landlord's title to the land is a good one, and therefore that the lease is competent. Further, all assignations of the lease should be checked as if these were normal dispositions. A search over the lease (not over the property which is a distinctly separate interest) should also be seen. Searches over both lease and property can of course be requested, but the sellers of the leasehold interest may not be willing to produce the latter which is not really their concern.

19.05 It was a requirement of the Leases Act 1449, s 18, that to qualify for the protection of that Act, the tenants must enter into possession of the land. This had the effect that a lease could not be used as security for money borrowed. This difficulty was circumvented by the Registration of Leases Act 1857, s 1, which provided that a probative lease for a period of 31 years or more might be registered in the General Register of Sasines, thereby giving the tenants a real right. Any lease of less than 31 years was regarded as not being of sufficient importance to be so registered, but LTR(S)A 1974, Sch 6, has reduced that qualification period to 20 years.

Conversely, however, LTR(S)A 1974, s 8, forbids the creation of future leases of residential property for periods exceeding 20 years. It is thus unlikely that residential leases will be registered any more, and the remarks that follow on registration would therefore seem to apply mainly to commercial leases.

19.06 It should be noted, however, that it is still competent to register long residential leases created before 1974 which have not yet been registered. If the lease is in an area which has been declared operational for land registration, the lease or a transfer of it for value must now be registered in the Land Register. The forms and procedures used are as for dispositions of feudal property.

19.07 The advent of land registration has thrown up another difficulty with long leases that was not appreciated before, and which is fully discussed by Colin Miller in his paper 'Conveyancing: Points to ponder' (Law Society PQLE Papers of missives and general conveyancing course, February 1985). Miller points out that the Keeper of the Land Register has taken the view that it is not, and never has been, competent to use a deed of conditions to regulate leasehold property, on a strict reading of C(S)A 1874, s 32. Further the Keeper takes the view that it is not competent to impose land obligations by reference in an assignation or partial assignation of a lease, as would be the case with a disposition. Any such obligations referred to in an assignation are therefore incompetent, and would be only personal obligations upon the tenants, and that the only safe way to proceed in such transactions is to set forth at length the conditions of title in each and every assignation—something which has never apparently been done.

19.08 The Law Reform (Miscellaneous Provisions) (Scotland) Act 1985, s 3, however, provides that it is retrospectively competent to impose conditions and make stipulations by reference to a previous deed which upon recording in the Register of Sasines or registration in the Land Register become binding upon singular successors of the tenants. Miller also points out that this piece of retrospective legislation is to cure difficulties raised by the Keeper, but it does not seem to apply to deeds of conditions.

19.09 An unexpected feature of long leases which cropped up in the last few years (note the quotation at the head of this chapter) has been the incidence of leasehold casualties. It should be explained that casualties were double payments of feu duty or rent which occurred every nineteenth year, or on the sale of the property. Feudal casualties were abolished in 1914, by the Feudal Casualties (Scotland) Act 1914. Unfortunately, however, this Act did not cover leasehold casualties. It had been generally assumed that these had been cancelled by the 1914 Act, or had otherwise dropped away, but this has not turned out to be the case.

A leasehold casualty is an additional payment of rent occurring on certain events. An example of this is as follows:

> 'As also to pay to the said (*Landlord*) and his successors proprietors of the said subjects or his or their assignees the sum of twelve pounds of additional rent for the first year's possession at the entry or succession of every heir to the said subjects and <u>one full year's rent or value of the said subjects including all buildings erected or to be erected thereon according to the actual value thereof at the time for the first year's possession or entry of every assignee or singular successor and that within a year and a day from the date of the heir assignee or singular successor succeeding or acquiring right or possession or of the right or possession opening to or devolving upon him, her or them</u>;'

You will note that I have underlined the part dealing with full year's rent or value, which is the critical part, it being claimed that this is intended to reflect inflationary changes, although at the time of the granting of the lease, inflation was not really known to any extent.

On the basis of this clause the landlord made a claim for a payment of several thousand pounds, on the basis of the 'full year's rent or value' being the amount of the rateable value on the property. In this case a member of the Keeper's staff had omitted the leasehold casualty from the land certificate, presumably believing it to be a matter that had then become redundant—this being several years ago, when virtually everyone would have thought similarly. It turned out not to be, and a claim was received from the landlord for the loss of the casualty payment, and was paid.

It is understood that there are many such casualty rights throughout Scotland, and that 'title raiders' were buying estates and enforcing these casualty rights. They were, of course, totally within their legal rights to do so, if the clauses supported them and were specific.

What was wrong was the legal position. These payments should have been abolished in 1914 together with feudal casualties, they caused much distress, and they were finally laid to rest by the Leasehold Casualties (Scotland) Act 2001, which makes such payments unenforceable.

Chapter 20

COMMERCIAL LEASES

'Lease Terms: The building is being offered to let on the basis of a 25 year full repairing and insuring lease with upward only rent reviews at five yearly intervals. The incoming tenants will be responsible for the landlords' legal expenses together with stamp duty and VAT incurred in connection with the grant of the lease.'

(Developer's Circular)

'A leading City (London) law firm is being sued for £7.5 million over a blunder allegedly made in drafting a guarantee. The action is being brought ... on behalf of 2,700 investors ... who complain that because of the guarantee they are only receiving a third of the rent promised.

The main purpose of the guarantee was to ensure that even if the buildings were not let, investors would still receive rental income for the first five years. In the event the guarantee failed to do the one thing it was supposed to do—protect the investors in the event of the developers of the building, who promised to pay the rent, going bust.'

(Financial Mail on Sunday)

'Apart from staff, property is the second-biggest expense for retailers. Store groups have long resented crippling "upward only" rent reviews. In London, for example, the average rise is ten per cent .... A spate of high profile retail collapses ... has resulted in a glut of space coming on to the market. Several retailers have taken advantage of the change to push for more flexible leases and are urging landlords to consider the American system where rents are based on the turnover rather than square footage.'

(Financial Mail, 30 April 2006)

20.01 The modern commercial lease is a repairing, renewing and insuring lease (RRI); that is, these obligations are placed on the tenants by agreement. This is a basic practice which has become customary (see quotation above). Whatever else you may be able to negotiate with the landlord, you are very unlikely to be able to negotiate out of this stipulation.

20.02 The modern commercial (or full repairing, renewing and insuring lease) is a formidable creature, and was, until recently, entirely unmoderated by any statutory relaxation of its strict terms, with the exception of the modest security of tenure given by the Tenancy of Shops (Scotland) Acts 1949 and 1964. The topic is a very complex one, and this chapter is only an attempt to explain the main principles of the subject. The contents of such a lease are entirely governed by negotiation between the parties. The terms are fixed usually by the landlord, and agreed by the tenants. There are none of the safeguards of security of tenure, and of compensation payable on outgoing afforded to tenants in England by the string of Landlord and Tenants Acts 1929 to 1988.

There was enacted the Law Reform (Miscellaneous Provisions) (Scotland) Act 1985, which protected tenants from an irritancy arising from late payment of rent, as in the case of *Dorchester Studios (Glasgow) Ltd v Stone* (1975 SLT 153). It also protected the tenants from an irritancy relating to non-monetary breaches of the lease. At section 5 it produced the most bizarre legal animal yet. Burdened and benefited proprietors, entitled spouses and non-entitled spouses, to name but four recently created legal animals, are fairly clearly definable legal concepts, but the concept of a 'fair and reasonable landlord' who 'in all the circumstances of the case' would not have terminated a lease, is vague beyond belief.

In his annotations of the 1985 Act, Professor Joseph Thomson says that 'it is to be hoped that the uncertainty surrounding "the fair and reasonable landlord" test will not be the occasion for protracted litigation'. This approach was tried successfully in *Lothian Chemical Co Ltd v City of Edinburgh District Council* (1995 GWD 4–197).

20.03 But what are fair and reasonable landlords? It could be argued that the landlords are merely attending to their duties on behalf of their investors, and it is right and proper that the landlords should follow a consistent management philosophy, and that they should not let the tenants away with too much for the sake of their investors, and indeed, for the sake of the tenants themselves. Alternatively, you could argue that fair and reasonable landlords are benign characters, not getting too upset about minor breaches of the rules, and turning a blind eye to breaches of the conditions of leases; but if a tenant neglects an essential repair, the whole property may suffer, and that is not being a fair and reasonable landlord at all.

20.04 And if LR(MP)(S)A 1985 does not create a matching concept of a 'fair and reasonable tenant' can we perhaps invent one? Tenants who always pay their rent in time, perform the various other obligations posed by the lease, are good traders and attract customers to the development, are an example of this. These tenants are otherwise known as a 'good covenant', and needless to say are a highly sought-after commodity. A good covenant can more or less dictate terms to the landlord, within the restraints mentioned above, whereas a lesser covenant has to take more or less the terms the landlord dictates.

20.05 Thus, when we have negotiations for a lease, much depends on the respective bargaining powers of the two parties. You may have two kinds of negotiation: (a) competitive, or win/lose, negotiation where one party is intent on imposing its will on the other party, and if it does not succeed in any respect, it will simply stop negotiations; and (b) co-operative, or win/win, negotiations where both parties are prepared to concede certain points to the other, and, without breaking the basic pattern of the leasing scheme, the landlord is prepared to allow certain deviations from it.

The former pattern of 'negotiation', which is less common nowadays, because leases that are too strict have proved to be counter-productive when they come to a rent review, requires the lawyer to do little more than to report to the client on the possible impact of the conditions imposed, and to outline the costs involved, which are liable to be extensive. But if we take the second possibility, of co-operative negotiation, it is here that the skilled leasing lawyers come into their own. Wit is pitted against wit, each striving to get the best deal for their clients, and at the end of the day both should feel that they have done a good job for their clients. You can take satisfaction that you have acted like good lawyers should, instead of like an unskilled office junior, whose only job is to take the bad news to the client.

20.06 What then, in sensible negotiations, are some of the major points that good lawyers should be looking for? First of all the lease should be clear and comprehensible, not repetitive or ambiguous, in a logical order, with an index and side-headings, and have a clear definition section at the beginning. Solicitors for both parties should keep their clients continuously informed of the progress of negotiations. You may feel that this is unnecessary, as the client does not understand what is going on, but it is very important to keep the client informed, in this sphere of law as all others. This is as much a matter of self-protection as anything else.

20.07 The rent payable is a matter for negotiation; the tenants should not necessarily be expected to accept the landlord's first figure. You will be kept advised on this, as on other matters, by a competent surveyor. Whether or not value added tax is payable on the rent is a competent matter for negotiation. Basically, to a VAT-registered company, whether or not it pays VAT on the rental is neither here nor there, because it can claim it back, and the only loss is that it had to pay the tax rather earlier, with a cash-flow benefit to the landlord, and detriment to the tenants. Where tenants are not VAT registered, as with a bank or other financial institution, it is distinctly detrimental to have VAT imposed, as it is just a straight 17.5% rent increase, which cannot be reclaimed. As such companies are generally good covenants, however, some solution can usually be found with co-operative negotiation. Rent reviews are generally made on an upwards only basis—that is to say the rents go relentlessly up, while sales maybe go down. This is unfair for the retailer, but landlords will insist on this stipulation. Perhaps a fair compromise might be to have the rent fixed on the turnover of the business, subject to a minimum figure. This method is not unknown in this country, but, of course, the landlord must have a foolproof method of checking the turnover figures.

20.08 Machinery for reviewing the rent must be established. Landlords are entitled to have the rent adjusted to cover the fall in the value of money, but the tenants should not yield completely to the landlord. This is purely a matter for negotiation—the length of the review break and so on—but there are important drafting considerations too. There should be resisted by the tenants any attempt to impose a condition that any restriction on use shall be disregarded on a rent review (see para **20.12**). On the other hand, the tenants should insist on the insertion of 'disregards' for rent review purposes of the tenants' occupancy and the goodwill the tenants have created, and of improvements made by the tenants. It is bad enough to improve someone else's property, without having to pay additional rent in respect of those improvements.

20.09 While on a longish lease it is quite acceptable that the tenants shall pay for repairs, there should be excluded repairs of latent defects that were not reasonably foreseeable at the outset of the lease, and which not even a competent survey of the premises would have revealed. These defects seem to arise mainly in the much maligned buildings of the 1960s when, as it turns out, all sorts of dubious materials were used and poor building practices followed. Asbestos and concrete which dissolved ('concrete cancer'), cladding which separates from the building, and high alumina cement are among the most likely building materials to cause latent defects.

20.10 The insurance provisions should be fair, and if in doubt the insurances of the property should be checked over by a broker. While the tenants can be reasonably expected to pay premiums, and while the landlords can fairly expect also to instruct the insurances, care should be taken that all risks that need to be covered are in fact covered, and that those that are not requiring cover, are not. The premiums should also be competitive, and the risks should be insured with a sound company. The position as to destruction of the property, and the insurance provisions against it, should be fair to the tenants. Ideally the tenants would want the Scottish law of *rei interitus* to apply, as in the case of *Cantors Properties (Scotland) Ltd v Swears & Wells* (1980 SLT 165), and to be able to abandon the lease in the event of destruction of the property, but it is now fairly well established that the landlord will wish to contract out of this provision. An unwelcome recent development has been the need to instruct cover against terrorist damage, and as one never knows where or when this may occur, comprehensive cover against this scourge must not be neglected. In the mainland United Kingdom, the government will not compensate for terrorist damage.

20.11 As heritable securities are generally taken over registered leases, the lending institutions will generally want clauses contained in the lease which will protect their interests in the event of an irritancy, or bankruptcy or liquidation of the tenants. These clauses will rarely be resisted by landlords, as the 'muscle' of financial institutions is hard to resist, and also because they would simply cease to lend if they lost their security in the event that the tenants became insolvent, or failed to pay their rent in time. It should be borne in mind that no security can be created over a lease that is not registerable, that is to say with a lease period of 20 years or less, as opposed to a lease for a period greater than 20 years, but which has less than 20 years of that period left to run.

20.12 The tenants must ensure that every contemplated use of the premises is allowed by the lease, and is permitted under town and country planning legislation. The tenants should ensure that not only does this permission exist, but is applicable to the whole length of the lease, and is not personal to another party. If planning permission is to be obtained, the lease should be made subject to the permission being obtained, and in terms acceptable to the tenants. Further the solicitors for the tenants should ensure that the use contemplated is acceptable in terms of the title deeds and that there are no restrictions which would adversely affect the use proposed by the tenants. From the landlords' point of view, restrictions on other uses should not be disallowed by the lease, lest this should affect the level of rent to be fixed on review, on the basis that the restriction makes the lease hard to transfer, and therefore of less value. If a restriction on use is imposed, this should not be stated in the lease to be disregarded on a future review of the rent, as the impact on the rent payable could be quite dramatic.

20.13 The tenants' solicitors should also inspect the title deeds, as if the property was being purchased, and searches should be obtained to show that the landlord truly is the owner of the property and that there are no securities over the property, or if there are that the consent of the security holder to the lease is obtained. The consent of the superior, or of any head landlord, to the proposed lease arrangement and to the proposed usage of the property should be obtained, if required. The same care should be taken when leasing a property, as when purchasing it, in seeing the appropriate planning and building certificates and any permission required from the superior

20.14 Details of the landlords' management charges should be obtained and be seen to be reasonable. Where, as the modern practice is, a shopping development contains, say, an ice rink, the tenants should not incur any share of the charges involved in running the rink.

20.15 From the tenants' point of view, there should not be too severe restrictions on assigning and subletting the lease. In addition, the tenants should be assured that in the event of an assignation of the lease being allowed that the original tenants are released from any further liability under the lease. In England there is a doctrine of privity, which imposes this liability on the original leaseholder. There have been distressing cases in England where the original tenant has retired, and sold his lease to a purchaser of the business. A few years later the new tenant cannot meet the rent, and under the doctrine of privity of contract, the original tenant is asked to pay. Landlords may well try to impose this concept to Scotland by negotiation and by inserting a joint and several liability on the original tenants and all assignees. It should be resisted, as the consequences for the original tenants can be very considerable.

From the landlords' point of view, it is also desirable to have a fair degree of freedom to assign or sublet, as if the lease is unduly restrictive in this regard, this too may have a detrimental effect on the level of future rent reviews. Landlords will, reasonably, wish to ensure that a future tenant is as good a covenant as the old tenant.

Generally, throughout the lease the tenants should be protected against any temptation on the landlords to spend the tenants' money freely, and safeguards should be built in that all expenditure should be incurred 'reasonably'. Further, the ascertainment of what is reasonable spending, and what is not, should be referred to an arbiter.

20.16 The tenants should be allowed quiet possession of the whole subjects of lease, provided that the terms of the lease are adhered to. The tenants should also reserve such rights over adjoining areas of ground, belonging to the landlords, as may be required, particularly from the point of view of access, and support of buildings, and for the leading of services to the premises leased.

20.17 It is certainly reasonable that the tenants should keep the subjects decorated, in a lease of any length. This obligation should not be too onerous, however, nor should it be inappropriate. If the tenants have a particular 'house style' the lease should not be framed in such a way as to be inimical to this. Also the tenants should not accept an out-of-date decoration clause, which requires them, eg to paint the woodwork with 'three coats of oil-based paint' and to apply distemper to the walls. Just try and get oil paint and distemper in your local supermarket!

20.18 The landlords may attempt to get personal guarantees from the directors of a company to a lease in favour of a limited company, if it is considered that the covenant of the company is not good enough, and that the company is not financially secure. This is a perfectly acceptable practice, and is not unfair. Having said that, the tenants' solicitors should automatically resist the attempt, but if the tenants are a small or newly-established company, it is not unreasonable for the landlords to protect their own interests if the tenant company is quietly dissolved at the first sign of trouble. What is important from the guarantor's point of view is that it is released when the tenants assign the lease, and that it be kept informed of any aberrant practices by the tenants which, if continued, might lead to an irritancy of the lease, such as slow payment of rent. A time limit on the guarantee may also be included.

20.19 The lease should specify the landlords' fixtures, bearing in mind that fixtures brought onto the premises may be deemed to have become heritable by the operation of the rule in *Brand's Trustees v Brand's Trustees* ((1876) 3 R (HL) 16) and *Scottish Discount Co Ltd v Blin* (1986 SLT 123). As should be the general practice disclosed in a number of conflicting cases following *Winston v Patrick* (1981 SLT 41), central-heating and ventilation plant should always be inspected before taking over premises, to ensure that they are in good working order.

20.20 The tenant should be taken bound in the lease to keep the premises well stocked, in order that the landlord may exercise a right of hypothec over moveables in the tenanted premises. Further the tenants should be bound to trade continuously throughout the terms of the lease, because there is nothing more depressing than an empty shop, even though rent is being received (see *Highland and Universal Properties Ltd v Safeway Properties Ltd* 2000 SC 297).

20.21 Lastly, after a long recital of the obligations of the tenants, all of which must be paid for by the tenants, the expenses of preparation of this document by the landlords' agent are fairly and squarely placed on the tenants' shoulders. Of course, you may console the tenants by saying that if they did not pay for these now, they would only have to pay for them in the future in the form of an increased rent, for in this world there is no such thing as a free lunch. The tenants will probably reply that while they admit that, were the case otherwise, the payment would probably be spread over a number of years. I would suggest that the tenants' solicitors attempt to limit these expenses at the outset, and tell the clients what they must expect to pay.

Better still, if you can negotiate out of paying the landlords' expenses at all, you should enjoy the gratitude of the clients. It really comes down to curbing the free spending of your clients' money, and your clients should not be expected to pay a very fancy price for a long, word processed lease.

Be sure to warn the tenants at the outset of the negotiations of the cost of all this: stamp duty, recording dues, landlords' expenses, management charges, VAT, your expenses, as well as the first rental payment due in advance, and the fitting-out costs. If you fail to do this you may find that the tenants seek to make a saving of the only thing under their control, and delay to pay your fee!

20.22 These are only some of the major considerations of negotiation and drafting a lease. No practitioner in this field should be without a copy of M J Ross and D J McKichan's invaluable *Drafting and Negotiating of Commercial Leases in Scotland* (2nd edn, Butterworths, 1993).

Chapter 21

SITE ASSEMBLY

'The next step was to buy all the land as quietly as possible. The site stretched for a quarter of a mile between the underground stations at Warren Street and Great Portland Street, along the north side of Euston Road, which until the 18th century had been the northern boundary of London . . . an area which Joe Levy (property developer) extravagantly describes as "a derelict bloody den of disease".

Joe Levy was forming a consortium of estate agents. He knew that if his firm alone were to attempt to buy from all the many different owners, freeholders, leaseholders, and subleaseholders, his intention might become apparent and there would be two great dangers. Owners might dream up an exaggerated idea of the value, to him, of their properties, or some small time property dealers might compete against him in order to hold him to ransom. In either case his ultimate profit on the redevelopment could either be slimmed down or wiped out entirely.'

(The Property Boom, Joseph Marriott, on the redevelopment of the Euston station site)

21.01 Commercial conveyancing is reasonably similar to domestic conveyancing, in that the same sort of documentation applies. There the similarity ends because commercial conveyancers handle huge sums of money, deal probably with several lenders, floating charges, ranking of securities, and go into other esoteric matters like leverage (borrowing) and mezzanine financing (a debt half secured by a security over the borrowers' assets and half by shares in the borrowing company). A good commercial conveyancer should, however, have a sound grounding in the basics of domestic conveyancing, and then the other bits can be grafted on.

While I feel that this chapter will introduce many basic concepts of commercial conveyancing, I should, however, stress that this chapter makes no claim to be anything but introductory, although I hope that it will be usefully so.

21.02 First it is important to note that the conveyancing aspects of commercial deals do not differ radically from domestic conveyancing. Residential conveyancers should, however, always be advised to resist the temptation to dable in commercial conveyancing unless: they know what they are doing; and (b) they have sufficient resources (and insurance cover!) to apply either to the commercial deal or have filled the gap to keep their residential transactions on target. There are the four main stages: (1) negotiation; (2) missives; (3) examination of title; and (4) settlement. The real difference lies in the fact that the lawyer in a commercial transaction must liase with a number of other people, and know fairly well what each is attempting to do. It should be remembered that it is the lawyers who must complete the evidence of the agreement, with their own signature on the missives, and therefore they must be amply satisfied that everything leading to the agreement seems to be in order.

I shall turn to the these aspects later, but first it may be useful to look at some of the metaphorical creatures in the metaphorical jungle of commercial conveyancing.

Landowner

21.03 The first persons with whom we must deal are the persons who own the land, and who are now being stalked by the developer. In most cases the developer will wish to acquire the landowner's interest absolutely, and the landowner will then be paid and will disappear. Developers do not like third parties to have any interest in their developments, as such interests may prove awkward at a future date. Some landowners, however, will not sell their land, but will grant a 'ground lease' to the developer. This lease will be for a long number of years and will require the developers to build the building and to pay a ground rent to the landowner. The developers then sublease the building to the tenants, and their profit is the difference between the two rentals (known as the profit rental), less, of course, the expenses of development.

The landowner will enjoy an annual rental income, probably increasing regularly, and at the end of the lease period, the land and buildings will revert to the landowner, or more probably to unknown descendants. This right is known as a 'reversion'.

As such arrangements tend to be for a period exceeding the normal lifespan, one may assume that in the intervening period the developers (who are not long-term investors) will have sold the reversion to a pension fund or similar body, which invests in the long term. The developers will then move on to the next development, or to a well-padded retirement. The small landowner is unlikely to reach such an agreement with a developer, and only powerful and experienced landowners are likely to reach such arrangements. For the rest, it is the case of a lump sum in their hands, and off to the Bahamas.

Developer

21.04 The developer is the person who makes the whole thing happen; the co-ordinator, profit maker, and let it not be forgotten, the risk taker. The developer runs considerable risks and will not get profit for several years and in return expects a substantial return. A sensible developer will employ a team of experts. They include:

(a) **Lawyer:** The lawyer completes all the documents and in such role should be the key adviser in the development. No detail should escape the lawyer's notice, for all may have a vital bearing on the documentation and, indeed, in any disputes that may follow. The lawyer should clearly establish the brief before commencing: is the lawyer engaged merely for clerical functions, or to provide commercial expertise? It is, I understand, a common source of liability claims when the lawyer thought that the job was to supply clerical services, but in fact the developer expected to be provided with commercial development expertise as well. When I talk of lawyers here I mean solicitors, but of course an advocate may also be called in at any stage to advise, or indeed may have to be. The lawyer is also responsible for the site assembly, where the development is made up of several parcels.

(b) **Valuation surveyor:** A valuation surveyor (as opposed to a quantity surveyor who provides a quite different service although belonging to the same professional body, the Royal Institution of Chartered Surveyors) is the expert on the price of land—the price at which it may be bought, and the price at which the development may be rented to provide the maximum return to the developer.

(c) **Architect:** The architect's primary task is to design and supervise the building of an attractive and useful development which conforms to all the requirements of the planning and building authorities. The architect may also provide useful advice on planning and environmental aspects, in conjunction with a planning consultant or otherwise.

(d) **Planning consultant:** The planning consultant and architect will negotiate with the council planning department, bearing in mind the requirements for a successful development, and also that it is unlikely that this can be completed nowadays in the teeth of opposition from the planning department. The planning position wished by the developer should be a material, suspensive, condition of purchase. The architect and the planning consultant will also deal with various bodies, such as

Historic Scotland and the Civic Trust, who will wish an input of any development involving buildings of significant interest, or if there are archaeological considerations.

(e) **Environmental consultant:** The environmental consultant will advise on the environmental audit to be carried out before purchase, and the carrying out of the required cleaning of a contaminated site. This process is referred to as 'best available treatment at not excessive cost' (BATNEC). The environmental consultant may come from any discipline, but most probably will have a planning, surveying, scientific, or engineering background. An environmental audit should be made a material condition of purchase, and be the subject of a suspensive condition.

The purchase of land should be the subject of a suspensive environmental clause, along the following lines:

'The purchasers shall receive, in respect of the site, ground support and geotechnical survey reports (all including soils and minerals survey reports and a site survey report in terms satisfactory to them) in which regard the purchasers will be the sole judge and whose judgement shall not be challengeable.

The purchasers will also carry out an environmental audit to allow them to satisfy themselves no dangerous or deleterious substances have been used on, disposed of, dumped, released, deposited or buried at the site and that the site is not adversely otherwise affected by the terms of the Public Health (Scotland) Act 1897, Control of Pollution Act 1974, Environmental Protection Act 1990 (all as amended or varied or substituted from time to time) or any other legislation concerning the protection of human health or the environment or the treatment or disposal of dangerous substances.'

(f) **Accountant:** The accountant will give advice generally on financial matters and particularly on the many complex taxation problems that may arise. The accountant is also responsible for due diligence reports on any companies bought as part of the site assembly.

(g) **Civil engineer:** Initially the engineer will take test bores and will assess the ground conditions both for contamination and building purposes. The engineer will sink test bores to make sure that the ground is sufficiently stable to support the building envisaged. No contract should be entered into by the developer without it being made a material, suspensive, condition that if test bores, or environmental audit, prove unsatisfactory, the developer may withdraw. The potential cost of making an unstable site suitable for building is horrific. After the site has been assembled the engineer may well work with the architect to ensure the structural safety of the building, and other matters like lift shafts.

In addition a mechanical engineer will be called in to assess moving plant, such as lift machinery, heating and air conditioning plant, and so on. It is a significant aspect of modern buildings that they are largely controlled by machinery.

(h) Mechanical engineer. The modern building is dependent on machines—to control the temperature, humidity, air quality and drainage. A modern building also requires to be computer friendly, which involves special wiring, and certainly more than merely several plugs. These are the responsibility of the mechanical engineer.

(i) Quantity surveyor: The quantity surveyor will again work with the architect. Broadly the architect will produce plans of the building and the quantity surveyor will prepare bills of quantities, which specify what work is to be done, and materials used, and these will be handed out to potential tenderers for the building work. A good quantity surveyor should be able to provide an accurate estimate of the costs of the building.

(i) Insurance broker: The insurance broker will advise on all insurance aspects from the first acquisition of property, through the building work, until the tenants are in possession of the new building. This covers an enormous range of potential insurable risks.

(j) Financier: The developer will have to buy the land, pay substantial professional fees, and then pay the cost of the building before any significant return is received. Temporary financing will therefore be necessary, and no doubt some form of security over the ground will also have to be given.

Planning and building departments of the council

21.05 The obtaining of a building warrant is relatively simple, provided the various complex building regulations are followed. This can be safely left to the architect, quantity surveyor and builders. Planning is much less simple as other considerations enter, particularly aesthetic and political considerations, which should quite properly enter, but which do not make life any easier, as they are imprecise and unspecified.

Thus the developer may find that the substandard building that is to be demolished is, in fact, a little-known work of someone famous, and that listed building consent is required, and various preservation societies are opposed to the development. The co-operation of a planning department is most important, without it being necessary to concede all their points. Basically these departments are reasonable to deal with, and they will not block a useful development—one which provides 'planning gain', in the form of cleaning up an eyesore or providing jobs etc—and which increases rates income. The council, possessing compulsory purchase powers as it does, may prove to be vital.

There was an example in Glasgow of the council saving a major development by compulsorily purchasing a small piece of land in disputed ownership, which dispute was preventing access to the development. There are also numerous other examples of councils helping the developer by stopping up streets or closing rights of way, and so on. As a *quid pro quo* for help rendered, the council may enter into an enforceable agreement with the developer under of the Town and Country Planning (Scotland) Act 1997, s 75. Thus the parties might agree that while the developer is building on the site anyway, something else, e g a public toilet, shall be built, thereby saving the council expense. The 'section 75 agreement' (formerly a section 50 agreement) is enforceable and can be recorded or registered.

An example of a very simple agreement of this kind follows:

'Section 75

WHEREAS the first party are planning Authority for the in terms of the Town and Country Planning (Scotland) Act 1997; AND WHEREAS the second party are the heritable proprietors of ALL and WHOLE that piece of ground part of the farm and lands of

in the Parish of and County of and comprising the south-east part of the field or enclosure? numbered on the Ordnance Survey Map of the said County of all as the said piece of ground is delineated and coloured red on the plan annexed and subscribed as relative hereto;

AND WHEREAS an application has been made to the first party by the second party for permission to erect a dwellinghouse on the said area of ground outlined in red on the plan annexed and executed as relative hereto;

AND WHEREAS the first party are disposed to grant the said planning permission subject to the second party entering into an Agreement with the first party in terms of section 75 of the Town and Country Planning (Scotland) Act 1997; THEREFORE the parties have agreed and do hereby agree as follows, videlicet:

(First) The second party hereby undertake that the dwellinghouse to be erected on the said subjects outlined in red on the said plan shall be used in all time coming by a person connected with or employed in agriculture and the dependents of any such person;

(Second) The second party further undertake that the said dwellinghouse shall not be sold in all time coming other than to a person so employed in or connected with agriculture;

The parties hereby agree that in the event of any disputes or differences of opinion arising as to the provisions of these presents or the interpretation thereof, such disputes or differences shall be referred to the Secretary of State for Scotland, or such other person or persons as may be nominated by him, and the decision of the Secretary of State, or his nominee as the case may be, shall be final and binding; But the provisions contained in this clause shall be without prejudice to the right of the first party to enforce these presents or any provision thereof or any condition of the planning permission to be granted in respect of the said dwellinghouse against the second party or anyone deriving title from him;

The second party hereby obliges himself to meet the recording dues of this Agreement and any other outlays and administrative expenses incurred by the first party in connection herewith;

The parties hereby grant consent to registration hereof for preservation and execution as well as for publication.'

There was an important litigation in England under almost identical provisions in the English Town and Country Planning Act. The case, known as 'the *Tesco Witney* case' was reported at [1995] 1 WLR 759. It concerned a planning application by Tesco for a development of an 'out of town' store at Witney in Oxfordshire. Tesco's application was accompanied by an offer to build a bypass road around the town, which was not particularly near the proposed store. This was a major planning gain for a council, as it would save them some £5m. Tesco did not get the permission, as the Council decided that the road was not sufficiently connected with the proposed development. The reporter appointed by the Department of the Environment agreed. The case was then considered by the House of Lords, who in long and carefully considered judgments dismissed the appeal.

As a result of this case, and the general feeling that planning permission was being bought in many cases, the Department of the Environment and the Scottish Office issued circulars dealing with planning agreements. The Scottish version is to be found in Scottish Office Circular 12.1996, and is indispensable reading for anyone concerned with such agreements.

Demolishers

21.06 The demolishers level the site for the builders. The developer should ensure that the price charged for this service reflects the value of any reusable material on the site, e g tiles, steel, wood, copper etc.

Builders

21.07 The builders are obviously in charge of building work. It is important that they do their work properly and promptly, under the supervision of the architect. The building contract is in standard form and should provide that the builders shall pay a penalty for every day late in completion. This should, of course, be a genuine estimate of loss incurred through lack of use, and consequently rental or deemed rental, it must not be merely punitive. Conversely, a bonus may be payable to them if they finish the work early.

Examples of typical, if simplified, clauses are given below:

Penalty (or properly 'liquidate damages') clause. The parties bind themselves and their respective representatives whomsoever to implement and fulfil the whole terms of this agreement, each to the other, under a penalty of £X sterling (or £X per day) to be paid by the party failing, to the party observing or willing to observe his part, and that over and above performance.

Force majeure. The sellers shall not be responsible for prevention or delay in production transport to and delivery into the XY Terminal, storage in the XY Terminal, loading into trucks from XY Terminal, transport to place of delivery of the goods, or any part thereof, whether in country of origin, in XY, in the country of delivery or in transit, occasioned by any executive or legislative act done by or on behalf of any government, act of God, war, blockade, hostilities, strike, lockout, riot, or civil commotion, combination of workmen, breakdown of machinery, fire, floods, earthquakes, or any other causes whatsoever beyond the reasonable control of the sellers or the producer. Sellers shall advise buyers if delivery is prevented or delayed by any such cause and sellers have the option either to cancel the contract or to extend the delivery period by such times as is required to effect delivery.

Arbitration. Any difference or question that may arise between the partners or their representatives or creditors or trustees in bankruptcy as to the meaning of the terms of this agreement, or as to the rights and liabilities of the parties to the agreement, or in the winding up of the partnership, or any other matter or claim relating to or arising out of the partnerships or any affairs thereof, whether during its subsistence, or after its termination, is hereby referred to the arbitration of (*here state a person's name or an office-bearer who shall choose an arbiter*); (*if the arbiter's decision is to be final state here* 'the terms of the Administration of Justice (Scotland) 1972, s 3 are hereby excluded from this agreement to arbitration').

Mediation. The parties attempt in good faith to resolve through negotiation any dispute arising out of or relating to the contract. If a dispute shall arise which cannot be resolved between the duty manager and the supervisor, the chief executives of the parties shall attempt in good faith to resolve the dispute. They shall meet within 5 days of the date (the 'breakdown date') of failure of the duty manager and supervisor to resolve the issue and if they are unable to resolve the issue within 10 days of the breakdown date either party may request to resolve the dispute through mediation conducted by a mediator appointed by the Law Society of Scotland by sending a written request to that body with a copy to the other party. The mediation procedure shall be determined by the appointed mediator in consultation with the parties. The fees and expenses of the mediator shall be borne equally by the parties. If the dispute has not been resolved within 14 days of the commencement of the mediation hearings or if no mediation has been commenced within 30 days of the breakdown date the provisions of this clause shall be of no effect.

Whether a dispute is resolved in court, by arbitration or by mediation is the question to be met by the parties. It is as well to think of this at the outset, when the parties are on co-operative terms, rather than when a dispute breaks out and they cannot even agree the time of day. Each has its merits, but, on the other hand, court proceedings are perceived to be expensive and too bound up in archaic rituals. Arbitration should be quicker and cheaper, but too often degenerates into a court without gowns. Therefore mediation would seem to be the ideal answer, but the concept has not fully caught on in Scotland yet, although it is enthusiastically used in the United States, and increasingly in England, at the instigation of the Lord Chancellor.

21.08 Letting agents These may be the same people as the valuation surveyors mentioned earlier, but not necessarily. They obtain tenants for the building. A really clever developer with a good development may 'pre-let' it, that is let it out before it is even complete. This will obviously make the developer's life much easier.

21.09 Tenants They provide the income which should reward the developer's efforts. Once the development is let, the developer will want as little to do with tenants as possible, and accordingly all maintenance and other obligations are passed to the tenants (see ch **20**). The only obligation remaining upon the developer then will be to ensure that the rent cheques arrive promptly.

21.10 Fund The development is now complete, and let. The developer is drawing rents. Developers, as a class, are not collectors of rent. They prefer to develop, sell, and move on to the next development.

On the other hand a good building, full of responsible tenants, all on full repairing leases, and subject to frequent rent reviews and an eventual reversion, presents an admirable investment opportunity to a pension fund or life assurance company with plenty of money to invest in solid investments, providing a good return, safety, and increasing rents. The developer therefore sells on to one such, and is happy. The acquiring fund is also happy for it has a sound investment with an attractive yield and prospects of increases. Further, if the leases are properly drawn up, it need never trouble itself with the tenants and can safely leave a managing agent in charge of the building—at the expense of the tenants naturally.

21.11 Development Having identified, I hope, the principal players, I would now like to look at the various problems which may face the developer. In the exercise at the end of the chapter, I have sought to provide examples of some of the simpler problems that face the developer.

It is implicit in the developer's job that a messy collection of buildings and pieces of land are acquired and bit by bit a site is assembled for development. This technique is known as 'site assembly' and perhaps the simplest example of this is to be found in the game of Monopoly™. You may remember that if you own Fleet Street you can demand a substantial rent; but if you also acquire The Strand and Trafalgar Square, you have all the reds, and the rents double. You can then start developing the site, and by the time you have built hotels, the rents are enormous. This is, of course, a simplification, but I hope you will see the point.

In real life the process is obviously much more complex. Sites have to be assembled laboriously, subject to many conditions of purchase and usually without letting anybody know that the process is going on. If the secret is released, prices will inevitably rise, and as the acquisition is nearly complete, the persons with the 'ransom strip' can demand almost anything they want, as they can otherwise block the development. For this reason the developer has to work in a cunning and covert fashion. Property and interests in property have to be acquired bit by bit, a property here, the landlord's part of a lease there (to await the termination of the lease). Businesses or property companies must be bought for their property content, and be run both to divert suspicion and to provide the developer with a bit of income. Properties must be bought in name of nominees or associated companies.

The properties have to be bought subject to suspensive conditions— conditions that suspend the implement of the agreement until the conditions are met—such as a grant of planning permission or the transfer of a licence, or satisfactory test bores or environmental audit (see para **22.05**).

At all time natural caution must be tempered with stealth and it may be that buildings may have to be bought without planning permission, as an application for this might reveal the master plan. Here careful advice on planning is certainly necessary. The duty of the lawyer in site assembly is to obtain for the developer a good and clear title to the entire development, with all third-party interests, so far as possible, eradicated.

21.12 The negotiations with the planning authorities do not primarily concern the lawyer, and I shall pass over these, as I will pass over the building of the property. The next problem is therefore to let the building to good tenants. It is a lucky developer who can get a single tenant for the whole development, and most have to be content with a number of tenants, and the standard lease of the development must therefore allow for multi-ownership.

The whole concept of ownership of commercial property subject to tenancies is, as I have attempted to point out, to shift the entire responsibility for the buildings to the tenants. Thus the practice has grown up in commercial leasing for the leases to be on a full repairing, renewing and insuring basis. Because of the immense power and ability of developers to choose their tenants at leisure, this is generally accepted practice.

21.13 There follows a fairly simplified example of a successful site assembly, which hopefully will show some of the problems that can arise.

You act for a Mr John Buzz, who has been engaged in property development on a small scale for several years. He now informs you that he wants to put through a larger development which will, if successful, provide a sum of money which will enable him to retire. For some months now Mr Buzz has quietly been acquiring a block at the corner of Sardinia Terrace and Lombardy Street (see plan A attached) which is in a rather run-down part of town, but which is nevertheless near a lot of housing. Mr Buzz has accordingly entered into a tentative agreement to build a supermarket on the cleared site and then to let this to Prontomart Ltd, a well-known national supermarket chain (see plan B attached).

Furthermore, assuming that everything else goes to plan, Mr Buzz has an understanding with the Long Life Assurance Company Ltd that it will buy the developed and tenanted site as an investment of pension funds, and will therefore then become the landlords of Prontomart. This will provide Mr Buzz with a sizeable sum which will enable him to retire in some comfort. There are, however, a number of problems to be overcome, and you are asked to provide general or specific advice on these.

(1) Referring to plan A, which shows the existing site, you will notice that there is at the corner of Sardinia Terrace and Lombardy Street a plot of ground with two large trees. These trees are the subject of a tree preservation order under the Town and Country Planning (Scotland) Act 1972, s 58. However, they overhang Lombardy Street, and the falling leaves in autumn make the road slippery. Furthermore, the roots are intruding under No 1 Sardinia Terrace causing difficulties in the foundations. Advise Mr Buzz as to the possibility of his being allowed to remove these trees legally, and substitute a landscaped area. (Hint: TCP(S)A 1972, s 58.)

(2) The bottom floor of the house at No 1 Sardinia Terrace is a shop which is tenanted by a Mr Hammer. Mr Hammer is opposed to the development as, he says, he will not be able to obtain a new shop property at an equally advantageous rent. Further, he says that the new supermarket will ruin his business anyway. Has Mr Hammer any security of tenure? (Hint: Tenancy of Shops (Scotland) Act 1949.)

(3) Between Nos 2 and 3 Sardinia Terrace, there runs a right of way to the public park. This is quite extensively used by children from the nearby school as a way to the swings. Mr Buzz wants to build over this right of way, and is quite prepared to provide an alternative route. Can Mr Buzz have the right of way closed? (Hint: TCP(S)A 1972, ss 203ff.)

(4) The public house, the Dog and Ferret, has two full-time employees, Ron and Fred (known to the clientele as Fido and Ferdie), whose belligerent and unhelpful attitude has ensured that over the years the public house has not been very successful. Can Mr Buzz ask the seller to dismiss Ron and Fred before Mr Buzz takes over, and, if not, what are Mr Buzz's liabilities in this matter to Ron and Fred? (Hint: see para **18.14**).

(5) The planning department of the district council has told Mr Buzz that if it grants planning permission for the supermarket it would 'very much like' if he would build a public toilet in the position shown on plan B, while he is building the store. If he agrees to do this, can that agreement be binding on Mr Buzz and his successors? (Hint: see TCPA 1997, s 75.)

(6) Advise Mr Buzz on his liability for: (a) stamp duty, (b) capital gains tax, (c) income tax on rental income received prior to the development being started, and (d) value added tax on the sales made in the public house and on any commercial rents received. (Hint: taxation textbook.)

(7) Advise Mr Buzz in general terms on the terms of the lease to be granted by him to Prontomart Ltd. (Hint: see ch **20**.)

The entire law of landlord and tenant is, therefore, completely replaced by the terms of the lease. Unlike in England there is no statutory interference with this process, barring the relatively mild security of tenure provisions of the Tenancy of Shops (Scotland) Act 1949 and the prohibition of automatic irritancies contained in the Law Reform (Miscellaneous Provisions) (Scotland) Act 1985. There is thus no security of tenure beyond the terms of the lease, no machinery for fixing fair rents, and no compensation for improvements made by the tenant. The lawyer for the tenant must therefore proceed with great care and try to get some sort of safeguard for the tenant if at all possible.

The entire topic of commercial leasing is a complex one, and is dealt with in a general manner in chapter 20, but for a fuller discussion I can confidently refer you to M J Ross and D J McKichan *Drafting and Negotiation of Commercial Leases in Scotland* (2nd edn, Butterworths, 1993). Any lawyer who embarks on commercial leasing without reference to this book is either very good or very foolish.

PLAN A

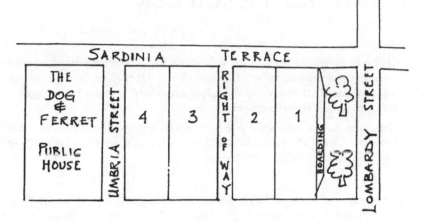

PLAN B

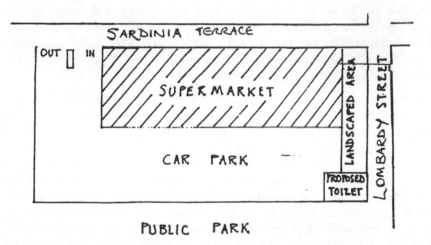

Chapter 22

BUYING FROM A BUILDER

'A Parliament spokeswoman said "We have consistently said that snagging is part of any new building process, whether it is a new home or a world-class Parliament building. It is important to stress that snagging involves no cost to the taxpayer".'

(The spokeswoman was speaking in February 2005 when it was announced that there were 'only' 74, snags out of 11,400, left to deal with. The following week, the roof of the debating chamber collapsed.)

22.01 We have until now been discussing the purchase of 'secondhand' housing. Your clients may well wish to buy a new house, and the procedure is similar, but there are some very important differences; for a start, the purchasers usually have almost no bargaining power, other than the power to try another building site, and have to sign a printed missive, produced by the builder. This document is not susceptible to any alterations, other than very minor ones. The terms of this agreement favour the builder, not unnaturally, and it behoves the solicitor to make sure that the settlement takes place on the date when it is agreed, otherwise strict penalties are incurred.

22.02 Before entering into an agreement, the purchasers should ensure that the houses are not built on an environmentally unsound site. This may sound rather dramatic, but there have been numerous instances of builders, even in good faith, building on sites which latterly turn out to be heavily contaminated. Builders are encouraged to build on 'brownfield' sites which have been used for other purposes. Such sites can frequently be contaminated by a number of very nasty substances, such as asbestos, petroleum, arsenic, explosives, radioactive substances, and chrome, or have been subjected to mining or quarrying, or waste tipping. It is estimated, by Landmark Information Group Ltd, who provide information about contaminated sites, that there are some 35,000 potentially contaminated sites in Scotland. It should be said that local authorities are now much more vigilant in giving planning permission for contaminated sites, and generally will not grant planning permission if the site is environmentally unsound. The following case, however, was cited in a pamphlet entitled 'Buyer Beware!' published by Friends of the Earth:

> '57 families were evacuated from a housing estate in Portsmouth. The families were given 24 hours to leave their homes after dangerous levels of asbestos were found in air and soil samples. The houses had been built on a former Ministry of Defence landfill site. The landfill had been covered with clean topsoil to prevent contamination but the capping proved inadequate.'

Potentially contaminative uses of the land are as follows: agricultural, extractive industry, energy industry, production of metals, production of non-metals and their products, glass-making and ceramics, production and use of chemicals, engineering and manufacturing processes, food processing industry, paper, pulp and printing industry, textile industry, rubber industry, infrastructure, waste disposal, gas work sites, landfill sites, metal industries, sewage works and sludge tips, chemical works, docks and wharfs, tar, oil and petroleum depots, scrap yards, tanneries, railway sidings and depots.

Even when the site appears to be an attractive 'greenfield' site, it should be remembered that it may have been used for some other purpose in the past, particularly in wartime. The history of 'brownfield' sites—that is sites that have been previously occupied—should always be carefully checked.

The builders should be able to provide sufficient evidence of the prior uses of the land, or treatment that has been done to the site, but if they do not, certain information as to past uses can be obtained from the local library, or from asking a specialist surveyor or environmental consultant to investigate the history of the land. The conveyancer may also be able to shed some light from the title deeds, but the ironic aspect of land registration is that the whole purpose of the land certificate is not to give the history of the title. Therefore, if you wish to find out who owned the site in years gone by, investigations have to be made in the old Register of Sasine.

If your clients cannot be satisfied as to the prior uses of the site by the information given by the builders, or from their own enquiries, they are better not to purchase. The purchase may prove to be an unpleasant one, and the house may eventually turn out to be unsaleable, or in exaggerated cases, explode through a build up of methane gas. Prospective buyers should also make enquiries about any history of flooding in low-lying areas. A 'home envirosearch' can be obtained from Landmark Information Group Ltd which gives a 500 metre search, discloses former uses, gives coal-mining areas nearby and subsidence risks, and gives details of flood risk and overhead transmission lines or pylons. The cost is, of course, borne by the purchasers but if they have any lingering doubts, that is money well spent.

22.03 The average new house is usually bought 'off plan' that is to say, before it is built, or only partially built. The services of surveyor are therefore not of much help, except to study the plans and form a valuation. A surveyor, however, will become vitally important when the snagging stage is reached.

22.04 The typical builders' missive describes a property, and the description of the property should be checked, and in particular the boundaries of the property. In land registration areas, considerable difficulty has been caused to the Keeper by properties not being laid out as they were stated to be in estate plans submitted to the Keeper prior to sales. For this reason, land certificates of new houses are often delayed until all the land certificates in the site are prepared, so that they can be fully consistent with each other. The plan of the house should not be a standard estate plan, with the relevant house coloured in—this is not sufficient for land registration, and remember that the whole country will be subject to land registration by April 2003.

The standard for descriptions is stated in an article by Alistair Rennie, the Deputy Keeper, in 1995 JLSS 16, where it is suggested that the appropriate obligation should read:

'In exchange for the price the seller will deliver a duly executed disposition in favour of the purchaser and will exhibit or deliver a valid marketable title together with a form 10 report brought down to a date as near as practicable to the date of settlement and showing no entries adverse to the seller's interest, the cost of said report being the responsibilty of the seller. In addition, the seller, at or before the date of entry and at his expense, shall deliver to the purchaser such documents and evidence as the Keeper may require to enable the Keeper to issue a land certificate in the name of the purchaser as the registered proprietor of the whole subjects of offer and containing no exclusion of indemnity in terms of section 12(2) of the Land Registration (Scotland) Act 1979: such documents shall include (unless the whole subjects of offer only comprise part of a tenement or flatted building) a plan or bounding description sufficient to enable the whole subjects of offer to be identified on the Ordnance map and evidence (such as a form P16 report) that the description of the whole subjects of offer as contained in the title deed is to include the whole of the occupied extent. The land certificate to be issued to the purchaser will disclose no entry, deed or diligence prejudicial to the purchaser's interest other than such as are created by or against the purchaser prior to the date of settlement. Notwithstanding the delivery of the disposition above referred to this clause shall remain in full force and effect and may be founded upon.'

Builders' solicitors may be reluctant to give such an obligation, but this is the standard of information that should be provided in every case.

22.05 The price is stated, and the date of entry is given, not as a precise date, but as the date on which it is certified as complete. A small deposit may be payable upon signing of missives, which deposit is subtracted from the final purchase price. It is generally provided that the settlement shall be by telegraphic transfer, and if the purchaser fails to make payment, interest is payable at a commercial price on the balance outstanding. After a certain time the contract may be brought to an end by the builder. No partial payment of the price is generally permitted, and the keys are not available until full settlement is made. Let this remind you at this point, that the expression 'telegraphic transfer' does not indicate any sense of urgency from the transferring bank.

22.06 The offer states briefly the principal feuing conditions, such as reservation of minerals, use of the house and garden, formation of roads, fencing, provisions as to the ownership, use and maintenance of open amenity spaces, reservation of servitude and wayleave rights for mains services, and the usual obligations of the seller in Sasine and Land Register transactions. To avoid disputes arising this selection of conditions is stated to be 'without prejudice to the generality': which is that the conditions to be included in the feu grant shall be 'in conformity with similar titles given off on this and other of (*the builders'*) estates and will be subject to a deed of conditions containing such conditions as (*the builders*) consider appropriate for the preservation of amenity'. A deed of conditions is prepared in terms of the Conveyancing (Scotland) Act 1924, s 9, and lays down the standard conditions for the whole estate. The disposition can, therefore, be kept relatively short, because it refers to the deed of conditions for the conditions contained.

22.07 The builders will usually apply for and warrant that necessary planning permissions, building warrants and the like have been obtained, but will not give an obligation to produce these. Furthermore, the neighbouring proprietors consent should also be obtained where an older building has been knocked down or converted and there is an old feuing condition that is inconsistent with the modern use that devolves from the superior to the *tertii* (ie those third parties having rights).

The builders, however, give an obligation to produce a completion or habitation certificate from the local authority. Settlement should not be made until this is exhibited, and the transfer from builder to purchaser is available for delivery. (See *Gibson v Hunter Home Designs Ltd* 1976 SC 23 for a case when it was not, and the terrible consequences that flowed from this failure, both for the purchaser who lost the house and the money, and for the legal profession generally.) The cases of *Sharp v Thomson* (1997 SC (HL) 66) and *Burnett's Trustee v Grainger* (2000 SLT (Sh Ct) 116) underline the importance of an early registration of the disposition.

22.08 The builders will reserve the right to vary the building materials to materials of a similar specification, in accordance with the circumstances, without affecting the price.

22.09 All extras on the building price, such as additional fittings to the basic specification, should be carefully checked, as should all discounts and incentives offered, in order that the purchasers may comply with the conditions for obtaining these.

22.10 The provision of searches in the Sasines Register is similar to the normal obligation. The obligation is the same as is normally given.

22.11 The builders will give a probable completion date, but they will not warrant this, nor pay any sort of damages if this date is not met. Thus a penalty clause and a force majeure clause are not appropriate, which would force the builders to pay damages if the house is not ready by a certain date ('penalty clause'), but exempting the builders for any failure caused by certain events such as war or strikes (force majeure clause).

22.12 Larger builders are usually members of the National House Building Council, and as such offer a buildmark certificate to cover the house against defects arising over a ten-year period (see para **4.24**). A small builder may not be a member of the NHBC, which implies no disrespect, in which case a certificate of inspection will be produced from the independent architect who supervised the development, stating that the development is complete in accordance with the plans. The architect should possess full indemnity insurance cover, in the event that a mistake is made.

The Council of Mortage Lenders, in the *CML Handbook*, suggest a certificate be given in the following terms:

APPENDIX 1

PROFESSIONAL CONSULTANT'S CERTIFICATE

Return To:

Name of Applicant(s)

....

....

....

....

Full address of property

....

....

....

....

I certify that:

1. I have visited the site at appropriate periods from the commencement of construction to the current stage to check:

(a) progress, and

(b) conformity with drawings approved under the building regulations, and

(c) conformity with drawings/instructions property issued under the building contract.

2. At the stage of my last inspection on the property had reached the stage of

....

....

....

....

....

3. So far as could be determined by each periodic visual inspection, the property has been constructed:

(a) to a satisfactory standard, and

(b) in general compliance with the drawings approved under the building regulations

4. I was originally retained by

....

who is the applicant/builder/developer in this case.
(Delete as appropriate)

5. I am aware this certificate is being relied upon by the first purchaser .....

....

of the property and also by

....

(name of lender to that purchaser secured on this property.

6. I confirm that I will remain liable for a period of six years from the date of this certificate. Such liability shall be to the first purchasers and their lenders and upon each sale of the property the remaining period shall be transferred to the subsequent purchasers and their lenders.

7. I confirm that I have appropriate experience in the design and/or monitoring of the construction or conversion of residential buildings.

Name of Professional Consultant

....

Qualifications

....

Address

....

....

Telephone No ....

Fax No ....

Professional Indemnity Insurer

....

8. The box below shows the minimum amount of professional indemnity insurance the consultant will keep in force to cover his liabilities under this certificate [£] for any one claim or series of claims arising out of one event.

Signature

Date

22.13 When a purchase is made from a large builder, a 'package' is being bought and stamp duty is payable on the total price of the heritage, less any moveable items included.

When a plot is bought separately, and a house is then later built on it, stamp duty is broadly only payable on the purchase of the land. Thus, if a plot is bought at £20,000 and a house is then built on it at a price of £150,000, stamp duty would only be payable on the price of the plot. As the current threshold for stamp duty is £120,000, there is therefore no stamp duty, instead of £1,700, which would have been payable if the items had been purchased simultaneously. This useful device must not, however, be used artificially, and the Stamp Office has produced a statement of practice (SP 10/ 87, 22 November 1987) restating the Inland Revenue's views on this matter.

A further complication arises with the introduction of the 3% (over £250,000) and 4% (over £500,000) stamp duty bands, when the stamp duty may be collosal, and the temptation to avoid it even greater. The Inland Revenue have introduced Stamp Duty Land Tax, requiring that details be given of costs in every transaction, which may be checked on. The ultimate sanction for any dishonesty is a criminal prosecution for tax evasion.

In the purchase of a new house each party will generally pay their own fees, but certain builders may offer incentives, including a contribution to the purchasers' fees. This should be carefully checked. Such an offer may hide a greater price for the property—remember, there is no such thing as a free lunch.

22.14 As the members of the Scottish Parliament found out, there may be snags that require to be sorted, such things as faulty paintwork, badly fitted doors and windows, floors that are not straight, and scratched fittings. A good surveyor will discover things that the purchasers could never dream of. The cost of a survey is money well spent, for the sooner these matters are attended to, the better it is. They should certainly be fixed before the tradespeople leave the site, never to be seen again. Anything serious that is not fixed should be reported to the NHBC or the insurers, who will, if the worst comes to the worst, pay for someone else to do the work.

Good builders will normally be careful about their reputations, but even good builders can be surprisingly difficult sometimes. In that case the purchaser can take direct action—letters to the papers, notices in the garden specifying the faults of the builder. If you do this, make sure your allegations are true, otherwise you might finish up defending a libel suit.

Appendices

Appendix I

SOME FORMS UNDER THE MATRIMONIAL HOMES (FAMILY PROTECTION) (SCOTLAND) ACT 1981

1 For use in both sale and security transactions where the subjects are not a matrimonial home within the meaning of the Matrimonial Homes (Family Protection) (Scotland) Act 1981, as amended by the Law Reform (Miscellaneous Provisions) (Scotland) Act 1985, s 13 (see 1986 JLSS 214).

Since the Civil Partnership Act 2004 came into force in December 2005 the term 'spouse' shall be taken to include persons who have entered upon a civil partnership.

I, AB (*design*), proprietor of the subjects known as *(*the subjects of sale/the security subjects*), do solemnly and sincerely swear/affirm as follows:

With reference to *the sale of the subjects of sale to

/*the grant by me of the standard security over the security subjects in favour of   the *subjects of sale/security are not a matrimonial home in relation to which a spouse (or civil partner) of mine has occupancy rights, the expressions 'matrimonial home' and 'occupancy rights' having the meanings respectively ascribed to them by the Matrimonial Homes (Family Protection) (Scotland) Act 1981 as amended. Sworn/affirmed by the above-named at

on   the   day   of   in   the presence

of XY (design)

Notary Public

(*Delete where inapplicable*)   (*Witnesses— see note 4*)

Notes: 1. The 'dealing' referred to in the forms of consent in respect of a loan should, for consents signed after 30 December 1985, be 'the granting of the security' as opposed to 'the taking of the loan'.

2. In cases where registration of title is applicable, the Keeper formerly required a statement from the applicant's solicitor to the effect that the relative consent, renunciation or affidavit was delivered at or before delivery of the disposition and standard security. Since the passing of the Law Reform (Miscellaneous Provisions) (Scotland) Act 1985 it has been competent to deliver consents retrospectively, and this question has been dropped from the new forms 1, 2 and 3.

3. The term 'notary public' includes any person duly authorised in the law of the country (other than Scotland) in which the swearing or affirmation takes place to administer oaths or receive affirmation in that other country.

4. A witness is also required if the Affidavit is to be registered in the Books of Council and Session.

5. It is not competent for an Attorney to grant the consent etc on behalf of the constituent.

6. Since the LR(MP)(S)A 1985 it has been competent to grant the affidavits and renunciations retrospectively.

Exempt from Stamp Duty by virtue of Finance Act 1949, Pt IV, s 35, Sch 8, Pt (1), (2).

2 For use where the title to the matrimonial home stands in the name of one spouse (or civil partner) only.

FORM OF RENUNCIATION OF OCCUPANCY RIGHTS

I, A (*design*) spouse (or civil partner) of B (*design*) hereby renounce the occupancy rights to which I am or may become entitled in terms of the Matrimonial Homes (Family Protection) (Scotland) Act 1981 as amended in the property known as being intended to become a matrimonial home as defined in the said Act: And I hereby swear/affirm that this renunciation is made by me freely and without coercion of any kind: And I declare these presents to be irrevocable.

Given under my hand at   this

day of   19   in the presence of (*design*)

Notary Public, and in the presence of these witnesses:

.... Witness

.... Full name

....

.... A

.... Address

...............................Occupation

[Notary's name and seal]

....NP

3 Consent by a non-entitled spouse (or civil partner) to a sale of the matrimonial home by the entitled spouse (or civil partner) (as provided in The Matrimonial Homes (Forms of Consent) (Scotland) Regulations 1982).

Schedule 1
Consent to be inserted in the deed effecting the dealing

(The following words should be inserted where appropriate in the deed. The consenter should sign as a party to the deed.)

... with the consent of A.B. (*designation*), the spouse (or civil partner) of the said CD, for the purposes of the Matrimonial Homes (Family Protection) (Scotland) Act 1981 as amended ...

[To be attested].

Schedule 2
Consent in a separate document

I, A.B. (*designation*), spouse (or civil partner) of C.D. (*designation*), hereby consent, for the purposes of the Matrimonial Homes (Family Protection) (Scotland) Act 1981 as amended, to the undernoted dealing with the said CD relating to (*here describe the matrimonial home or the part of it to which the dealing relates: see Note 1*).

Dealing referred to:

(Here describe the dealing: see Note 2.)

[To be attested].

Note 1: The expression 'matrimonial home' is defined in s 22 of the Matrimonial Homes (Family Protection) (Scotland) Act 1981 as follows:

'"matrimonial home" means any house, caravan, houseboat or other structure which has been provided or has been made available by one or both of the spouses (or civil partner) as, or has become, a family residence and includes any garden or other ground or building attached to, and usually occupied with, or otherwise required for the amenity or convenience of the house, caravan, houseboat, or other structure.'

Note 2: The expression 'dealing' is defined in s 6(2) of the Matrimonial Homes (Family Protection) (Scotland) Act 1981 as follows:

'"dealing" includes the grant of a heritable security and the creation of a trust but does not include a conveyance under s 80 of the Lands Clauses Consolidation (Scotland) Act 1845.'

Note 3: The consent is not liable to stamp duty.

Appendix II

ORGANISATION OF THE REGISTERS OF SCOTLAND

With the introduction of registration of title into:

(1)   the County of Renfrew on 6 April 1981;

(2)   the County of Dumbarton on 4 October 1982;

(3)   the County of Lanark on 3 January 1984;

(4)   the County of the Barony and Regality of Glasgow on 30 September 1985;

(5)   the County of Clackmannan from 1 October 1992;

(6)   the County of Stirling from 1 April 1993;

(7)   the County of West Lothian from 1 October 1993;

(8)   the County of Fife from 1 April 1995;

(9)   Aberdeen and Kincardine from 1 April 1996;

(10)   Ayr, Dumfries, Kirkcudbright and Wigtown from 1 April 1997;

(11)   Angus, Perth and Kinross from 1 April 1999;

(12)   Berwick, East Lothian, Peebles, Roxburgh and Selkirk from 1 October 1999;

(13)   Argyll and Bute from 1 April 2000;

(14)   Inverness and Nairn from 1 April 2002;

(15)   Banff, Caithness, Moray, Orkney and Zetland, Ross and Cromarty, and Sutherland from 1 April 2003;

The land registration scheme is complete.

The department now comprises the Land Register of Scotland and the 14 other registers which already existed.

Register of Sasines

Register of Community Interests in Land

Register of Deeds in the Books of Council of Session

Register of Protests

Register of European Judgments

Register of the Great Seal

Register of the Quarter Seal

Register of the Prince's Seal

Register of Crown Grants

Register of Sheriffs' Commissions

Register of the Cachet Seal

Register of Inhibitions and Adjudications

Register of Entails (now closed)

Register of Hornings (abolished by the Debtors (Scotland) Act 1987, s 89)

Appendix III

PROFESSIONAL INDEMNITY INSURANCE

'Welcome to the world of professional claims—a world where your worst nightmares come true—a world full of snakes and very few ladders—a friendless world of reporters, notoriety—and financial ruin—and it could all be so different—friends, riches, acclaim.'

(Neil Douglas, indemnity solicitor, talk to diploma students)

'Sometimes, at the back of your head, you take your foot off the gasometer.'

(Ally McCoist)

To err is human and most solicitors will have had at some time— whatever they may say—the horrible feeling that they may have done something, or not done something else, that may give rise to a claim in professional negligence.

At such times it is reassuring to know that you have your indemnity policy standing between you and a financial chasm. The minimum cover per solicitor is currently £1.25m but this may not be enough. I believe that some larger firms insure for much larger sums per partner, but of course the bigger the firm, the bigger the business and volume of business, and thus the possibility of a bigger mistake. In any event it is really not a good idea to try to save expense by cutting down this cover. The premiums are obviously expensive, but thanks to careful management, have not reached the levels ruling in England, which in 1995 were 4% of the firm's turnover. In many cases this is a huge sum.

Examples of conveyancing mistakes that have occurred in the past and should not therefore recur, but probably will, are as follows:

1. The very worst mistake a solicitor can make is to forget the strict provisions of the Companies Act 1985, s 410, relating to the registration of charges created by a limited company. This covers not only floating charges, but also fixed charges, such as standard securities. Thus if a limited company grants a standard security over its land, the lender's agent must first record this document and obtain a date of recording from the Keeper. The recording date, in either the Register of Sasines or the Land Register, is the date of creation of the security, and within 21 days of that date the lender's agent must register particulars of the charge with the Register of Charges, kept at Companies House, 37 Castle Terrace, Edinburgh EH1 2EB. Failure to do this will mean that the charge is void against a liquidator or creditor of the company, and the lender will rank only as an ordinary creditor instead of being secured. The loss due to the solicitor's error is potentially huge.

2. Another point to watch, in General Register of Sasines titles, is when you send your standard security to be recorded in the General Register of Sasines and you receive a recording date, and you then duly lodge your particulars of charge. Then disaster strikes, and the Keeper returns your standard security for correction. When you have made your corrections, you must then re-record the security, and *again* register details of the charge. The first notification is invalid. Fortunately this cannot happen in the Land Register.

3. You sell land for a client and allow the client to grant absolute warrandice, even though you know that ownership of part of the land is doubtful. The new owner is then interdicted from building on the area of doubtful ownership, and claims against your client under absolute warrandice. As a result your client has to buy the land in question at an extortionate price and looks to you for recompense.

4. All boundaries, rights of access, and servitude rights should be checked. Failure to do so, may result in extremely expensive remedial action … at the conveyancer's expense. Such things should be more easily detected with registration of title, and on digitised Ordance Survey maps, instead of the haphazard methods of description which previously existed.

5. Great care should be taken to check all planning permissions and building warrants for work done.

6. The letter of obligation should not contain any obligation that you may be unable to deliver. Thus, you should not undertake to deliver a clear planning report—you may not get one. Also do not undertake to deliver a letter confirming that the roads are publicly maintained—they may not be. See an article by Professor Robert Rennie on this topic in 1993 JLSS 431. See also *McGillivray v Davidson* 1993 SLT 693.

7. When acting for a mortgage lender, read the lender's instructions carefully and follow them to the letter. If you have difficulty in doing so, report the problem immediately to the lender and follow their directions.

If that involves declining the instructions, so be it. See Rennie 'Negligence and the Expanding Duty of Care' 1995 JLSS 58.

8. When acting for a lender, read the lender's instructions carefully and follow them. See Rennie 'Negligence, Securities and the Expanding Duty of Care' 1995 JLSS 58.

For your own sake and for the sake of the profession, who have to pay sharply increased premiums each year please try and avoid mistakes like these.

In a publication prepared by the Law Society and the Indemnity Insurance Brokers, entitled *Better Practice in Practice*, certain guidelines are laid down for solicitors. While, hopefully, all of these have been stressed throughout this book, these guidelines present a useful summary:

- Take clear instructions from all your clients direct—that is to say, not solely through intermediaries.
- Record properly all communications, all meetings, all telephone calls, in writing.
- Enforce a good diary system—a double diary system, if necessary.
- Read and check the file, and think before taking a decisive step.
- Review all files regularly.
- Always know what your assistants are doing.
- Copy all important correspondence to clients immediately.
- Only provide letters of obligation that you can personally meet (see above).
- When going on holiday, leave adequate file notes.
- Where reliance is placed on words, express them clearly, fully, and accurately and, wherever possible, in plain English.
- Take expert advice in areas of uncertainty—legal or otherwise.
- If you are using a lawyer in another town as a correspondent, bear in mind your responsibility to your client is nevertheless not reduced.
- Similarly, if you are acting as correspondent to another lawyer, keep the instructing solicitor constantly advised.

Every practising solicitor should be familiar with the contents of this booklet.

To these guidelines, I would add another:

- Never forget that you are responsible for all documents that you prepared. You should, therefore, check every document that you have prepared, before it leaves the office and is signed. It is not enough to leave the checking to staff, especially junior staff who may have just left school and who are set to comparing documents between making tea and doing the deliveries, and who cannot be expected to have any idea of legal terminology.

As an example of this, I saw a deed from a respected firm which stated 'I grant drainage rise' instead of 'I grant warrandice'. Such intelligent, but totally wrong, guesses of bad writing are always the hardest to spot, simply because they are so plausible to the untrained eye. (See also *Hunter v Fox* 1964 SC (HL) 95).

Written amendments on typed or word processed documents should also be carefully checked. One such mistake through a misreading of poor writing—I'm sorry to say it was my own—was to transform the term 'three miles' into 'three metres'. Had it not been caught in time, the result could have been hideous, as this was the area in which the seller of a business was not allowed to trade for a certain number of years.

When drafting deeds, approved styles should be used wherever possible. Conveyancing styles may be found in the excellent style book issued to diploma students, or in most conveyancing texts. Much useful information may also be gained from consulting English style (or 'precedent') books, most particularly Butterworth's Encyclopaedia of Precedents. Care must however be used when following a style, and this must never be done uncritically, particularly in the case of English styles. A cautionary tale unfolds in *Tarditi v Drummond* 1989 SLT 554- a style from *Halliday Conveyancing Law and Practice* (vol II 15.138) was followed, but the court ruled that it was 'difficult to understand, and should not be followed slavishly in future'. This excellent advice applies to all style books.

In a speech reported briefly in the *Glasgow Herald* of 9 November 1985, Judge David Edward QC is reported as saying to newly admitted solicitors that they should not imagine that they could get through their professional lives without making mistakes, and it was important to admit when they had been made. He continued to say that 'clients and insurers are surprisingly sympathetic to the lawyer who admits to his mistakes'.

This is sound advice, for if an attempt is made to hide a mistake, it only gets worse. One would, I think however, have to be careful about the exact admission made in case this prejudiced a valid insurance claim.

343

It is a constantly recurring theme of damages cases that the innocent parties are pursuing matters to the bitter end 'because they didn't even apologise'.

Appendix IV

PROPERTY SALE QUESTIONAIRE

PROPERTY ADDRESS..

SELLER(S) ....

General Note

- Please complete this form carefully. Your solicitor or estate agent will help you to fill it in. If you are unsure how to answer any of the questions, ask them to explain more fully before you do this.
- The following information is necessary to ensure that the sale of your property goes smoothly.
- Where necessary, please give more detailed information.
- It is important that your answers are correct. If you are still unsure you should not complete the answers. Your solicitor or estate agent will advise you on what to do about this.
- If anything changes after you fill in this questionnaire but before the Date of Entry, tell your solicitor or estate agent immediately. This is important as giving the correct answers in the first place.
- Please give your solicitor or estate agent any formal Notices you have received which affect the property as soon as possible, including any Notices which arrive at any time before the Date of Entry.

1.	Council Tax	
	Which Council Tax band is your property in? A B C D E F G H	

2.	Parking	
	What are the arrangements for parking outside your property? Please give details:	
3.	**Alterations/Additions**	
(a)	Have you made any structural alternations or additions to the property since you bought it? **If Yes:** (i) please describe the changes.	Yes/No
	(ii) did you obtain Planning Permission, Building Warrant, Completion Certificate and other Consents? **If Yes,** these will be needed by the purchaser and you should give these to your solicitor as soon as possible for checking. If you do not have these please note below who has these documents and your solicitor or estate agent will arrange for them to be obtained:	Yes/No
(b)	Have you had replacement windows, doors, patio doors or double glazing units installed in your property? **If Yes:**	Yes/No
	Were the replacements the same shape and type as the ones you replaced?	Yes/No
	If Yes, please describe the changes (made approximate dates when the work was completed)	Yes/No
	Please give any guarantees which you receive for this work to your solicitor or estate agent so that they can check whether they can be transferred to the purchaser(s).	

4.	**Central Heating**	
(a)	Is there central heating in your property?	Yes/ No/ Partial
(b)	**If Yes/partial** – what kind of central heating is there? (eg gas fired, solid fuel, electric storage heating, gas warm air)	
(c)	Do you have a maintenance contract with Scottish Gas or any other registered firm? **If Yes,** please give details: We would recommend that if the heating system has not been serviced within the last 12 months that this is done prior to completion of the sale.	Yes/No

5.	**Services**			
(a)	Please tick services are connected to your property and give details of the supplier:			
	Services	**Connected**	**Supplier**	
	Gas/Liquid Petroleum Gas			
	Electricity			
	Water mains/private			
	Mains Drainage			
	Septic Tank/Soakaway			
	Telephone			
	Cable TV/Satellite			
	Broadband			
(b)	Do any drains, pipes or wires cross any neighbour's property? **If Yes,** please give details:			Yes/ No/ Don't Know

(c)	Do any drains, pipes or wires leading to any neighbour's property cross your property? **If Yes,** please give details:	Yes/ No/ Don't Know
6.	**Shared Services**	
(a)	Are you aware of any responsibility to contribute to the cost of anything used jointly, such as the repair of a shared drive, boundary or drain? **If Yes,** please give details: If your property is a flat, is there any responsibility to contribute to repair and maintenance of the roof, common stairwell or other common areas? **If Yes,** please give details:	Yes/ No/ Don't Know
(b)	Do you contribute to the cost of repair of anything used by the neighbourhood, such as the maintenance of a private road? **If Yes,** please give details:	Yes/No
(c)	Is there a maintenance contract in respect of grass cutting and maintenance for common garden areas, playground or verges **If Yes,** please give details:	Yes/No
(d)	Do you need to go on to neighbouring property if you have to repair or decorate your property or maintain any of the boundaries? **If Yes,** please give details:	Yes/No

(e)	Do any of your neighbours need to come on to your property to repair or decorate their building or maintain their boundaries? **If Yes,** please give details:	Yes/No
(f)	So far as you are aware, do any of your neighbours or any member of the public have the right to walk over your property, for example to put out their rubbish bin? **If Yes,** please give details:	Yes/No
(g)	Do you have the right to walk over any of your neighbours' property for example to put out your rubbish bin? **If Yes,** please give details:	Yes/No
7.	**Specialist Works**	
(a)	In the past 20 years, has treatment in respect of dry rot, wet rot, damp or any other specialist work been carried out to your property so far as you know? **If Yes,** please say whether you carried out the repairs or if they were done before you bought the property:	Yes/No
(b)	Do you have any guarantees relating to this work? **If Yes,** these will be needed by the purchaser and should be given to your solicitor as soon as possible for checking. If you do not have these yourself please state below who has these documents and your solicitor or estate agent will arrange for them to be obtained. You will also need to provide a description of the work carried out – this may be shown in the original estimate.	Yes/No

8.	**Others Guarantees**					
(a)	Are there any guarantees or insurance policies of the following types:					
	(i) Electrical Work	No	Yes	Don't Know	With Title Deeds	Lost
	(ii) Roofing	No	Yes	Don't Know	With Title Deeds	Lost
	(iii) Central Heating	No	Yes	Don't Know	With Title Deeds	Lost
	(iv) NHBC	No	Yes	Don't Know	With Title Deeds	Lost
	(v) Damp Course	No	Yes	Don't Know	With Title Deeds	Lost
	(vi) Anything similar? (eg cavity wall insulation, underpinning, indemnity policy) **If Yes,** please give details:	No	Yes	Don't Know	With Title Deeds	Lost
	(vii) Do you have any written details of the work that this guarantee(s) relates to? **If Yes,** please give details:					
(b)	Have you made or considered making claims under any of the guaranteed listed above? **If Yes,** please give details:					Yes/No

9.	**Boundaries**	
	Do you know of any boundary of your property being moved in the last 10 years? **If Yes,** please give details:	Yes/No
10.	**Local Authority Notices**	
	In the past 10 years have you ever received a Notice from the Council: (a) advising that a neighbouring property has made a planning application?	Yes/No
	(b) that affects your property in some other way?	Yes/No
	(c) that requires you to do any repairs or improvements to your property?	Yes/No
	If the answer to any of the above is Yes, please give these to your solicitor or estate agent or advise them who has these.	
11.	**Factoring/Managing**	
	Is there a factor or property manager for your property? **If Yes, p**lease give details of their name and address together with details of any deposit they hold for you and the approximate annual charges: Is there a common buildings insurance policy? If your property is factored by the residents, who is responsible for dealing with this? If there is a common fund, how much is normally paid into the fund and how often?	Yes/No

12.	Residents' Association	
	Is your property within an Estate which has an established Residents' Association? **If Yes,** please give details (including approximate annual charges):	Yes/No
13.	**Loan Finance**	
(a)	Other than your mortgage, have you taken out a loan from any other company? (for example, for the installation of double glazing, kitchen or bathroom units etc)	Yes/No
(b)	**If Yes,** is this loan or loans secured on your property (ie a second mortgage over the property)?	
(c)	Please give details of this loan or loans:	
14.	**Hire Purchase, Credit Sale etc**	
	Are you still paying for any of the moveable items (for example, kitchen appliances or carpets) to be included in the sale price for the property under a Hire Purchase, Credit Sale or other form of Credit Agreement? Please give details:	Yes/No
15.	**Occupiers**	
	Please state the full name(s) of the owner(s) of the property?	
	Is your spouse or civil partner a joint owner of the property?	Yes/No
	Does your spouse or civil partner live in the property with you?	Yes/No
	Please state the full names of any other occupants of the property (eg a tenant) and details of any agreement (eg a lease) or other arrangement that allows them to live in the property:	

I/We hereby confirm that the foregoing is true and correct to the best of my/our knowledge and belief.

....
(Signature)
....
(Signature)

Date..

....
(Signature)
....
(Signature)

Appendix V

ENFORCEMENT OF STANDARD SECURITIES

References are to the Conveyancing and Feudal Reform (Scotland) Act 1970, SC – Standard condition of loan under Sch 3 to Act.

1. Calling-up notice	2. Notice of default	3. Insolvency of proprietor	4. Petition to sheriff to exercise remedies
ss 19, 20; Sch 6, Form A SC 9(1)(a)	ss 21–23; Sch 6, Form B SC 9(1)(b)	SC 9(1)(c)	ss 24, 29(2)
Debtor does not comply / Debtor redeems loan and creditor grants discharge; s 17; Sch 4, Form F	Debtor remedies default / Debtor appeals notice to sheriff and is upheld / Debtor does not comply	Apparent insolvency; Trust deed; Arrangement with creditors; Judicial factor appointed; Company wound up or liquidator, receiver or administrator appointed; Possession taken of assets under floating charge	Application specifies nature of default. Additional or alternative to notice of default if granted

At this stage the borrower, or certain other people, may petition the Court to suspend procedures under the Mortgage Rights (Scotland) Act 2001. Please note that this applies only to residential properties, and it does not apply in cases of apparant insolvency. See chapter 10.

354

DEBTOR IN DEFAULT - CREDITOR'S REMEDIES

Traditional Remedies: 1. Personal action; 2. Adjudication; 3. Poinding of the ground.	Any remedy outwith Act given by standard security: SC 10(1).	Sale of security subjects: SC 10(2). If sale is not possible then the remedy is **foreclosure**: SC 10(7). (sheriff court action)	Entering into possession and letting: SC 10(3)–(5). **Note:** this remedy may be accompanied by a court warrant for ejection in terms of the Act of Sederunt 1990 SC 1990(6). It is not strictly necessary on the expiry of a calling-up notice but may in practise be desirable. In most cases possession is sought first before exercising any other remedy	Repair reconstruction and improvement: SC 10(6).

Appendix VI

MAPS OF SCOTTISH LOCAL GOVERNMENT AREAS

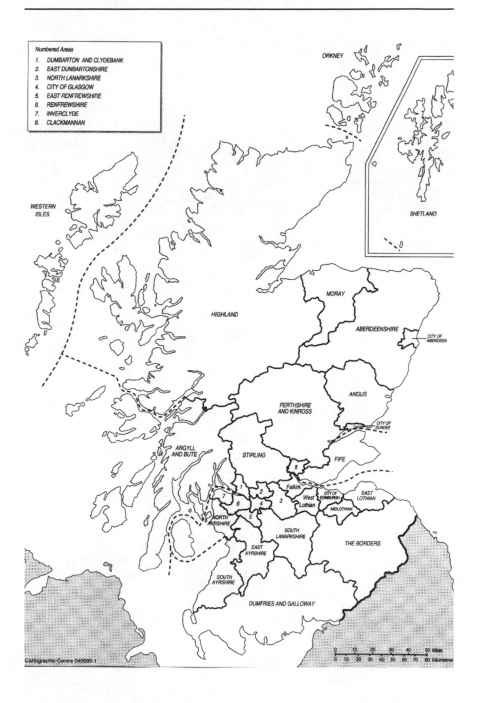

Numbered Areas

1. DUMBARTON AND CLYDEBANK
2. EAST DUNBARTONSHIRE
3. NORTH LANARKSHIRE
4. CITY OF GLASGOW
5. EAST RENFREWSHIRE
6. RENFREWSHIRE
7. INVERCLYDE
8. CLACKMANNAN

ORKNEY

WESTERN
ISLES

SHETLAND

HIGHLAND

MORAY

ABERDEENSHIRE

CITY OF
ABERDEEN

ANGUS

PERTHSHIRE
AND KINROSS

CITY OF
DUNDEE

ARGYLL
AND BUTE

STIRLING

FIFE

8

Falkirk

West
Lothian

CITY OF
EDINBURGH

EAST
LOTHIAN

MIDLOTHIAN

NORTH
AYRSHIRE

SOUTH
LANARKSHIRE

THE BORDERS

EAST
AYRSHIRE

SOUTH
AYRSHIRE

DUMFRIES AND GALLOWAY

Cartographic Centre 040595-1

INDEX

Law Society of Scotland
generally 1.03–1.08
Leases
marketable title, and 8.29
Legal Defence Union (LDU)
generally 1.08
Legal Disciplinary Partnerships
generally 1.15
Letter of engagement
generally 4.05
Letter of obligation
marketable title, and 8.38
Letter writing
addressees 2.02
addresses 2.02
brackets 2.02
colons and semicolons 2.02
commas and apostrophes 2.02
content 2.02
dashes 2.02
ending the letter 2.02
full stops 2.02
grammar 2.03–2.05
introduction 2.01
jargon 2.06
Latin terms 2.06
modes of address 2.02
punctuation 2.02
Liability for debts
regulatory controls, and 1.11
Licensed conveyancers
generally 1.13
Licences and franchises
sale and purchase of business,
and 18.11

Lifetime mortgages
borrowing on heritable
property, and 10.10
Limitation of claims
Glasgow Standard Clauses,
and 4.34
Limited companies
marketable title, and 8.32
Limited liability partnerships
generally 1.03
regulatory controls, and 1.11
Liquidators
marketable title, and 8.22
Litigation
Glasgow Standard Clauses,
and 4.19
Loan to value (LTV)
borrowing on heritable
property, and 10.01
Lochs
marketable title, and 8.25
Long leases
registration of land, and 14.10

Management charges
commercial leases, and 20.14
Marketable title
access rights
generally 8.18
new homes 8.19
adjudication titles 8.33
adjudications 8.39
administrators, and 8.22
alterations to the
building 8.17
background 8.01
bankruptcy, and 8.22

Valuation
sale and purchase of business, and 18.13
Value added tax
settlement, and 9.21
Vassal
abolition 15.01
Vehicles
sale and purchase of business, and 18.08
Verification of identity
generally 4.07
Volume conveyancing
generally 1.15

Walls
marketable title, and 8.24
tenement property, and 16.02
Warrandice
marketable title, and 8.05
Warranties
sale and purchase of business, and 18.16
Water supply
marketable title, and 8.20
Work-in-progress
sale and purchase of business, and 18.06